92 WOOD 2009
Rulli, Marti
Goodbye Natalie, goodbye
  Splendour

Southwest   04/05/2010

SOUTHWEST REGIONAL

GOODBYE NATALIE
GOODBYE *SPLENDOUR*

GOODBYE NATALIE
GOODBYE *SPLENDOUR*

MARTI RULLI
with
Dennis Davern

MEDALLION
PUBLISHING, INC.

ISBN-13: 978-1-59777-639-4
ISBN-10: 1-59777-639-4
Library of Congress Cataloging-In-Publication Data Available

Book Design by Marti Lou Critchfield

Printed in the United States of America

Medallion Publishing, Inc.
9465 Wilshire Boulevard, Suite 840
Beverly Hills, CA 90212

10 9 8 7 6 5 4 3 2 1

Dedication

This book is dedicated to the unforgettable
Natalie Wood, an icon during her lifetime
and a legend forever beyond.

Table of Contents

PART ONE

The Call

And the dirt of gossip blows into my face,
And the dust of rumors covers me.

—Bob Dylan ("Restless Farewell")

Sunday, November 29, 1981

Just past dawn, off the coast of Santa Catalina Island's Blue Cavern Point, a search helicopter pilot noticed a small red "bubble" of color in the gray ocean, eerily conspicuous yet forlornly small, a silent signal to tragedy. The pilot swooped in for a closer look, then immediately radioed the sighting, ending a brief but grim search for the missing legendary film star Natalie Wood.

The chilly morning intensified the despair felt by those who had been looking for the forty-three-year-old actress, wife, and mother. Early risers amongst the holiday weekend boaters worried because helicopters normally did not hover above the coves and circle the moorings of the Island at this early hour. Natalie Wood's husband, Robert Wagner, and their boat captain, Dennis Davern, had been waiting aboard the Wagners' yacht, *Splendour*, for word from the search crews since 1:30 a.m. when Wagner had announced over *Splendour's* radio, "Someone is missing from our boat."

Splendour had been moored since Saturday afternoon at Two Harbors at Catalina Island's Isthmus—the quiet western part of the island where Doug's Harbor Reef was the lone restaurant. Robert Wagner, Natalie Wood, Dennis Davern, and Wood's co-star, actor Christopher Walken—the Wagners' guest, on break from filming *Brainstorm* with Natalie Wood—had dined at the restaurant Saturday evening before returning to *Splendour*. Soon after donning her flannel nightgown and removing some of her jewelry, Natalie went missing, along with the Wagners' thirteen-foot, motorized dinghy, *Valiant*.

Paul Miller, who would later draft a report on Wood's death, was moored near *Splendour*. Don Whiting, the Harbor Reef restaurant manager, along with Miller, had heard Wagner's vague distress call. Whiting returned the call and agreed to help with Wagner's request for a low-key search. Whiting set out by boat with his friend, restaurant cook Bill Coleman, to look for Natalie.

An island campground worker, Paul Wintler, also picked up on the call, and cruised to *Splendour* to help. He returned to the island with Wagner, but there was no sign of Natalie in the dark beach area, and the restaurant was closed. Wintler took Wagner back to *Splendour*.

Upon learning of the situation shortly after 2:00 a.m., Doug Bombard, owner of Doug's Harbor Reef, drove to the harbormaster's house and explained the trouble. Harbormaster

Doug Oudin followed Bombard back to the pier, where he started up Patrol Boat 10 and cruised to *Splendour*.

Oudin strongly suggested to a drunken Wagner that a call be placed to the Coast Guard. Wagner reluctantly agreed. Oudin returned to his Two Harbors office and placed an official call. The Coast Guard responded at 3:25 a.m., but a fully equipped, professional search could not be launched until 6:00 a.m., approximately seven hours after Natalie disappeared.

Oudin cruised Patrol Boat 6 back to *Splendour*. Wagner and Davern, both drunk, met Oudin at the stern. Oudin let them know a search effort was underway. Wagner told Oudin that Natalie was dressed in her nightgown.

Just as darkness lifted, Whiting and Coleman came upon the missing dinghy nestled in kelp in a cove about a mile from where *Splendour* was moored. The dinghy was empty, its oars in place, its engine in neutral, and its ignition key in the off position. Whiting and Coleman decided to use the dinghy so they would have a two-boat search effort.

About a half hour later, the helicopter pilot spotted the "red bubble." Doug Bombard—also searching by boat—was nearest to the reported sighting. He cruised toward Blue Cavern Point to investigate. His heart sank at the sight of a woman wearing a red jacket that held her afloat in a virtually upright position. The woman's head was tilted forward, her face submerged in the water, with only her dark hair visible on the water's surface.

Natalie.

Bombard had been ordered by lifeguard Roger Smith not to touch the body because homicide might be involved, but Bombard couldn't allow Natalie to wait: What if she was just unconscious, and there was still a chance to save her? Bombard reached for Natalie just as Smith arrived to see her ice-white body slip from her red cloak. Bombard grabbed Natalie and pulled her and her coat into his boat.

Natalie's eyes were fixed and open. She was dressed in only the red down jacket, a flannel nightgown, and blue wool socks—a bedtime outfit adorned by a bracelet, four rings, and a necklace.

Smith reported the recovery of the body. He also notified the homicide division of the Los Angeles County Sheriff's Department.

The details Bombard and Smith knew thus far only distorted the already out-of-focus view. If Natalie left her yacht willingly, why was she in nightclothes? If she left in the dinghy, how had she fallen out of it? Why was the dinghy key in the off position? Why did Natalie have bruises on her legs and arms and a facial abrasion? What possible explanation could account for Natalie Wood's dead body, dressed in a wet nightgown, now on the floor of a boat and on its way back to the island for official identification?

Robert Wagner declined to view his wife's body when a small group of officials boarded *Splendour* to inform him of the grim discovery. Wagner dropped his head, and with emotion and drama, cried out, "She's gone, she's gone, oh, God, she's gone. Why?"

Dennis Davern embraced Robert Wagner, as if to keep him from falling over.

"Will you please identify her for me, Dennis? I can't, I just can't," Wagner pleaded. The extraordinary request seemed to deepen everyone's compassion for Wagner, but no one considered, even briefly, that the terrible task of identifying Natalie Wood's body would haunt Dennis for the rest of his life.

When Christopher Walken came out of his stateroom and saw the strange entourage on board, he stopped short of asking questions. He put his hand over his brow and moaned, "Oh no, oh no."

With sympathy, authorities complied when Wagner insisted on escaping the island. A shore patrol boat cruised Wagner, Walken, and Davern to the nearby island where Natalie's body waited. An official led Davern to Natalie. Wagner and Walken were quickly escorted to a waiting helicopter provided by the authorities.

A distraught and despondent Wagner, heading home to the quiet security of his bedroom on tree-lined Canon Drive in Beverly Hills, saw that he would be detained as he stepped out of the chopper in Newport, back on the mainland. Just fifty feet from the landing pad stood Detective Duane Rasure from the Los Angeles County Sheriff's Department. Rasure wanted answers.

Rasure's "What happened?" drew faltering responses: "a pleasure cruise....rough seas...she's gone...we don't know...." Wagner's distress left Rasure calculating the man's obvious grief and despair as a "two-plus-two" case—the easy answer equaling pure accident. Because Wagner appeared so unstable, Rasure decided that he would get back to him. He excused Wagner and Walken after getting their brief, corresponding answers.

Wagner headed home to contact attorneys—the proficient, expensive kind who could take over: one for himself and one for his boat captain.

Detective Rasure flew to the island to talk with the captain.

Davern had just left the decompression chamber, used on the island by divers, where Natalie's body lay on a cold metal table with her red down jacket placed across her chest. Devastated by the sight of Natalie, bruised and dead, Davern was in no mood for Rasure. Rasure pressed Davern further than he had Wagner, but Davern's responses to Rasure's questions invariably echoed Wagner's. Rasure had no reason to suspect that Wagner and Davern might have contrived the similarities.

Rasure asked Davern if he had spent Friday night on the island in Avalon with Natalie. Davern, on the defensive, gave two different answers before realizing the detective had been talking to some islanders. He said, "I want to talk with R.J. or see my attorney."

* * *

That unthinkable Sunday, just three days after Thanksgiving, brought the start of the holiday season to a tearful juncture as fans paused to grieve for an American sweetheart. We thought about little Susan Walker, *Miracle on 34th Street*'s young character who had launched Natalie Wood's world fame. We pictured Natalie Wood as Maria, dancing and in love in *West Side Story*. We wondered how *the* Natalie Wood could possibly have come to such a frightful end.

Natalie's loved ones suddenly were faced with an endless tragedy, for the circumstances surrounding her death were far too questionable ever to allow them true closure. The night Natalie Wood died, a mystery was born—and it would produce a ripple effect for decades to come.

* * *

When network television interrupted regular programming throughout the afternoon and evening of November 29, 1981, to report that Natalie Wood had drowned, I was, like most people, stunned and saddened by the news. I was taunted by the scant details, the conflicting reports, and the lack of an explanation for this tragedy. And although I didn't know it at the time, I—a person remotely connected to the tragedy—was about to embark on a quest for truth that would change my life.

Chapter 1

August 17, 1983, 11:30 p.m., Pacific Time. Nearly two years after Natalie Wood's death, Dennis Davern sat on the edge of the bed in *Splendour's* master stateroom—formerly Natalie's room—and painfully relived, perhaps for the thousandth time, the day he had identified her body. Dreading sleep, he filled a glass with scotch—a nightly ritual in which both he and Robert Wagner (known as R.J.) had indulged, often together, since Natalie's funeral.

Dennis feared sleep without the booze that usually helped to muffle his recurring dreams of Natalie's face—alive and dead—as raging thoughts tortured him with the knowledge that nearly two years before, on November 29, 1981, he, Dennis Davern, the proud and conscientious skipper of *Splendour*, had made a terrible, terrible mistake.

Dennis's memories suspended him in a time warp he could not escape. He continually visualized Natalie sitting in her wheelhouse settee—"Natalie's perch" they had called it—creating her needlepoint pillows or reading her scripts. He had long ago cleared *Splendour* of Natalie's personal belongings: her oriental face mirror, her music box, her beautifully stitched pillows, and her earring found in the corner of the stateroom that matched the pieces-of-gold chain she had given him the night before she died—the chain he still wore around his neck. Even with the yacht cleared, Natalie still filled the space around him.

Natalie had turned her husband's sport-fishing boat into a haven, a home on the sea that had received many of the most celebrated people of the entertainment industry. Dennis recalled how Natalie had poured herself into decorating the yacht's interior in a blue color scheme, tastefully caught in the fabrics and wallpaper. The exception to the blue motif was the master stateroom, where Dennis now slept, still surrounded by Natalie's subtle peach and soothing earth-toned choices. For him, those colors were anything but soothing; they were just another reminder of the tragedy in which Dennis had played an unwilling part.

Dennis refilled his scotch glass and carried it to the open rear deck. The still night was a stark contrast to the night when Natalie had met her death through her greatest lifelong fear—deep, dark water.

Dennis was approaching a breaking point. For nearly two years, he had held a secret inside him—a horrible secret that he wished to God he did not know. The very keeping of it went against everything he knew was right, yet at the crucial moment he could have revealed what he knew, his fear and confusion in the midst of an unbearable tragedy had immobilized him. Keeping the secret had seemed not only the right thing but the only thing to do. The secret now churned inside him like a living thing that clawed desperately for a way out.

He paced the deck, then rushed back to the stateroom and randomly pulled open a drawer. Pencil drawings of Natalie's two young girls, which Dennis had deliberately kept on board, transported him to a long-ago cruise when Natalie had sketched her daughters, Natasha and Courtney. Dennis lay on the bed, motionless, and recalled another time:

There's Natalie, nestled into her settee in the wheelhouse—a stack of unread scripts beside her, with one in her lap. She's rubbing her dark eyes. She takes a sip of Pouilly-Fuissé, her favorite wine.

Dennis struggled to focus on the memory, but tonight the scotch failed him. Dennis closed his eyes against hot tears—tears that no longer took him by surprise.

* * *

Same night, different coast, 2:30 a.m., Eastern Standard Time. From a sound sleep, my eyes sprang open. Ironically, within a minute, the startling ring of the telephone confirmed my uneasiness, and I jumped up, ran to my desk, and grabbed it before it awakened my husband.

"Marti, Marti, I need your help…to talk…to tell you. Please."

It was my friend Dennis Davern.

Now living aboard *Splendour*, he called a lot lately, without regard for the east-west time difference—I lived in New Jersey. I had never heard such distress in his voice. I knew, before he said another word, what the call was about.

Dennis agonized constantly over Natalie Wood's death. He had tried to hide his difficulty in coping with the tragedy, but there was no concealing his pain. We had discussed it occasionally but briefly over the past twenty months. It was his determined avoidance of the subject and his recent, drastic weight loss that told me how deeply he was wounded. Now, tonight, I could tell from his voice that Dennis, anesthetized with booze, was about to perform drunken surgery on himself. My immediate thought was to stop him.

"Denny, where are you?"

"I'm on *Splendour*...the murder yacht, that's where I am," he answered sarcastically. "People call it the murder yacht, and the tabloids are calling me the death-yacht captain."

"I'm sorry, Den. I know you're hurting. Has the therapist you've been seeing helped at all?"

"I've been seeing Wagner's doctor. I can't talk there. I'm going to burst," he cried. "I'm ready to burst...I can't take it anymore."

I wouldn't take advantage of Dennis's drunkenness, and I wasn't so sure I wanted to hear his obvious, enormous burden. But Dennis, even in his most inebriated state, knew that I would listen to whatever he had to tell me and that I would do anything in my power to help him.

"I'll never regret telling you, Marti," he continued. "Tape me so I can never take this back. I'll shock you with something you...that you won't...."

"Stop, Denny!"

Despite *preferring* to believe that Natalie Wood's death had indeed been accidental, I suspected there was a dark side to the story. The subject was widely discussed among my circle of friends and family. Dennis, to this point, had not spoken of the details of that night, and more than the contradictory news stories, more than the downward turn Dennis had taken since Natalie's death, it was his silence that bothered me. This night, as he sobbed on the telephone, I feared he would say too much, and my stomach churned with anxiety for him.

"I won't tape you like this, Den," I told him. "You're dealing with enough. When you wake up tomorrow and realize what you said—well, this is serious."

"It's beyond serious, Marti. It's beyond your worst thought. It's eating me alive. Identifying her body.... You know I had to identify her," Dennis sobbed.

I stayed quiet. Quiet and numb.

"Marti, ask me anything, so I can answer. Take this out of me, please."

I fought temptation and said, "Den, I just can't. Right now, I don't care how she died. I just care that you—"

"*Everyone* cares how she died!" he vehemently interrupted.

"Denny, I need you sober for this."

"I'm never sober anymore," he yelled. "If I'm not drunk on scotch, I'm drunk on fucking bullshit! It's all total bullshit, and I can't stand it!"

He mumbled more, and I waited with no idea what to say.

Finally, Dennis said, "I want this story in a book, Marti, and I want you to write it. The strangers and reporters who hound me, they just care about getting it first, but I need it explained right."

I sandwiched the receiver between my shoulder and jaw and grabbed a pen and paper, as if I could finish a book by daybreak. Natalie Wood's death had become one of many intriguing Hollywood mysteries, and I was talking to a witness—a desperate one. Had I any inkling that I was facing decades of frustration, disappointment, outrage, and consuming work, I still would not have put down that pen.

"Marti, will you answer me?" Den asked.

"You've never told me what happened that night, and your whole demeanor since then leaves me imagining the worst. That's scary."

"Remember the night we met? What I told you?" Dennis asked.

"Of course, I do. You said we would do something big together one day."

"Well, this is it, Marti. This is our something big. The big truth."

Chills ran through me. I had no clue what secrets Dennis would reveal, but I trusted him. To be privy to something as shrouded in mystery as Natalie Wood's death overwhelmed me, but there was more at stake: I thought about the word "justice" and now suspected that Natalie hadn't received it.

"Den. I can't just say 'yes, I'll write a book' at three in the morning."

Dennis was prepared to tell me every detail of the weekend Natalie Wood died. I sensed I might regret what I said next, but at the moment, it seemed the only right thing to say. "Den, you're in no state of mind to relive that weekend tonight, so tell me something nice about your relationship with Natalie instead."

"She knew she would die in water, Marti. Natalie knew it—even said it. That's two predictions made years ago, and here we are."

"Den, we'll talk about all that later. Tonight, go lighter."

Perfect medicine. His voiced cleared to a less burdened tone. He seemed to sober up. "I got along great with Natalie," he said. "We spent a lot of time together on the boat. I was their friend, not just an employee."

"I've talked to you enough through the years to know that much. But are you still friends with Wagner?"

"The world should know just how much of a friend I've been to him."

His strange response startled me. "Meaning?" I asked.

"Meaning I lied for him, like friends do. Like I was told to do, anyway. But what about Natalie? Is it okay to lie because she's dead and doesn't matter?"

I stayed quiet as Dennis yelled out the answer to his own question, "No!"

"Den, please, just tell me about a boat outing or something."

He paused and took a deep breath. "We would sit in the wheelhouse, just hanging out. I knew when to leave her alone and when to start a conversation. Sometimes, I'd say, 'Hey, Natalie, wanna listen to some music?' I'd throw in the Doors or a Jimmy Buffet tape, but she would say, 'Take that out and put on Dylan.' She loved listening to Bob Dylan. Sometimes we'd dance around and sing. One day, I made her feel ten years younger. I was thinking about that cruise right before I called you. I told her she would never drown out there."

* * *

The Wagner family set out aboard *Splendour* for a day of shopping the boutique-lined streets of Avalon on Catalina Island, but when they moored, the brutally hot sun persuaded everyone to stay with the yacht.

Natalie lounged lazily on her corner settee and read a script. Her jeans obviously irritated her legs, and she shifted about constantly. She glanced over at Dennis, where he dozed in his captain's chair at the wheel. He lifted an eyelid each time she stirred.

"Dennis, it's hot," she complained. "I can't move, I can't read, I can't even think. Would you please get me a glass of ice water?"

"Ice water isn't good for you in this kind of heat, Natalie."

"Maybe we do need air conditioning," she suggested.

"Like R.J. would go for that," he grinned. "He thinks he'd be laughed off the boat by his fishing buds, but I'm with you, Natalie," Dennis agreed, wiping his brow with his forearm.

Courtney's, Natasha's, and R.J.'s voices, sounding from the rear of the boat where they played and swam, reverberated against the thick calm. Natalie delighted in hearing her husband's teasing laughter mixed with her daughters' playful squeals. She closed her eyes and tuned in.

Dennis watched Natalie's face. Never was she more serene and beautiful than on days like this one. Her smile grew wider with each burst of laughter from the stern.

"Dennis, why don't you take some pictures of all those children out there?" she said, smiling.

R.J. and his stepdaughter, Natasha, treaded the crystal blue water as four-year-old Courtney watched from the deck. Courtney would not budge toward the water as her father coaxed her to the swim step, but no one teased her. Instead, R.J. asked Natasha to come on deck while he gathered tackle boxes and poles for fishing. The girls were excited to help reel in dinner.

Dennis returned to Natalie, who'd lost concentration on her script. She stood up as he entered the wheelhouse.

"These things aren't helping today," she complained, looking down at her blue jeans. "Dennis, did you notice those girls back at the marina, how skimpy their cut-off jeans were? Their cheeks showed!"

Dennis grinned.

"What if I cut these like that? Am I too old for that look?"

"You'd look great in anything, Natalie."

Her lethargy disappeared as she rushed off to her stateroom. A few minutes later, she returned, frustrated, with scissors in one hand, a glass of ice water in the other.

"I ruined them," she whined, looking down at the ragged, uneven edges of her jeans, which barely allowed her knees to peek out. Her untucked tee shirt made her look almost frumpy.

Dennis burst out laughing. "If you were after the long, leggy look, Natalie, you missed it."

She tried not to laugh while defending her attempt. "I buy clothes. I wear them. I don't alter them! Can you cut them, Dennis?"

"Yeah, I'll fix them."

Natalie squirmed out of her homemade knickers, down to her bathing suit bottom, and reluctantly handed over her jeans. As Dennis reached for them, she clutched them back. "Be careful!"

Dennis cut just below the crotch, ignoring Natalie's "Wait! Not so short!"

"Here, put these on. They'll be perfect," he assured her.

The custom cutoffs revealed Natalie's smooth, tanned legs. She did a slow pirouette, confident she triumphed over the scantily clad marina beauties whom she, of all people, had envied.

"Now, hand over that glass of ice water," Dennis reprimanded.

She threw back her head and filled the wheelhouse with her laughter.

The day lingered on as Natalie read scripts, and R.J. fished with the girls. At dinnertime, R.J. barbecued steaks on deck while Dennis prepared a salad in the galley. When Dennis went to call Natalie for dinner, he noticed her pensive expression. "I just love coming out here," she said. "It's a balm for my spirit." Then she leaned forward, looked at Dennis, and admitted, "Only two things scare me, though. What if I have a heart attack? What would happen, Dennis? Help couldn't get here in time."

"We could be on the island, to a hospital, within minutes, Natalie," Dennis assured her.

She wasn't satisfied.

"What brought this on?"

"I'm under a lot of stress, and I just worry about heart attacks. I just want to be cautious. Maybe we should all take CPR training. You should know CPR, Dennis."

"I'll check into it," Dennis promised, "but I don't see you having a heart attack. You're worrying for no good reason."

"Okay, Doctor Dennis, but what about drowning?" she asked.

"Drowning? You're sure high on anxiety today."

She exhaled loudly, telling Dennis she was perturbed at his dismissal of her fears.

Dennis sat quietly at the wheel. The melodic wash of water lapped at *Splendour's* hull.

"Natalie, check out the sunset," Dennis finally said.

Side by side, Natalie and Dennis watched the sun's orange wings spread across the island and horizon. A rosy glow hid Catalina's hilltops and spread across the sky. As golden sparkles danced off the calm water's surface, Natalie drew in a deep, peaceful breath, and Dennis knew she felt better.

"You'll be fine out here, Natalie," he assured her.

Natalie gave him a beaming smile. "Okay, Dennis, let's go eat."

At the dinner table in the galley, Natalie cut Courtney's portions into tiny, tiny pieces.

"The sunset was awesome tonight," R.J. commented.

Natalie agreed, then teasingly asked her husband, "So, where are the fillets to complement our steaks, R.J.? Catch anything other than the sunset?"

Natasha burst into a fit of giggles. Courtney, following her older sister's cue, laughed along. As conversation drifted lazily over dinner, Courtney dozed off. Natalie carried Courtney to the sofa in the adjoining main salon, then asked Natasha what she wanted to do.

Natasha pleaded, "Mommy, will you draw a picture of me? Please?"

Natalie attached a few sheets of cream cotton paper to a clipboard. "Now, stay still, Natasha," she instructed.

Natasha loved the attention and repeatedly asked to see the work in progress as her mom's pencil moved in downward strokes and upward sweeps across the paper. "You'll have to wait until I'm done," Natalie insisted.

When the sketch was completed, Natasha beamed at her mother's rendition of her pretty young face and long, flowing hair. "Now draw Courtney, too, Mommy," Natasha insisted.

Natalie continued, exerting less effort, but sketched her sleeping toddler as Natasha peeked over her shoulder. "How's this?" Natalie asked, holding up the finished sketches for R.J. and Dennis. Then she commented, with reflective expression, "I always wanted to be an artist."

R.J. smiled and raised his eyebrows, then replied, "Nat, darling, you *are* an artist."

Chapter 2

Three hours after Dennis's call, I was still at my desk, writing every word he had divulged. His frantic words stayed fresh in my mind: *It's beyond serious. It's your worst thought. It's all bullshit. The truth has to come out. I'm on* Splendour…*the murder yacht.*

When my husband, George, got up for work, he asked, "Is Den okay?"

"George, I don't know if we can help him with this. Something strange happened the night Natalie Wood died. He asked me to write a book!"

"Seriously? Did he tell you what really happened?"

"No, and I never thought he would be willing to tell anything, but whatever secret he's keeping is torturing him."

"Let's just be there for him," George said. "But I wish he'd start calling in the daytime."

I smiled. After George left for his construction job, I fell into a restless sleep, awoke within two hours, and called in a personal day at my newspaper job. I pulled a box from the bedroom closet where I had saved, for whatever reason, all the initial newspaper, tabloid, and magazine reports on Natalie Wood's death.

The United Press International's November 30, 1981, report offered the basics:

Natalie Wood Found Drowned

AVALON, Calif. (UPI)—The body of actress Natalie Wood was found floating Sunday in a shallow lagoon off Santa Catalina Island, where she was spending the holiday weekend with her actor husband Robert Wagner, authorities said.

County lifeguards and sheriff's deputies said Miss Wood, 43, apparently drowned accidentally. Coroner's officers investigated the scene and the body was flown back to Los Angeles where an autopsy will be performed. Miss Wood, a brown-eyed beauty who starred in "*West Side Story*" and "*Rebel Without a Cause*," was found fully clothed about 200 yards offshore at the base of a small cliff at 7:45 AM PST officials said.

The actress and her husband had sailed to the island 26 miles off the coast from Los Angeles on their yacht, and had been celebrating the holiday weekend with friends. Wagner returned to his Beverly Hills home after positively identifying his wife's body. He was joined there by Elizabeth Taylor and Roddy McDowell.

Wagner issued a statement through his attorney, "Mr. and Mrs. Wagner had dinner last night in a restaurant on the Isthmus on Catalina Island," attorney Paul Ziffren said, "after which they returned to their boat—the *Splendour*.

"While Mr. Wagner was in the cabin, Mrs. Wagner apparently went to their state room. When Mr. Wagner went to join her, he found that she was not there and that the dinghy also was gone. Since Mrs. Wagner often took the dinghy out alone, Mr. Wagner was not immediately concerned," Ziffren said.

"However, when she did not return in 10 or 15 minutes, Mr. Wagner took his small cruiser and went to look for her. When this proved unsuccessful, he immediately contacted the Coast Guard, who then continued the search and made the discovery early this morning."

A Coast Guard spokesperson said they received a call at 3:20 AM notifying them that Miss Wood was missing. Other witnesses said Miss Wood had been celebrating with friends Saturday night when she wandered off by herself about 1 AM PST, said Lt. Gary Crum of the County Lifeguard Department. The friends grew concerned and notified lifeguards about 5:15 AM, he said.

The body, clothed in a dress and red jacket, was discovered floating just under the surface of the lagoon in an area that a county lifeguard said was inaccessible by foot. The temperature of the water was about 57 degrees. A small inflatable boat equipped with an outboard motor was found near the body.

Granted, the report was but a day removed from the tragedy, but the article failed to mention that Natalie's "dress" was a nightgown. Nor did it correctly report who had identified Natalie's body—important details that went unverified and were erroneously reported on the front pages of newspapers worldwide. Readers were fed the subliminal image of a devastated Robert Wagner bearing the torture of identifying his wife's dead body.

The article painted a picture of Natalie socializing with friends, then wandering off and disappearing, her worried friends deciding more than four hours later to call for help. But Paul Ziffren, who as Wagner's attorney certainly must have scrutinized his client's words before relaying them to the press, presented a different picture: Robert Wagner, within fifteen minutes of discovering Natalie was not in their stateroom, frantically racing around in his small boat to look for her. It seems safe to assume that Ziffren did not invent the details he provided to the press.

Robert Wagner wanted the world to believe that Natalie Wood, who just weeks earlier had told the New York *Daily News*, "I'm frightened to death of the water.... I can swim a little bit, but I'm afraid of water that is dark," went unprovoked to the dinghy in the dark of the night, in the cold rain, dressed in jacket, nightgown and socks, untied the dinghy, tried to board it, and fell silently into the water to her death.

Wagner's explanation went unquestioned by all media institutions except the tabloids. The tabloids wanted to know: What husband would not immediately be concerned upon noticing his wife is missing, especially from a boat? What husband would not be terrified—and would not immediately seek assistance? Wagner's "knowing nothing" was further puzzling because it seemed all the more reason to have acted immediately rather than to forestall a call for help, but it worked in his favor by serving as an acceptable excuse for having delayed a professional search. Los Angeles Coroner Thomas T. Noguchi had headed up Natalie's autopsy. Noguchi had joined the Los Angeles County medical examiner's office in 1961 and was the county's chief coroner from 1967 to 1982. In 1982, the county Board of Supervisors decided that Noguchi's ego interfered with his professionalism, and he was forced from his position. Noguchi had earned the nickname "Coroner to the Stars" for his high-profile autopsies and investigations of celebrity deaths, including those of Marilyn Monroe, Robert F. Kennedy, Sharon Tate, Janis Joplin, Freddie Prinze, and William Holden.

In an ironic twist of fate, Holden, who was Stefanie Powers's companion, had died two weeks before Natalie Wood. Powers—Robert Wagner's friend and costar in their hit show *Hart to Hart*—had just been consoled by Wagner as she grieved for Holden. Holden's body had been found by a building worker in Holden's Santa Monica apartment on November 16, 1981, after Holden was presumably dead for days. Toxicology reports showed Holden's blood alcohol level at 0.22 percent, more than twice the legal driving limit. Noguchi publicized that Holden, drunk, had tripped on a rug, hit his head on a teak bedside table, and then passed out and bled to death. Noguchi had taken a verbal beating for publicly announcing his findings. Some celebrities, Wagner and Powers among them, felt that the unpleasant, personal details of Holden's death should have been withheld.

Two weeks later, Noguchi had Natalie Wood's death to answer for, and he ruled the death accidental, claiming Wood must have untied the dinghy, slipped, hit her head, and then fallen into the water and drowned. Although he left it undetermined why Wood untied the dinghy, he released a report of an argument between Christopher Walken and Robert Wagner that may have prompted Wood to leave the boat. The evidence upon which he based his speculation of an argument was not made public. His office quickly modified the statement when homicide detective Roy Hamilton said, "I don't know where the coroner got that information. We talked to Wagner and Walken, and there was no indication that there was any argument. I think he (Noguchi) was juicing it up a little bit."

Assistant Coroner Richard Wilson toned down Noguchi's statement with, "We think 'argument' might be too strong a word. It might have been an animated conversation…heated conversation…a lot of conversation over a number of hours."

Questions blared in concerned minds: Why would Natalie, dressed in a nightgown, leave *Splendour* so late at night on a remote part of the island?

Four weeks after Natalie's death, to explain her manner of dress, Wagner's theory was publicly offered that perhaps the dinghy was banging on the side of the boat, keeping Natalie awake, so she tried to secure it and slipped from the swim step into the water. Natalie's jacket must have weighed her down.

That theory raised yet more questions.

Why would she have gone out on a rain-soaked deck wearing socks but no shoes? Were shoes missing? Why had Natalie not asked Dennis, whose job it was to maintain the boat and who happened to be fully clothed, to secure the dinghy? Dennis was paid well to be at Natalie's beck and call—to bring her tea at any hour; to cook her dinner; to taxi her to and from the island; to shop for her; to baby-sit her children; to put on music; to turn down the volume; to adjust the heat; to perform any number of tasks, menial or large—most certainly, securing a banging dinghy that disturbed Natalie's sleep would be a routine task. Dennis was also her friend—a friend and employee of whom she asked plenty.

If the banging dinghy was a common problem, as Robert Wagner stated much later, why did investigators first surmise that she had left the boat? Further, after six years in the Wagners' employ, would Dennis not have been aware of a banging dinghy problem and have established a routine of tightly securing it? Had that night's wind levels been checked and confirmed?

The final word was that Natalie Wood's death was caused by accidental drowning. Case closed after ten days. Unsettling questions remained, and Dennis's conversation from last night confirmed that every question was valid. They ricocheted through my mind. By the time I spoke with Dennis the next evening, I was loaded like a machine gun with questions to fire at him. I had said I would call him, but he called me early in the evening.

"Marti, I'm looking at the sketches Natalie drew of Courtney and Natasha. They're the victims of this whole mess. They lost their mother. They worshiped her, and she loved them so much. Why in God's name didn't R.J. and Natalie think of what they were doing to their babies?"

"I don't know, Denny. My heart goes out to them. But you've really got my head spinning."

"I'm holding so much in, and the truth would have made things even worse, especially for the girls. Now I'm confused and scared."

"But you want the truth out now?"

"Out of me, for now. It belongs in a book where Natalie can get the dignity she deserves. I don't know if I can go public—if I'd have the guts—or if Wagner would go nuts on me and try to stop it. Maybe you can publish it after I'm dead." He gave a humorless laugh.

"Den, I've written little newspaper entertainment pieces and one manuscript—which was rejected. I've addressed small issues, but I'm mostly in marketing now, and doubt I can handle something this serious."

"Remember my poetry booklet? You got right into my head and helped me arrange the poems," Dennis reminded me.

"Den, your teenage love poems don't compare to what you're asking now."

Dennis had studied lithography in the early 1970s before moving to California and had printed his poems in a booklet. One of his poems about the sea always stuck with me, and I made a mental note to find his booklet.

Dennis continued. "You can help me be believed. Everyone knew me as the happy-go-lucky boat skipper before Natalie died, and now as the surprise actor on *Hart to Hart*, the after-hours friend who gets drunk with R.J."

"Den, I'm astounded after reading the newspaper report again—did Wagner take out his own cruiser to look for her?"

"Wagner didn't have a cruiser to take out. He lied from day one."

"I'm already frustrated by this, Den."

"Just help me. You *know* me. I need you."

"I have to think things over," I said. "I'll call you back."

Chapter 3

I thought about what Dennis had asked of me, then thought mostly about our relationship and about how our paths had crossed. We had been born and raised about seventy miles apart in New Jersey; Dennis near "America's Favorite Playground" in Margate, a suburb of Atlantic City, and I in a metropolitan town, Cherry Hill, just across the Delaware River from Philadelphia, Pennsylvania.

Dennis was born ambitious. On September 25, 1948, Ruth Davern lay exhausted in her bedroom at home where Dennis was born. She gazed adoringly at her newborn son and recognized his eager restlessness. She smiled, then whispered, "Dennis Girard Davern, you're going to be a star."

But Dennis liked boats. He played day in and day out with his cousin Jimmy Giblin, building the confidence that they would eventually need to get their small rowboat past the Atlantic Ocean breakers. After summers of having to continually surf the boat back to the shoreline, Dennis's affinity with the sea and boating was permanently rooted when, near his eighth birthday, he finally passed those breaking waves.

Dennis's parents, Matthew and Ruth Davern, loved all of their children equally and raised them—Rita, Maureen, Matthew, Dennis, and Paul—in an average, Catholic, happy home environment. When the family of seven moved to the fast-growing suburb of Willingboro, about an hour from the seashore, Dennis missed the salt air and often daydreamed in class about boats and the sea. Nonetheless, he maintained an average grade level through Catholic elementary school and kept it consistent through public middle school and high school.

Congenial and outgoing, he established many friends— lifetime friends—but Dennis was always the "different one." Friends noticed it and envied his independent way of thinking. Although adventurous and prone to daydreaming about world travel, Dennis never labeled them dreams. He was steadfast about his goals.

The military service, with the security of a paycheck, seemed a good option for an unemployed teenager itching to leave home. The tragic loss of Dennis's older brother, Matthew, in the Vietnam War had ruled out the Army or Marines. Losing Matthew crushed each Davern family member, especially Dennis, who had been Matthew's shadow growing up. Ruth and Matthew Sr., as a couple, did not survive the pain of their son's death. Their marriage deteriorated, so they split up and lived in separate homes. To ease family worry and because of his love for the sea, Dennis joined the Navy. He enjoyed the travel and independence, but in 1971, with his Navy tour of duty honorably fulfilled, he looked forward to civilian life again in his home state, New Jersey.

His complexion had become lined with a seaman's creases from the ocean sun. His lanky, small frame had bulked to that of a man, and he had matured. He was handsome, about 5'10", with brown tousled hair, a beard, and prominent eyes, distant and cavalier, like the sea he loved.

While Dennis had been away, his parents' divorce was finalized. His two older sisters, Maureen and Rita, had married, started families, and moved on. Dennis, his younger brother Paul, and their mother remained at home. Dennis became restless.

* * *

Dennis had already bonded with the sea by the time I was being named Margaret Matilda Carter in 1952, two counties east of him, in Camden, New Jersey. My mom, Jenny, at age forty, gave birth to twins, Jimmy and me, the "babies" of the family. We had three older siblings.

My father, Horace, terminally ill by the time I was two, had accepted an offer from a dear family friend, James Dill, to help our family move to upscale Cherry Hill, a town away. "Uncle Jim" moved with us and promised my father he would take care of us.

I was four years old when two family members left: my oldest half-brother, John Bice, joined the Navy, and my father died. Too young to deal with loss, I accepted my father's death with little pain and contemplation. Life went on, and growing up in Cherry Hill was just plain great, but I enjoyed it only temporarily: when I was twelve, my mother and Uncle Jim both passed away of natural causes, just weeks apart. I thought a whole lot more about these devastating, life-altering losses.

My older sister Mary, married with two young daughters, was unable to take on two twelve-year-old, orphaned siblings. My eighteen-year-old brother Horace "Dave" Carter, whom I idolized and wanted to live with, was away in the Navy. So, my twenty-seven-year-old half-brother Jack, out of the Navy but whom I barely knew, took Jimmy and me in to live with him and his wife, Ruth-Ann, and their two young daughters.

A year later, my new family moved to a new housing development in Edgewater Park, across Route 130 from Willingboro, where Dennis and his family lived in Burlington County.

School remained important to me. I read constantly and was especially interested in books and articles on Hollywood celebrities because so many of them had played a small part in my young past. Cherry Hill was famous in the 1960s for the Latin Casino, a trendy nightclub that hosted big stars. By age ten, I had met dozens of celebrities and megastars as they came and went from the Country Squire, a modest hotel where most of the Latin Casino's performers stayed during their nightclub gigs.

For the public, fifty cents bought a day of swimming at the hotel's pools, one indoors, and one outside that was situated near the back parking lot where the Latin Casino's latest stage act usually arrived by helicopter from the nearby airports. The celebrities usually spent an hour with fans. Peter Lawford, Joey Bishop, and Sammy Davis Jr. as well as many others had given me autographs.

I grew up fast. As a teenager, I longed to be on my own, always wanting the past or anticipating the future, so I hardly felt a part of the present. In high school, I became pregnant and gave birth to my first son, William, named after his father, who had graduated high school and soon afterwards left for the Vietnam War. I used pregnancy as a ticket to freedom to ensure my early independence, and I married to secure that independence. I took my 6-month-old son to meet his father, who was on R&R in Waikiki, Hawaii—afraid it might be the only time the two might meet. Fortunately, my husband survived the war, but as is typical of teenage unions, our marriage failed.

At eighteen, I rented an apartment, worked two service jobs, was raising a baby, and had little time for attending school, so I enrolled in correspondence high school, psychology, and writing courses, and I studied at night.

My twin brother, Jimmy, frequently visited me, always with his friends. He introduced me to John Foster, the first legally blind student to enroll at Rider College in New Jersey. John needed textbook readers, which I enthusiastically volunteered for, grateful for the opportunity to help him study his majors, psychology and philosophy, and to be able to experience college in exchange.

Soon after I befriended John, Jimmy introduced me to Paul Davern, whom I instantly hit it off with as a friend. Paul, my age, wanted to set me up on a blind date with his older brother, Dennis, just discharged from the Navy. I said no way to a blind date and stuck to it. Although Dennis and I lived only minutes apart, ironically, it would be in Florida where Dennis and I would first cross paths.

* * *

Paul, Dennis, and their mother, Ruth Davern, moved to Seminole Beach, Florida. Jimmy kept in touch with Paul and decided to move to Florida. My friend Laura Mansberger and I joined Jimmy, and we anticipated Paul Davern's assurances of "jobs galore" in Jacksonville Beach as we cruised down Interstate 95 in 1971 toward a new life in the Sunshine State.

We arrived at Ruth Davern's home around ten on a warm February night. After introductions and a brief, pleasant visit at Ruth Davern's kitchen table, Paul and Dennis were eager to show off their new town and beach. We piled into Jimmy's Chevy Impala and ended up on the beach with Paul's new friends.

Taken by Dennis's charisma, Laura flirted, and she and Dennis gabbed on and on, but I noticed Dennis's peculiar glances my way. Sitting around the campfire, Dennis and I across from one another, his eyes caught mine in a power lock—an intense, unnerving, but somehow comfortable stare. Before we each looked away, Dennis said, knowingly, directly into my eyes, "One day, we're going to do something big together." It wasn't a pickup line.

"I know that," I answered with naive confidence. The witnesses to this tête-à-tête quietly watched for what was next. But it was over. Said and yet to be done, if ever. After all, we were kids on a beach at night, with cheap wine.

The day after our beach party, Jimmy and I ended up in jail with Dennis. We were driving along the sandy beach in Dennis's little Austin Healy, Laura in the front passenger seat and Jimmy and I scrunched into the back. A cop stopped us and said Jimmy and I were "dangerously out of the car." We got out of the car until the officer left, then hopped back in to ride home. The same cop stopped us on the street. He was pretty mad. Jimmy and I were charged with riding on the exterior of a car, Dennis charged for allowing it, and Laura released.

Scared to death despite the trivial nature of our "crime," Dennis and I opened up, telling each other our life stories as we sat on a hard bench in a holding room, waiting to be thrown into jail cells. I told him about my parents' deaths factoring into my marrying too soon. I wanted to learn more and to write journalistic articles—or maybe just song lyrics. Dennis wanted to travel the world. Yes, our different aspirations might one day cross. We covered the basics of our young, maturing lives before being led to our separate jail cells because our $30 bail money, which would settle the case, would not post until morning.

In the next months, I got to know Dennis better. A dear friendship developed before my extended Florida spring break grew old. Those "jobs galore" Paul had boasted of primarily consisted of transient positions.

My permanent return to New Jersey coincided closely with the Davern family's return. I moved into a rented apartment with my son, about a mile away from the Daverns' new apartment in Burlington Township, and Dennis and I saw each other nightly. We considered becoming romantically involved but we wanted an honest relationship without the strains of romance. A family attachment existed that we were smart enough to leave alone, and to keep. We bonded with a pact to always be there for one another. Friends often become mere memories—but Dennis and I vowed to never let that happen.

Dennis introduced me to his friend George Rulli, who had just left the Navy. George and I hit it off romantically, and we married. We named our first son Matthew, and Dennis considered it a tribute to his brother lost to war. Dennis surprised us with a box full of gifts for Matt and showed the same generosity when our daughter, Jeannine, was born two years later. Among Dennis's gifts was something for me—an ocean-blue, tri-folded, heavy plastic notebook with pockets inside; a white dove, taking flight, was pictured on the cover.

George established a construction business, and I waitressed evenings until my kids started school, then secured the job I had coveted. When hired by a Greater Delaware Valley newspaper corporation, I learned every aspect of the business while freelance writing for the editorial department. I loved my multifaceted job.

Dennis worked for a lithographer while attending graphics arts school, and he printed his poetry as a lithography assignment. Nearly every weekend, George and I socialized with Dennis, fun get-togethers with lots of laughter. George and I shared a special bond with him because he was our one friend who had not been acquired for either of us through our marriage. We shared Dennis equally and identified with him separately, for we each carried our own histories with him. Dennis was family, our best friend. I valued our friendship, and now, over a decade later, Dennis knew that I would never put a price on it.

I made a trip to my attic. When I called Dennis back, I told him, "I found your poetry booklet. Listen to this part of a poem you once wrote...*Stars will find their faces In the sea, And the answer will shine down On you and me.* You probably meant sky stars, but it's eerie," I said. "I'm so partial to you, no one would believe me any more than they believe you if I take on this project."

"Not if, Marti. *When.* You wouldn't believe the extremes reporters go to. I'm close to saying 'Okay! You want the truth? Here it is!' But I can't risk that."

"I found the notebook you gave me when Matt was born too. I already put all my Natalie Wood information in it. I'm nervous, but want to help."

"Thank you," Dennis said, with relief.

"Is the truth really that bad?" I asked.

"It's bad, all right. I can take a lot, but not this. And neither can R.J. That's why he's going cold on me. I'm a reminder. Just months ago, we were still crying on each other's shoulder in his trailer on the *Hart* set. R.J. would tell others to not bother us in there. Now, it's me who knocks and is told to go away."

"I thought you and Robert Wagner were inseparable."

Dennis explained that for the first year after Natalie Wood's death, he and R.J. depended on each other for comfort and support. They drank scotch almost every night in R.J.'s den, never talking about *that night.* But, that night lingered, continually darkening, like a cloud collecting moisture—one bound to eventually pour down.

After Natalie died, Wagner lined up acting parts for Dennis and paid for his membership in the Screen Actors Guild. Acting provided a challenging diversion for Dennis. Although a peculiar thing for R.J.'s longtime, professional friends to witness, they saw firsthand how Dennis became R.J.'s lifeline, and vice versa. R.J. and Dennis ate together, drank together, drove to and from work together, and Dennis lived at R.J.'s house for months after Natalie died. For a few hours a night, Dennis would travel across town to visit his girlfriend.

The first time George and I saw Dennis after Natalie died was the first anniversary of her death. After eight years away in Los Angeles, Dennis visited for a Thanksgiving reunion with family in New Jersey. George and I were invited for Dennis's welcome home. Dennis and I had stayed in touch through the years, and a photo Dennis had sent me just three months before Natalie died was the mental image I carried of him. Nothing could have prepared me for the skeleton of a man I saw walk through the door that Thanksgiving Eve. Dennis, bone thin, looked like a lost soul. I told him he looked good but meant it only in the sense that I was happy to see him.

Dennis seemed on edge for the first two days of the visit, but by Saturday of the holiday weekend he loosened up and started calling old friends. For five days, George and I made the rounds with Dennis, visiting people. Seeing his friend Chuck Esser, who had become a homicide detective, proved the antidote to Dennis's gloom. The Denny we had known was back—at least for a few days—until he talked to Robert Wagner by phone.

When Dennis phoned R.J. a week into his trip, after R.J. had returned from Switzerland, R.J. offered Dennis extra money to prolong his New Jersey visit. Wagner had already paid for Dennis's trip and had given him a thousand-dollar check. Dennis stayed only two days after the phone call, insisting he had to get back to L.A. to be by Wagner's side.

Now, approaching the second anniversary of Natalie's death, R.J. was drawing away, leaving Dennis bewildered and hurt.

"Sometimes," I told Dennis, "a tragedy draws people closer at first, then it changes. Like with your parents, after losing a child, they became reminders to each other of the pain."

"Exactly. I'm a constant reminder," Dennis said, "but R.J. has no reason to doubt me. I've been dodging reporters for two years. They've tried to dupe me, seduce me, and buy me. I never breathed a word. Just a month ago, some distinguished-looking guy with an English accent approached me as I worked on *Splendour*. He said he wanted to buy it. What happened next was incredible."

Wagner, instead of procuring a selling agent, had agreed to let Dennis try to sell *Splendour*. The yacht had been on the market with a price tag of $350,000. Dennis stood to receive a 10 percent commission upon her sale. There was little interest in *Splendour*, however, other than from curiosity seekers and reporters, so Dennis was cautious with prospective buyers.

The interested buyer introduced himself as Peter Williams, a representative of an East Coast–based whale-watch operation that needed a West Coast fisherman's yacht. Dennis became suspicious when Peter Williams's first request was for inside pictures of the yacht. Dennis wouldn't allow it. Williams took Dennis to lunch and covered the tab, which Dennis, as the selling agent, would normally have incurred, yet Williams was quite convincing as the "whale-watch" prospect. Over several weeks, Peter Williams treated Dennis to more lunches, dinners, and nights on the town. One afternoon, at the Red Onion restaurant, a woman named Elizabeth joined Dennis and Peter for lunch. Blonde and leggy, Elizabeth flirted with Dennis. Williams made an excuse to leave, and Elizabeth asked Dennis to take her to see *Splendour*. She, too, wanted "business-related" photographs of *Splendour's* interior. Dennis refused, but Elizabeth invited him back to her apartment for dinner.

"We were on the sofa in her apartment," Dennis recounted, "and she put her hand inside my shirt. She suggested we go skinny dipping at the boat, but I didn't answer. Then she kissed me. I didn't kiss back. She started to take off her clothes, so I took off mine. We went at it."

"Geez, Denny, did you feel vindicated?" I asked.

"No, there was nothing pleasant about it at all. I felt really disgusted. When it was over, I said, 'So put that in your newspaper, Elizabeth.' She says, 'You're pretty smart,' like she tossed me some kind of compliment. So, I said, 'Nah, you're pretty stupid, Elizabeth. Thanks for dinner and dessert.' Then I walked out."

"Did you see her again?"

"I knocked on her door two days later, and no one lived there. They had rented and furnished her an apartment just to get to me. I found out later that Williams is from the *National Enquirer*. I was so upset that I called my mother and asked her to keep a record of this kind of harassment. I'm getting scared. My mom was shocked. She totally thinks Natalie's death was an accident."

"Did you tell R.J. about this?"

"Yeah. I wanted to find out if there was any legal recourse. R.J.'s response was typical. He asked me, 'Well, did you fuck her?' I told him I did, and he said, 'Then let that be revenge enough.'"

"I can't believe they went through all that just to get pictures of *Splendour*," I commented.

"Marti, they're after me all the time. One night, at the docks, a reporter opened a briefcase filled with cash. It had to be over fifty thousand. It was mine if I opened my mouth. I just walked away."

"Well, how do they know there's anything more?"

"We'll get into details another night."

It was like swallowing bullets, but I stifled my questions. "Den, where are you going to live after *Splendour* is gone?"

"I can't even think about that. I'll miss this boat almost as much as I miss Natalie."

* * *

Dennis's *Splendour* years carried an endearing history. Although Dennis was not destined to stardom, as his mother had predicted, he would eventually be surrounded by the best of them—Sir Laurence Olivier, Sean Connery, David Niven, and Sidney Poitier are just a few of those whose safety Dennis would one day guard on intimate cruises aboard the Wagners' yacht.

The exciting journey began in 1974 when Dennis again left New Jersey, Florida-bound for Fort Lauderdale, accompanied by his girlfriend, Debby Lister. With little money to tide them over, Dennis and Debby's priority was employment. Dennis's love for water and boats drew him to the local marinas. One morning, after filling out a job application, Dennis met Phil Bloom, a charismatic, energetic entrepreneur who bought yachts at East Coast market prices, refurbished them, and then sold them at profitable West Coast value. Between the purchase and sale, hard labor was required, but the promise of a thrilling cruise from the Atlantic Ocean to the Pacific Ocean compensated. Phil had just purchased a sixty-foot sport fisherman yacht named *Dizzy Izzy* and hired Dennis and Debby to work on it.

Then, as unmerciful as fate can be when life is on an upswing, Debby received word that her brother had died. Dennis accompanied his grief-stricken girlfriend to New Jersey, but when it was time to return to Florida, Dennis and Debby amicably parted ways.

Phil was pleased when Dennis returned. "I was afraid you might be another marina drifter," he told Dennis. "But I can tell you enjoy yourself even when the work is hard."

Phil hired Helen Ludy, a perky blonde in her forties, as cook/general assistant, and Bill Jones, another seadog, as engineer. Dennis was half the age of his fellow crew members, but they all got along fabulously.

Without an inkling of the pleasures and pain toward which *Dizzy* carried him, Dennis relished the cruise, one day at a time, and he learned what a strong boat *Dizzy* was after experiencing a horrible storm that almost capsized the boat not long into the trip.

Dennis marveled at the Panama Canal, but noted Costa Rica as his favorite stop and vowed to return one day. He was full of hope and anticipation when they first docked in San Diego. Bill and Helen ended their tour of duty and left with Phil, who had two weeks of business in Los Angeles. Dennis, for his first stint in charge, alone with *Dizzy Izzy*, enjoyed himself while he could.

When Phil returned to take the yacht up the coast, he caught Dennis in the midst of a small party on board—Dennis with a blonde dancer he had met at the Alley Cat. Phil had given strict instructions to allow no one on board. To Dennis's great relief, Phil let it slide. The next morning, Phil and Dennis cruised *Dizzy* to her destination, Marina del Rey—the world's largest man-made harbor. As Dennis saw the thousands of sparkling yachts and boats resting in their slips, he hoped to stick around for a long time, possibly a lifetime, if all went his way.

They docked at Dolphin Marina. It was mid-March; the coast-to-coast trip had taken over after two and a half exciting, unforgettable months. With Phil's mission completed, he introduced Dennis to Bob Rose, whose yacht, *Ramblin' Rose*, was docked a few slips away from *Dizzy Izzy*. Bob Rose offered Dennis a cabin aboard *Ramblin' Rose*, and Dennis gratefully accepted. Since there was work yet needed on *Dizzy Izzy* in preparation for her sale Dennis still had a job. Phil changed *Dizzy's* name, for show rather than for legalities, to *Challenger*, to enhance her salability. Dennis painted the new name on the back of the boat.

Dennis lived aboard *Ramblin' Rose* and took odd jobs around the marina. On Dennis's twenty-seventh birthday, September 25, 1975, Phil sold *Challenger*, nee *Dizzy Izzy*, to Robert Wagner and Natalie Wood. A notice of the sale was posted at the docks and published in local newspapers.

"They were married on my yacht a few years ago," Bob Rose told Dennis. "It was their second marriage to each other. The Wagners have been yacht-hunting for some time now, driving the local yacht brokers crazy, looking for the perfect boat. Now that they've found it, I'm sure they'll be spending a lot of time around here. You'll meet them."

Dennis felt proud that *Dizzy Izzy* was the perfect yacht for the Wagners. So much of his effort and skill had helped to make the boat desirable.

When Bob Rose moved *Ramblin' Rose* to a new marina in October, he invited Dennis to go along, but Dennis chose to stay at Dolphin Marina. Craig Cosentino offered Dennis his docked, floating dome for a mere slip fee, and Dennis accepted. *Home* magazine of the *Los Angeles Times* published a feature on the unique dome boat, and Dennis now lived aboard the most talked about boat at the marina.

Ken Adams, skipper of Robert Wagner and Natalie Wood's yacht, newly named *Splendour*, hired Dennis because of Dennis's familiarity with the boat, so Dennis continued to work on the yacht that had carried him to California. As Dennis painted *Splendour's* deck one late morning, he was startled by a man's voice from behind.

"Hello, how's it going today?"

Dennis turned around, and there they stood: Robert Wagner and Natalie Wood.

"Hello," Dennis responded. "I'm Denny Davern. Your skipper, Ken, hired me to work on *Dizzy*...uh, *Challenger*, or," he corrected, "now, *Splendour*."

Everyone smiled.

"I'm Robert Wagner, and this is my wife, Natalie Wood. It's good to meet you."

Dennis shook hands with each. "It's good to meet you too," he said.

Robert Wagner and Natalie Wood were a stunning couple, standing there, dressed casually in their slacks and pullover tops.

"Why did you call the yacht *Dizzy*? Did you work on it before?" Robert Wagner asked.

"I've been working on this yacht since last year," Dennis said proudly. "I'm one of the crew members who cruised *Dizzy Izzy* from the east. The name changed to *Challenger* for market."

"How'd she fare, cruising that long a distance?" Robert Wagner asked.

"She's a fine boat, Mr. Wagner. Through sun or squall."

"Will Ken have you paint our new name on the back of the yacht?" Natalie asked Dennis.

"Yes, Mrs. Wagner. Ken said he had to talk to you about that. When I have the design, I'll start."

"If you'll be here this afternoon, I'll go over the design with you," Natalie said.

"That's fine with me. I'll find Ken and let him know."

"Where is Ken?" she asked.

"Around the marina somewhere. I believe he's preparing for a charter. I'll find him."

"There's no need for that, Denny," Natalie said. "I can surely go over details with you if he's unavailable. After all, you're here and he's not."

Dennis detected her irritated tone but knew it was not directed at him.

"Is your real name Dennis?" Natalie asked. "Would you mind if I call you Dennis?"

"Not at all," answered Dennis.

"Dennis, my favorite color is pelican blue, but I would have to see the color before approving it. We're off for lunch now, but we'll return in a few hours. Would it be possible to find pelican blue paint in the meantime?"

"No problem."

"Thank you, Dennis," she said. "Dennis DaVern," she repeated, liking the sound of his name and placing the accent on the last syllable of his last name.

Dennis liked that Natalie wanted to use his formal name, and he liked the way she pronounced it. Anything altered by Natalie Wood was okay by him, so he immediately adopted the new version. The Wagners strolled down the dock, and Dennis hurried off to the paint store. To his great relief, a color he had never heard of—pelican blue—was available.

When the Wagners returned later that afternoon, Natalie sat with Dennis at the galley table and sketched her vision for *Splendour's* name design.

Dennis had seen Natalie Wood on television and in movies but never realized how petite she actually was. Her small frame and delicate features were the ultimate in femininity. Her voice was soothing. Natalie was a remarkably stunning woman.

"Let me show you the paint, Mrs. Wagner," Dennis said, as he pried off the lid of the paint can.

"Oh, that's it. That's the perfect color, Dennis!" she exclaimed. Her big, deep brown, beautiful eyes looked into his. "I want to thank you, Dennis, for your efficiency. I admire efficiency." Her smile already melted him.

Dennis wondered if Natalie was still annoyed with Ken and felt a stab of guilt for having pleased her. He reasoned, however, he had little time left with the yacht he had come to love, so he would take advantage of every opportunity to still work on the boat.

Over the next few weeks, the Wagners frequently visited *Splendour*, always to find Dennis lovingly tending her. Ken Adams was rarely around. When Robert Wagner offered Dennis the job of *Splendour* captain, Dennis expressed his concern over replacing Ken. The Wagners convinced him that he had earned the position. Dennis proudly, happily accepted.

Chapter 4

Dennis and I were on the phone every night, but his emotional state was so fragile that I tiptoed through conversations.

Nearly two years had passed since Natalie's death, ordinarily enough time for the grieving process to have reached the final stage of acceptance. Dennis had always been a stable and reasonable man, able to handle life's crises. When his brother was killed in Vietnam, Dennis mourned him, but he was not rendered dysfunctional and self-destructive by it. Now he remained on the desperate edge of despair, unable to let go of his heavy grief for, technically, an employer—it was plain abnormal.

Although the truth existed in the form of a tortured, drunken Dennis Davern, I poured through articles, old and new: the media was not leaving this story alone. The articles, both speculative and official, doubly fueled my despair. A woman was dead, under no less perplexing circumstances than if she had fallen from an airplane. There had to be an explanation.

Unprepared, with no resources, no knowledge of where or to whom to turn, I stuck to basic common sense while analyzing the rumors and theories thus far presented. No doubt, I would hear more, because speculation was all that existed apart from a reluctant skipper's hints.

Scenario One: Robert Wagner was furious because Natalie had left the yacht with Christopher Walken the night before she died and had slept with Walken in a motel. The Wagners fought about it the next night, leading to Natalie's disappearance.

Common Sense: Not likely. On a four-member cruise, how could two people disappear for the night without an explanation? If Natalie had spent Friday night on the island with Walken, R.J. would not have waited until the next night to object.

Scenario Two: A distraught and drunken Natalie, torn between her husband and her costar, Christopher Walken, committed suicide.

Common Sense: Natalie had a long history of psychoanalysis, but in 1981, she had everything to live for: fame and fortune, a lifestyle unrestrained by financial concerns or limited choices, a strong marriage, and ageless beauty combined with the wisdom of maturity. She had yet to complete the shooting of what she considered her comeback film, *Brainstorm*, and she had been cast for the lead in her stage debut of *Anastasia*. Above all, Natalie Wood now had her daughters. She would never, ever have taken her life from her young daughters.

Scenario Three: Robert Wagner and Stefanie Powers, married as characters on their hit show *Hart to Hart*, fell in love and plotted to kill their respective real-life mates so that they could be together.

Common Sense: Absurd. The two unnatural deaths, occurring so close in time, may vie for one of Hollywood's strangest coincidences, but this kind of innuendo was obviously nothing more than pure blather.

Scenario Four: The "banging dinghy" theory Robert Wagner mentioned, then put forth by coroner Thomas Noguchi and his assistant, Paul Miller. Miller wrote an advisory report on Natalie's death, as he had been moored near *Splendour* the night she died. Noguchi's report speculated that Natalie had fallen into the water while trying to secure the dinghy, which may have been banging on *Splendour's* hull and annoying her. He suggested that Natalie had clung for hours to the dinghy and had tried repeatedly to climb into it before succumbing to hypothermia. Noguchi believed that Natalie would have had to propel the dinghy, given the tides and wind, for it to have reached its final destination. Alleged fingernail scratches on the dinghy's rubber sides supposedly supported the theory.

Contradicting his initial report, Noguchi used Miller's ideas for his pending book, *Coroner*, already being promoted in the tabloids. Noguchi claimed that algae on *Splendour's* swim step was undisturbed, indicating that Natalie perhaps had tried to *board* the dinghy, it slipped away, and she drifted with the float-away dinghy rather than try to make it back to the boat because the saturated weight of her jacket started to drag her down. Trying to mount the dinghy supposedly accounts for the bruises on her arms and legs.

Common Sense: This banging dinghy theory came to focus only after the media questioned Natalie's bedtime attire. Most importantly: How could Natalie's wool socks possibly have remained on her feet as she desperately kicked over a mile through the water?

Nothing I had read thus far had even raised a question about Natalie's socks. I couldn't imagine that such a glaring flaw had not occurred to Noguchi or to anyone—professionals whose careers centered on searching for and analyzing the subtlest details of a case. The undisturbed algae made no sense in relation to

Noguchi's theories of whether Natalie had attempted to board the dinghy or to secure it. *Perhaps Natalie had attempted neither.*

Because nothing else clicked, I kept returning to the coroner's retracted information about a fight. I called Dennis. "Did Natalie and Chris Walken spend the night alone on the island?"

Silence.

"Okay, explain the coroner's undisturbed algae discovery."

"Marti, we cruised to Catalina. The force of the water at the stern would have cleaned that swim step like a car through a carwash. Algae doesn't collect on the swim step. We boarded the dinghy several times that day and night. If algae existed, wouldn't it have been disturbed when we returned from the restaurant?"

"What about the argument the coroner mentioned?"

"We—R.J., me, and Christopher—all said we didn't know what happened to Natalie. Someone like R.J., with his status and power, didn't have to answer hard questions, and by association, neither did I. There was no reason for authorities to not believe us. I thought I'd be in the hot seat for weeks, and I probably would have talked. But that hot seat never even got warm. They believed us! But, of course, there was trouble that night."

"Did you lie about who Natalie slept with in Avalon? The room clerk said he smelled pot when he went to the room to fix a heater," I mentioned.

"Just more bullshit, Marti. Natalie didn't smoke pot that night. I know, because it was *me* she spent the night with."

"Oh, my God, Denny!" The obvious thought went through my mind, and I blurted out, "Were you two having an affair? Were you in love with her?"

"It wasn't like that at all. The tension was so bad that night that Natalie couldn't stand to stay on the boat. We left together and went to the motel. I went to watch over her. I slept in the same bed with her, but we didn't have sex. And, of course, I loved her, but I wasn't in love with her. She was my friend."

"So, the investigators knew you spent the night with her and didn't think anything of it?"

"They accepted the truth that I was with her in a bodyguard capacity. What gets me is that they didn't pursue *why* she left *Splendour* that night. R.J. lied and said that the water was rough, and Natalie was feeling sick, so the words 'rough seas' came out of that fib."

"I read about an 'animated conversation' between Wagner and Walken relating to both nights, Den."

"The animated conversation thing was reported as a political argument that annoyed Natalie, and then became some bullshit about Walken defending Natalie when R.J. complained about her being away from home too much. Maybe a few words about Natalie's work schedule were mentioned, but the truth is, R.J. wanted to move the boat Friday night to go over to the Isthmus—over ten miles away in the pitch black night—and Natalie wouldn't hear of it. We didn't get there until Saturday, and I wish we'd never gone at all."

"Why did Wagner want to move the boat Friday night?"

"Who the hell knows? I think he wanted to get away from having to have breakfast in Avalon the next morning. He didn't like hanging with Walken and Natalie in public. He was the third wheel."

"So, why not just move the boat early, before Natalie woke up?"

"That's what Natalie wanted to know. She couldn't understand—neither could I, and I don't think I ever saw that kind of look on her face. She was completely flabbergasted. It was about ten-thirty that Friday night, and R.J. was running around like a madman—up to the wheelhouse, gunning the engine, back down to the deck, messing with the rigging, you name it. His face was so red, it looked like a tomato. Natalie was in her stateroom, packing a bag. She was furious and embarrassed. It was just crazy."

"Where was Walken?"

"In his room. He went to bed before all this, but I figured he heard the arguing. I went to ask Chris to interfere, and he told me to never get involved in the middle of a married couple's argument. But I couldn't let R.J. move the boat at night. It wasn't safe. I kept saying, 'Come on, Chief, let's wait until morning, let's just go to bed now,' but he wouldn't budge. He was drunk and mad."

"And the officials bought the rough seas explanation? Even with a dead Natalie Wood come Sunday morning?"

"What else could they do?"

"Well, if they knew she had left the boat with you Friday night, what made them think she would try to leave alone on Saturday night—wearing only a nightgown?"

"Two plus two. It could have been that easy. Instead, two plus two equaled a bullshit story about a banging dinghy. I tied the lines tight that night—the dinghy wasn't banging. We were down for the night."

"Unbelievable," I mumbled. Then I angrily went off. "Den, this is an atrocious insult to Natalie Wood that her death was so quickly dismissed. She's looking like the crazy one. I know you feel loyalty to Wagner, but, please, what about your loyalty to Natalie?"

"I identified her."

"Then clarify—justify—her death, Den!"

I felt a stab of guilt for putting Dennis under fire, but who else would ever be accountable for truth? Robert Wagner? What an everything-to-lose, nothing-to-gain situation he had on his hands. His legal staff fronted the questions, and worse yet, his boat captain assumed the gruesome task of identifying his wife's body. The story ended as well as he could have expected as far as blame went. He wasn't about to come clean with incriminating truth.

Christopher Walken? He had bowed away quietly, hoping to leave the incomprehensible mess behind him. Walken, already a best supporting actor Academy Award winner for his role in *The Deer Hunter* and on the brink of a promising film career, did not want his career marred by a weekend he only wanted to forget. This was not *his* tragedy.

The coroner? The final, official word on Natalie Wood's death came from Dr. Noguchi, who, after being fired, retracted information and tucked away—or never started—a psychological report. He was under heavy fire for having leaked honest information in the first place. Questioning discrepancies or further discussing the tragedy was not in his best interest.

The public? People wondered: Is there more to Natalie Wood's death? Answering that question, however, is the responsibility of law-enforcement officials, who are paid by a public that deserves truth and justice without having to raise a collective demand for it. In this case, such a demand might have put some pressure on authorities, but there was no public outcry for justice.

The media? The tabloids continued to eat up the Natalie Wood mystery, looking for scandal with every bite. Details were too scarce, however, to enable reports to include anything beyond speculation and innuendo. Credible publications and newspapers were virtually forced, by mere lack of evidence, to leave the story alone.

The investigators? The case was closed before the right questions were even framed, let alone asked or answered. But authorities need to start with facts. Apparently, they believed the three *Splendour* weekend survivors, all of whom agreed it had been a pleasant weekend. When attorneys got involved, it was pretty much a wrap-up. Authorities do not like to reopen cases, especially high-profile cases that can cause embarrassment.

Who, then, would come forward?

It all came down to Dennis Davern.

Chapter 5

No matter how unfair or unbalanced the burden, it appeared that Dennis Davern was left holding the proverbial bag. Dennis stood alone as the sole participant, the only motivated conscience, who might ever offer hope to solving the mystery surrounding Natalie Wood's death.

Dennis, torn between his loyalty to Robert Wagner, who was alive and present in his life, and to Natalie, who haunted his dreams with a call for justice, searched for the courage to release his secret. Although I had challenged Dennis's loyalty to Natalie, she was not alive to nurture it. The likelihood of Natalie's memory rivaling the constant reality of Robert Wagner's powerful hold over him was now Dennis's inner, day-to-day struggle.

Dennis agonized over the pain his confession would invoke for Natalie's daughters. Natalie had wanted her girls to live normal childhoods and did not want them raised at the studios as she had been. She wanted her daughters to be happy. Dennis could give Natalie that by remaining silent. Deep down, Dennis wanted to tell his secret, but he continued to let it fester inside of him.

Every life holds value, and to witness the slow deterioration of my friend's quality of life disturbed me. Dennis had been an average if somewhat cavalier guy, prone to average faults but certainly not deserving of the tragedy he found himself in the midst of. In the public eye, he was no match for Wagner. But Dennis's burden was a heavy one, so he unloaded part of it on me. It felt like lugging cement around. I called him and said, "Den, I'm not going to push it. I know it's hard for you, and I'll help you through it, book or no book."

A month later, in October, he called, frantic.

"Marti," he explained, "I promised Randy I'd be his deckhand for a fishing charter tomorrow. Randy captains a yacht for John Davidson—the host of the show *Real People*. We'll be cruising to White's Cove at Catalina, and I can't do it. And I promised—"

"Well, White's Cove is a different part of the island, right?"

"I can't even look out toward the island. Will you call Randy for me?"

Dennis's request only proved his desperation. I suggested that he call Randy and be truthful that it's too soon to return to the island.

The island's magic was gone. Catalina was now synonymous with Natalie Wood's death—reduced to a ghost island for Dennis. Catalina's beauty, with its scenic coves and jutting cliffs, and Avalon's blend of fine restaurants and charming village stores had once wrapped up entertaining afternoons for the Wagners and their guests. It provided a haven for the Wagners, a serene and beautiful setting close enough to get to on a whim—twenty-two miles from Marina del Rey—yet a world away from the hustle-bustle of Hollywood.

The small island is a mere twenty-one miles long and less than a mile wide at its narrowest point, the Isthmus; its elevation varies from sea level to 2,000 feet. The island cost George Shatto and Charles Sumner $200,000 in 1887. Hoping to attract visitors from the mainland, they laid out the site for the City of Avalon. By 1919, however, Shatto and Sumner had lost their majority interest to William Wrigley Jr., who improved roads and water systems, and in 1928 created the world-famous Casino at Avalon—which to this day offers no gambling—and the Bird Park as tourist attractions. After Wrigley's death, his son Philip placed Catalina in a conservatory to protect its wildlife and beauty forever.

During World War II, the island became part of the war effort and was restricted to the public. At the war's conclusion, moorings were installed in a number of coves to encourage boat owners to use the harbors and island facilities. One of the developments was the town of Two Harbors, at the Isthmus, approximately ten miles west of Avalon, on the same side of the island where *Splendour* moored the night Natalie drowned. The two towns, Avalon and Two Harbors, remain the only towns on the island, with 95 percent of Catalina's approximate three thousand residents living in Avalon.

Two Harbors was used as the setting for Director Frank Lloyd's 1935 version of *Mutiny on the Bounty*, starring Charles Laughton. The palm trees, planted to enrich the film's authenticity, still wave in the breeze, inviting boaters to the tropical atmosphere of the small, rustic village.

Two Harbors consists of a general store, a snack bar, a dive shop, restrooms and showers, and administrative offices for the company controlling the business ventures at the west end of the island. Its only restaurant is Doug's Harbor Reef, where Natalie Wood ate her last meal. Close to the water is a building that houses a decompression chamber for divers, where Natalie Wood's body was placed for Dennis to identify her.

Natalie had always loved to visit Avalon's curio shops, jewelry stores, and boutiques and to lazily stroll through the colorful, enchanting streets. The El Galleon restaurant was her choice spot—a special restaurant for her and R.J., as they had visited it on each of their two honeymoons.

Although Dennis now avoided Catalina, from the docks at Marina del Rey he could see the distant, misty mound of the island.

Dennis's state of mind began to take a toll on me. Normally a relaxed person, I began to suffer anxiety attacks, one night so badly I was hospitalized. Natalie's death cried out for an answer, and finding that answer had become not just a passion but an overwhelming responsibility for me.

I mentally visualized her death even though I knew only the barest details of her final moments. I didn't need a vivid imagination to understand the darkness and fear of drowning. The summer before Natalie died, I experienced a near drowning during a tubing trip with friends on the Delaware River, which flows with strong currents, undertow, and rapids along the entire winding New Jersey–Pennsylvania border. A thermal lunch container, tied to my tube, had snagged on a rock after I went over an eight-foot drop on Windfall Dam, roaring that day from a recent, heavy rainfall. The white water had turned to whirlpools, and I was stuck in the middle of a forceful one. Water gushed down my throat, choking me, reaching my lungs, and I started to black out. I realized I was probably going to die, and my last thought, as darkness closed in, was *drowning's not that bad*. The words were literal: blacking out had not been physically painful. Being in death's grip, however, was terrifying. My twelve-year old, Billy, somehow yanked me out of the whirlpool and rescued me.

I sometimes obsessed over what Natalie's last thought had been. She might have been conscious, after all. A new report surfaced, via tabloid, offering another reason Noguchi may have changed his theory. Investment banker Marilyn Wayne, who was moored near *Splendour* the night Natalie died, claimed to have heard a woman's cry for help around eleven o'clock. Wayne said she heard pleas for help and then heard a man's voice saying something to effect of "Hold on, I'll get you." Sounds from a nearby party were reported, and after hearing about Natalie's death the next morning, Wayne claimed that it was probably Natalie she had heard. Wayne's story confused me all the more.

I asked Dennis about Marilyn Wayne.

"I don't know. Wagner says she's someone who wants her name in the paper," he said.

"The coroner believes her, Den, but according to what's published, the lead detective, Rasure, dismisses her the same way Wagner does. Why wouldn't he want to talk to her?" Then I dropped it. "So, how did it go with Randy?"

"He completely understood. He offered me a bay fishing charter instead."

"Good. Did you do a lot of fishing with R.J.?"

"He loved fishing and fished every chance he had. It was his favorite pastime." Dennis's voice picked up a positive tone. "Natalie usually stayed in her perch when R.J. fished. She always teased him when he caught nothing. And she couldn't understand why he loved fishing, so one day he told her not to knock it until she tried it. So she tried it. R.J. got a pole ready, and she caught one—a nice one—right away. It wasn't real big, but to her, it was the biggest fish that ever swam the Pacific," Dennis laughed. "She bragged all day and into the next and made me use two rolls of film on that fish.

"Some of R.J.'s friends had those eighty-foot or bigger sport fisherman boats, but R.J. knew that *Splendour* was the perfect size for him. He tried to get more involved in boating, like when he bought that five-thousand-dollar sonar we never used..." Dennis broke off, laughing, before continuing. "The sonar was supposed to be used for fishing. You could get a reading up to hundreds of feet away, and you could set it on different depths, depending on what kind of fish you were hunting. It's attached to the bottom of the boat and scans underwater, like a camera, and images are transferred to a screen at the control panel in the wheelhouse. But the only thing we ever used it for was to look for the pilings when we pulled into the docks. The pilings are planted in the ground and marked underwater, dock A, dock B, dock C, and so forth. That expensive piece of equipment was a joke, and we laughed our asses off, using it to find our dock listing underwater, that we could see right in front of us."

"You were really close to them, weren't you, Den?"

"Yes. And they liked me. When they would be away at various times, I'd even get letters from R.J. telling me that Natalie and the girls say 'hi' and that they all can't wait to get back to the boat. They would actually miss me! I can't believe it ended this way. If you could have seen them together. It was during the fishing trips that R.J. and I really got to know and like one another. I'll never forget the first time I took him out by himself. It was the first time I was invited to their house too. Natalie was into home decorating then—her home was awesome."

* * *

R.J. and Dennis stayed in the wheelhouse, cruising the ocean. R.J., in his glory, said, "I love this boat. It's perfect."

When Dennis replied, "You're lucky to have her, Mr. Wagner," R.J. asked Dennis to call him R.J., "like my other friends do."

The restrictions of their employer–employee relationship receded as smoothly as the rising mist from the ocean water that morning. Their mutual interest in and enjoyment of *Splendour* carried them past the early barriers usually encountered by developing friendships.

Dennis would never have met Robert Wagner if not for *Splendour*, and their friendship now grew beyond the boat. Perhaps it was the rarity of sharing solitude—a need so exclusive and personal—without being infringed upon by each other. Perhaps it was the understanding that they each derived the same replenishment of spirit from the power and beauty of the sea. Whatever inspired the friendship, it was palpable, and Dennis was grateful for it.

The pleasurable fishing cruise ended late afternoon with R.J. inviting Dennis to dinner at his home. Dennis's old Volkswagen van followed R.J.'s sparkling Mercedes to Canon Drive, a Beverly Hills street lined with majestic trees hovering over exquisite homes, all cushioned by lavish landscaping and sculptured hedges. Expensive, mirror-polished automobiles lined the brick and cobblestone driveways. Dennis saw no people, though, and thought the absence of life eerie and sad. This wasn't your average neighborhood with people bustling about. When this elite class of people ventured out, it was usually behind the tinted windows of custom automobiles or chauffeured limousines.

Dennis followed R.J. through wrought iron gates that led up the lamppost-lined circular driveway to the Wagner's front door. Brightly colored flowers smothered the inviting front porch of the huge, colonial/cape house.

The foyer was as large as a typical living room. In the living room, R.J. introduced Dennis to Willie Mae Worthen, the housekeeper who served as Natasha's and Courtney's nanny. Dennis liked Willie Mae's smile. Dozens of flowered and checkered throw pillows swallowed the elegant, French furniture. Deep-colored oil paintings contrasted perfectly with the overall pastel theme. The glistening oak bar, twelve feet long, situated in an alcove between the living room and den, offered a bowl of mixed nuts in front of every other leather-backed barstool.

Natalie walked into the room. "Hi, Dennis," she cheerfully greeted him. "Nice to see you. What can I get you?"

Dennis took a seat at the bar and asked for a Coke. He thought he may have overdone it when he said for the fourth time, "I've never seen a home as beautiful as this," but Natalie loved his compliments.

"I help a lot of my friends decorate their homes," she told him, "And I love when someone appreciates my efforts." She smiled the most beautiful smile.

The den, behind the barstools, featured a red and blue Scottish plaid sofa and a round, dark wood country table with captain's chairs. Dark wood trim surrounded the den's red used-brick fireplace, and the jungle of plants and potted trees warmed the atmosphere. So, far, Dennis had spotted three fireplaces.

Dennis said it again, "Mrs. Wagner, your home is beautiful."

Natalie smiled and said, "Dennis, please call me Natalie, or Nat, or anything but Mrs. Wagner. We're friends, and friends don't need formalities."

"Okay, Natalie it is." He chose her full name because she had preferred his when they had met.

Proudly, Natalie led Dennis up the stairway, eager to show her home to new and appreciative eyes. Dennis mused over the timing that, on this same day, both R.J. and Natalie had removed the social barrier. Up the staircase, Dennis walked on air. The spacious master bedroom, done in blue floral prints and white lace, contained a fireplace of white marble. At the foot of the bed, a pillow-covered sofa and two white-wicker chairs surrounded a glass coffee table, topped by dozens of brass-framed family photographs. An area near the windows facing Canon Drive served as Natalie's white-wicker bedroom office.

The tour through the second level revealed no exception to Natalie's preference for blue until they reached Natasha's and Courtney's bedrooms. Courtney's pink brick fireplace had a mouth filled with a colorful menagerie of stuffed animals.

"I'm the stuffed animal nut, Dennis," Natalie admitted. "When I was growing up, I couldn't bear to go to sleep before holding actual conversations with my stuffed friends—I never felt alone because of them." She grinned and added, "Courtney loves hers too. Natasha and Courtney are staying with friends this weekend. You'll meet them soon."

Natasha's room, a mixture of green and pink, featured a canopy bed. The two girls shared a bathroom and a playroom, centrally located between their rooms. The toy-stocked playroom contained every child's delight.

Of the six bathrooms, Natalie's was most lavish, including a French bidet and a huge whirlpool tub. Downstairs, on the way to the kitchen, they passed through the dining room, done in darker blue walls, stark white woodwork, and crystal chandeliers.

With a room for every mood, the Wagner home was a creation of masculinity and femininity combined to perfection, a distinction Dennis saw evolving aboard *Splendour*. After the tour, Dennis and Natalie joined R.J. in the kitchen. Willie Mae dressed a green salad, then excused herself and went to her quarters, a room off the kitchen. The table was set for three.

When Dennis commented on how much he liked the big brick country kitchen that featured an eight-burner island gas range, Natalie assured him, "You can cook up a storm there any time you'd like, Dennis."

His first meal with the Wagner's, he knew, would become a special memory. Dennis was overwhelmed that Natalie and R.J. had allowed him into their lives—their hearts. He cleaned his plate. It was not the beef, potatoes, and salad he so heartily consumed— it was the friendship. For as long as R.J. and Natalie would serve it, he would happily and gratefully devour it.

Chapter 6

During most phone conversations about Dennis's tenure as *Splendour* captain, I at first couldn't ask enough about his famous employers. What do they drive? *Mercedes. His and hers.* How do they get along? *Great.* Do you visit their house? *All the time.* Are their kids spoiled? *Of course, but sweet.* Are they like regular people? *Yes, but rich and famous.* Do they have pets? *Lots. Natalie loves pets.* What do you do on cruises? *Hang out.* What's their favorite ice cream? *Häagen Dazs, any flavor, always on board.*

Dennis suggested I visit his mother to borrow the volumes of Wood/Wagner articles and photographs she had amassed. Ruth Davern's pride in her son being a yacht captain was heightened by the world fame of his employers, and she had admired Natalie and R.J. long before meeting and socializing with them on her vacations to visit Dennis in California. Ruth unequivocally adored the Wagners. Her deep concern over my intention was obvious as I stood in her cozy living room, waiting for her to hand over her cherished collection.

"R.J. and Natalie were a special couple," Ruth told me. "Robert Wagner is the nicest man, most wonderful man. Please keep that in mind," she cautioned.

"I don't know him, Mrs. Davern," I answered, "but I trust your judgment."

Published information agreed with her. Almost everything I read about the Wagner family proved complimentary—especially since their second marriage. The more I read, the less I comprehended November 29, 1981. They were billed as *the* Hollywood couple. They had it all. But I reminded myself that media viewpoints can derive from carefully planned and selected interviews. I wanted behind-the-scenes information that I wasn't going to find in magazine articles.

I called Dennis. "Everything I've read confirms Natalie and R.J. as the toast of the town. Denny, what do you think happened to them? If theirs was such a good marriage, how could one episode end so tragically?"

"Their second marriage was good, but there were some problems that carried over from their first marriage—one of them being R.J.'s drinking and jealousy. R.J. was afraid Natalie and Chris were having an affair. Before Natalie started filming *Brainstorm* she seemed restless. Maybe R.J. thought she was unhappy with him. She put a lot of unnecessary pressure on herself. After Courtney was born, she had been pretty inactive at the studios— by her standards, anyway. Then she suddenly had a new, handsome leading man—and younger—whose attention she loved, and R.J. was threatened."

"Was she a perfectionist?"

"With everything. Especially with her girls. Natalie wanted Courtney's diapers changed hourly, wet or not. Her kid never had a rash."

"That's a conscientious mother. Was she as compulsive about herself?"

"She was fanatical about keeping everything immaculate; her home, her kids, her boat, and she and everything around her was always sparkling."

"Who was her best friend?"

"Mart Crowley." He was once Natalie's secretary, and then he produced *Hart to Hart*. Years ago, Mart wrote *Boys in the Band*. Natalie loved Mart. He was pompous and had a holier-than-thou attitude sometimes, but she loved him."

"How did Mart react to her death?"

"Devastated like the rest of us. Mart wasn't around too much right after Natalie died, but then he started seeing R.J. on occasion. Natalie's sister Lana wanted to produce *Hart*, but R.J. insisted on Mart after he wrote some good episodes for it.

"R.J. always played Peter Allen's music when Mart was on board. He played the tape so much that I had to replace it because it wore out," Dennis laughed. "R.J. fished, jet-skied, dove, and liked the water. Natalie liked to socialize. They enjoyed the boat in their own ways.

"So many fans picture R.J. like his role in *Hart*, as Jonathan *Hart*, but R.J.'s private role is different. Everyone loves him, though. They loved Natalie, too, because she was a perfectionist. When you spent time with Natalie, she would make sure you had a perfect time. R.J. was more laid back. A boring cruise wouldn't bother R.J., but it would drive Natalie insane—if guests were on board. On private cruises, she loved to kick back, read scripts, and do her needlepoint."

"Would R.J. join in Natalie's fun?"

"Oh, yeah. He liked a good time too. We all drank, laughed, and had lots of fun. We drank a lot. Once, I told R.J. I might be drinking too much and needed to cut back. But he encouraged me to drink more. He said, 'Don't worry, Dennis, I'm sure you're overreacting.' When I said I was up to a fifth of scotch a day, he brushed it off and said that wasn't much at all. R.J. drank more than any of us. I cut back on the hard stuff and started having only a few beers on outings."

"Did Natalie drink a lot?"

"No, not really. She knew how to have a good time. She'd have a couple glasses of Pouilly-Fuissé or champagne, and she'd relax."

"Were there drugs on board much?"

"This is L.A. Some guests had pills, but no big thing. Pot was as common as cigarettes. Cocaine was big, too, but no one announced it. You could tell who used and who didn't. R.J. and Natalie didn't get into street stuff. R.J. wasn't into drugs at all. He just drank, but Natalie did use a lot of prescription pills."

"Did you interact a lot with the guests during cruises?"

"Sometimes. Once, during a cruise with some of their celebrity friends, someone brought up *Apocalypse Now*. When I mentioned my brother was killed in Vietnam, everyone turned to stone. No one had the slightest idea how to react to that. Later that night, Natalie took me aside and said she would like to talk to me about Matthew one day. She cared about people.

"I learned fast that actors live stressful lives. They work long hours and don't want to be bothered with heavy subjects during free time. They like to talk about their studio lives and the fun they have on the sets. They get a kick out of playing practical jokes on each other—some pretty outrageous things. Once, for R.J.'s birthday, Lee Majors hired an overweight hooker to show up at R.J.'s studio motor home. R.J. was mad, but never told Natalie about it."

"What were Natalie and R.J. passionate about?"

"Their marriage and their girls. They were the ideal family, but Natalie always loved her birth family too. Her father's death crushed her. He was a quiet man I saw only a few times. He drank a lot, and Natalie told me her parents sometimes fought like cats and dogs, but Natalie was loyal to them. I didn't see Natalie for a long time after her dad died. She went to Russia with her writer friend, Tommy Thompson, and R.J. I helped watch the kids while they were away. She called them every night—really missed them."

"Den, I read that Tommy Thompson died of cancer soon after Natalie."

"He really loved her. Natalie said she wouldn't have gone to Russia without him. It meant a lot to her to visit her heritage, and she liked the people she met, but she was happy to get back home. She seemed more down to earth for a while after that trip and even did the shopping at Boy's Market for a few cruises and went with me one afternoon to pick up burgers at Mr. D's, a popular marina coffee shop and lounge.

"I'd told Natalie that every day, without fail, Mae West pulls up at Mr. D's in her black Cadillac limousine, sends in her driver for takeout, sits in her limousine, and eats her lunch from Styrofoam containers. Natalie didn't believe me. We weren't there five minutes when, sure enough, in pulls Mae West. Even Natalie was star-struck, but she said, 'So this is what happens to old Hollywood sex goddesses? Afternoons with greasy burgers?'"

"Did you ever talk to Mae West?"

"No. I talked to her driver and saw him after she died. She left that gorgeous, classic Cadillac limousine to him."

"Generous. Did Natalie leave anything to you?"

"No. I wouldn't have expected anything. Natalie left everything to R.J. with provisions for the girls. She left her clothes to her sister Lana. Her mother, who Natalie called Mud, can live rent-free in the condo Natalie bought for her. Mud pushed Natalie into acting, and Natalie wanted to be different with Courtney and Natasha, swearing they'd have to wait until they were older before working in the business. R.J. seemed mad when Lana came to pick up Natalie's clothes. R.J. paid Lana for some fur coats he wanted to keep."

"Why was he mad?"

"Because Lana sold the clothes, but I don't blame her. What else was she supposed to do with them? That's what R.J. would have done. I think Lana picked up the clothes as soon as she could because *she* didn't trust R.J. Natalie *willed* those clothes to Lana. R.J. almost seemed mad at Natalie for that, like he didn't want Lana to have anything. Lana and her mother were devastated. Natalie was their rock. Then, Natalie's just gone, and R.J. was really insensitive to them.

"Natalie's mom is a strange flashback to old Russia. She's hard to be around. When you look at her, you never know what she's thinking, so you watch your step. Her eyes put you on guard. She hated the boat. Natalie wouldn't invite her on board because of what a gypsy once predicted.

"The gypsy said that Natalie's mom would die in dark water, but Mud was afraid that Natalie might die in water too. The gypsy also predicted that Natalie would be a star, which came true. But maybe Mud made her a star because of the prediction. Natalie might have been a regular person if Mud hadn't ever seen that gypsy. But because stardom came true, Natalie feared the water prediction. Natalie was deathly afraid of drowning."

"Did Natalie talk much about her sisters?"

"Her older sister, Olga, lives in northern California, married with kids. Natalie visited her the summer before she died. R.J. bought an R.V., right when his driver went on strike, and asked me if I'd drive that big thing up there, but I told him I was too busy at the marina. Natalie once said she envied Olga's normal life, but Natalie loved being a star. As for Lana, Natalie loved her a lot, but R.J. just didn't go for Lana, so Natalie didn't bring her family on the boat much. R.J.'s stepson, Josh Donen, from his marriage to Marion, came on board a lot."

"Did it bother R.J. that Natalie named the yacht *Splendour*? It's odd that she'd name it after *Splendor in the Grass*, a constant reminder of her relationship with Beatty."

"Natalie told me she added the 'u' to the spelling of *Splendour* to change it enough to appease R.J.—just in case—but not enough to take away its meaning for her, but *Splendor in the Grass* was a special movie to make. She was real disappointed at not winning the Oscar for it. But who knows, maybe it did bother R.J. He went along with the theme, though, and named the dinghy *Valiant* after one of his earlier films, *Prince Valiant*—though he laughed at that movie."

To understand Natalie Wood as an adult actress and woman, Dennis said, you needed to know that she had been around the block enough times, personally and professionally, but that she "always showed up at the front door." She had dated many men, but that was typical Hollywood fare. Some of the dates, such as with Tab Hunter, were arranged for studio publicity.

According to Dennis, Natalie was the consummate professional. As a young child, she was the family breadwinner, with a strict stage mom who planned her young life. Natalie may not have been forced, but she was definitely pressed, to work long, hard hours, and she did so without complaint, because complaining was never worth Mud's wrath.

Her rebellious teens got her out from under Mud's rule, but Natalie had grown up in an adult world and had handled youth with rare maturity, able to hold comprehensive adult conversations with producers and directors at an age most children were just learning to dial a telephone. Her teen and early adult years revolved around a Hollywood circle when late-night parties ruled the scene and when chic meant carousing at a party with a cocktail in one hand and a cigarette in the other, and leaving with whoever could best advance your career.

Although Natalie preferred a career independent of easy breaks, her widely publicized May–December romance with Nicholas Ray, who directed *Rebel Without a Cause*, stirred rumors to the contrary. The film had taken her from "Pigtail Girl" to adult commodity, and Nick Ray helped that transition along. Because Natalie was her family's primary source of income, Mud may have cared about Natalie's romantic choices, but as long as the career did not falter, and the money kept coming in, she hardly interfered with Natalie's freedom.

In the 1950s, Hollywood studio conduct was laid out in contracts. But Natalie was not the kind of person to dress, walk, talk, or act non-independently. She was a rebel but *with* a cause. She defied the nonsense studios expected of their stars, including publicity shoots and fake dates, curfews and bad roles. Natalie was a trendsetter, which infuriated Mud. When Natalie did not want to be owned by a studio any longer, Mud threw a fit. But Natalie had outgrown Mud's management and convinced the studio to provide juicier roles. Goodbye pigtails forever.

Natalie found great satisfaction in her career, but when her daughter Natasha was born, Natalie embraced motherhood with joy and commitment. Her priority was to provide as normal a home life as possible for her family.

Robert Wagner had worked hard to establish himself in Hollywood but openly deferred to Natalie's status. He talked a lot about how important it was to own a percentage of the work he starred in or produced. Natalie had the good sense to have accepted a behind-the-scenes percentage of her hit movie *Bob & Carol & Ted & Alice*. Natalie had made smart investments and wisely had not squandered her riches. She helped R.J. and other friends financially on several occasions. Dennis once overheard an argument when Natalie said to R.J., "If not for my investments and ability to know who to have advise me, things would be different."

R.J. scoffed back, "Bullshit, Nat, TV bought this boat."

"Well then, let's enjoy it!" Natalie exclaimed and laughed. Which they both did, and that's how Dennis thought most of their arguments went: a little tiff, then a big laugh.

Early in R.J.'s career he had signed with an agent, Henry Willson, who also handled Rock Hudson and other actors rumored to be homosexual. It was a time when celebrities who were gay primarily needed to remain in the closet. But signing with Willson was considered a definite suggestion of your sexual preference. I asked Dennis his opinion.

"R.J.'s a guy who turns his head at a pretty girl. R.J. and Natalie had many gay friends, but if R.J. had any tendencies, I never saw it."

I told Dennis, "I'm sorry I never took you up on those offers to visit Los Angeles. I wish I had met R.J. and Natalie."

"Marti, you would have been in awe of Natalie."

"I always was," I answered. "I saw *Miracle on 34th Street* lots of times as a kid, but who checks out the credits at seven years old? My first powerful connection with her was in *Gypsy*, and I was infatuated. The next day, I cleared off a big old desk in our upstairs playroom to use as my burlesque stage. I wore a leopard, two-piece bikini under my clothes, and the closest thing I could find to compare to the circular 'puff' *Gypsy* used in her act was a toilet seat cover," I confessed, laughing. "I charged a quarter admission and put on a '*Gypsy* show' for my twin brother and his friends. My mother would have killed me if she'd known. My audience of ten-year-olds was pretty bored."

Dennis laughed, as I continued, "I doubt I'm the only one who mimicked her *Gypsy* act. Then I saw her in *Inside Daisy Clover* with Robert Redford, and I just wanted to be her. Her onscreen relationship with Redford was so convincing that I later always confused Wagner with Redford. *West Side Story* was terrific."

"She used to walk around the boat, singing songs from *West Side Story*. It bothered her that she was dubbed in it, and we'd tease her and say, 'Natalie, one day we'll tape you and play it back so you'll never again question it.' She took it good-naturedly, but I think it bothered her."

"Was Robert Redford ever on the boat? They were a good screen couple, and that's why, when you started working for them, I was confused with the Redford/Wagner thing."

"No, I never met Redford, but Natalie was pretty upset when she wanted to rev up her career, and Redford was directing *Ordinary People*. Natalie read the book and loved it. She said Redford chose someone else and didn't give her a chance. A lot of people confused Wagner and Redford, and I always had to say, 'I work for Wagner, *not* Redford.' But not after *Hart to Hart*."

* * *

Natalie Wood, born on July 20, 1938, in San Francisco, California, as Natalia Nikolaevna Zakharenko, called Natasha, was destined for stardom. Her parents, both Russian immigrants, had fled the tyranny of their homeland. Natalie's mother, Maria, met Natalie's father, Nikolai Zakharenko, in San Francisco. Maria divorced her first husband after her first daughter, Olga Tatuloff, was born, and married Nick, who Americanized the family by adopting the surname Gurdin.

Because Maria Gurdin had been convinced by a gypsy that her second daughter would become a world-renowned star, she trained little Natasha from the time she could walk and talk to prove the gypsy correct. Eight years later, Natalie would have a younger sister, Lana, born March 1, 1946. Lana lived a less colorful childhood next to the shining star, Natasha, whose new stage name became Natalie Wood. The Gurdin family revolved around Natalie. Maria Gurdin insisted upon it, and the family adapted and obliged.

Maria served as young Natalie's manager, accepting as much work for Natalie as was offered, and Maria went looking for work at slow times. Natalie, a natural talent, became very quickly the family commodity. Although Nick Gurdin worked on and off in maintenance, even securing a few jobs through Natalie's studio connections, Natalie made in one hour what the traditional head of household brought in weekly.

Happy Land, released in 1943, was Natalie's first film with a small part as a crying little girl who dropped her ice cream cone. Audiences fell in love with her big, round, deep, dark eyes.

When the family moved to Los Angeles, with hopes of furthering Natalie's film career, it took a few years to get Natalie accepted and established at the studios, but once she made it in, the rest was history.

In 1947, *Miracle on 34th Street* became an instant holiday classic. Natalie, as little Susan Walker, who didn't believe in Santa Claus, stole Americans' hearts and never returned them.

Educated primarily on the lots of Universal, Fox, and Warner Brothers, it took Natalie seventeen years to lose the little girl roles before landing the lead as Judy, a rebellious teenager, in *Rebel Without a Cause*, which earned Natalie her first Academy Award nomination for Best Supporting Actress. She starred with James Dean, Sal Mineo, and Dennis Hopper. Natalie's friend Nick Adams also played a small role in this movie about teenage renegades. Ironically, Dean, Mineo, and Adams, like Natalie, met with tragic, untimely deaths. Dean was killed in an automobile accident, Mineo stabbed to death by a stranger, and Adams overdosed on pills.

Throughout the 1950s, as the queen of fan magazines, Natalie was as popular as Elizabeth Taylor. Her second Academy Award nomination, for Best Actress, came in 1961 with *Splendor in the Grass*, starring opposite newcomer Warren Beatty. It was an accomplishment accompanied and complemented by her becoming the 138th actor to be immortalized at Grauman's Chinese Theater. *West Side Story* premiered that same year. Although Natalie was not nominated for her leading role as Maria, the film won Oscars for Best Picture, Best Direction, Best Supporting Actor, and Best Supporting Actress.

Natalie's third and final chance for the Best Actress Oscar came with 1963's *Love with a Proper Stranger*, costarring Steve McQueen. Natalie lost to Patricia Neal in *Hud*.

With three Academy nominations under her belt, Natalie, after filming *This Property Is Condemned* in 1966, took a break and did not return to a serious role until 1969, as Carol Sanders in the smash hit *Bob & Carol & Ted & Alice*. Her next award came just before her death as the Golden Globe for Best TV Actress: Drama, in 1980 went to Natalie for her part as Karen Holmes in *From Here to Eternity*.

Maria Gurdin's gypsy predictions were not lost on Natalie and carried through her film career, dating back to 1949 in *The Green Promise*. When running across a bridge that had been rigged to collapse after she made it safely across, the bridge prematurely fell and sent Natalie plunging into dark water. She had to be rescued from drowning and suffered a wrist injury of which she was so self-conscious that she always covered the slight disfiguration with her trademark wide bracelet.

Off Catalina Island in 1952, filming *The Star*, Bette Davis came to Natalie's defense when director Stuart Heisler insisted Natalie leap from a yacht into the Pacific Ocean. Natalie obliged, but the scene needed to be shot over, and Natalie was too terrified to do it. Bette Davis, sensitive to Natalie's genuine fear, threatened to quit if a stand-in wasn't brought in for the reshooting.

When *Splendor in the Grass* director Elia Kazan stood fast on his decision that a reservoir scene would not be shot from a studio tank, Natalie obliged the director by challenging her fear and acted the scene in a natural environment of water, which terrified her.

Natalie launched Robert Redford's career by demanding him for her leading man in the film *Inside Daisy Clover*. During filming, Santa Monica Bay was the setting for a scene that trapped the costars in a drifting small boat. The incident sent Natalie into a frenzy.

Just two years before Natalie died, her scene in *The Memory of Eva Riker* called for her to run on a beach and then into the ocean. She refused. The scene was finally realized by a double, with close-up water shots filmed from a studio water tank. Natalie's character drowns in Eva, and Natalie had acted the scene convincingly. She had, eerily, practiced the scene over and over, at her home and aboard *Splendour*, though not in water.

Few who ever worked with Natalie were unaware of her fear—she was terrified of water, especially sea water—and she was never embarrassed to admit it. Everyone admired her as a devoted, class-A actress for each time she had braved her fear for the sake of a film.

Although not all of Natalie's films were big hits, her few embarrassments pale next to the successes of her career, remarkably one of Hollywood's lengthiest for her short life. Natalie played quality parts or starring roles in fifty big-screen films, and she had accomplished acclaimed television work between the big-screen projects.

Natalie Wood's level of achievement and audience approval was not as easily obtainable for Robert Wagner. He made his mark in television, but not until the 1970s. Before then, many people mistook him for other Hollywood Roberts. Although extremely well known and instantly recognized, invariably busy, continually visible, often finishing two or three films per year, he had not stirred the film industry or captured the hearts of audiences, as had Natalie Wood.

Robert Wagner, born in Detroit, Michigan, on February 10, 1930, moved to Los Angeles at a young age with his family. He began his acting career at age seventeen as a general extra under contract with Fox Studios. He had many fans, but his overall public appeal proved less than spectacular until his television series *It Takes a Thief*, from 1968 to 1969. His popularity increased with *Switch*, from 1975 to 1978, and then soared with his most successful endeavor, *Hart to Hart*, costarring Stefanie Powers, airing in 1979.

Robert Wagner and Natalie Wood combined their talents and starred together in *All the Fine Young Cannibals* in 1960 and for a television production of *Cat on a Hot Tin Roof* with the brilliant Sir Laurence Olivier as costar in 1976. Natalie had a cameo on *Hart to Hart* in 1979.

When Natalie was a mere eleven years old, she had "chosen" her husband. A young, handsome actor in his late teens walked past her on a Fox studio set one afternoon. She turned; her eyes followed her dream husband until he faded out of sight, then she proclaimed to her mother, "When I grow up, I want to marry him." That handsome young actor was Robert Wagner.

Her wish came true.

She was stunningly gorgeous at eighteen when she went on her first date with R.J. He proposed the next year by slipping a huge, freshwater pearl and diamond ring into her champagne glass at Romanoff's restaurant. They married on December 28, 1957, in a formal, private ceremony in Scottsdale, Arizona, where Wagner's parents lived. They honeymooned with a train trip and then a week spent on R.J.'s boat, *My Lady*, off the coast of Catalina Island.

The Hollywood media called the union "the most glittering of the twentieth century." For a while their relationship seemed perfect, and then the world's vicarious thrill went kaput when they separated four years later. Natalie then dated her *Splendor in the Grass* costar, Warren Beatty, as Wagner went on to marry Marion Marshall. The highly publicized divorce saddened all who had rooted for the couple.

The Wood–Beatty romance did not survive Beatty's philandering, and Natalie respected herself too much to put up with anything but honesty. At this frustrating chasm in her personal life, she was determined to find the love of her life, so she got back out there, after heavy psychoanalysis, with the courage and pride of a warrior defending the essence of love. She socialized and dated, consorting with old and new male friends, but found herself constantly measuring men to the happiness she missed as being a wife. Before Wagner, Natalie had been no stranger to serious dating and to marital engagements. Gossip columnists had romantically linked her to actors Scott Marlowe, James Dean, Frank Sinatra, Steve McQueen, Dennis Hopper, Raymond Burr, and Robert Vaughn, as well as various directors, producers, and tycoons.

She dated Elvis Presley, of whom she said: "Elvis was so square, we'd go for hot fudge sundaes. He didn't drink, he didn't swear, he didn't even smoke, it was like having the date that I never had in high school. I'd never been around anyone who was that religious. He felt he had been given this gift, this talent, by God. He didn't take it for granted. He thought it was something that he had to protect. He had to be nice to people, otherwise God would take it all away." Natalie enjoyed meeting and getting to know Elvis, but that was the extent of her interest in him.

But Wagner, apparently, had captured Natalie's heart, though it would take fifteen years for them to reclaim their love. When she saw Wagner again at a party one night, they rekindled the flame, and gave marriage a second shot.

Natalie, thirty-four, and R.J., forty-two, exchanged wedding vows again, this time determined to make a go of it. They remarried on July 16, 1972, during a casual ceremony held on Bob Rose's yacht, *Ramblin' Rose*, moored off Paradise Cove in the Pacific Ocean. Only a handful of family members and friends attended. They were absorbed in their love for one another. Natalie paid off all financial debts to clear the path for a new union. They pooled their finances from that day forward. Experience and expensive analysis contributed to their development and balance in adulthood.

During the intermission between their first and second marriages to one another, each had married and become a parent. Robert Wagner and wife Marion Marshall Donen had Katie, short for Katherine. Natalie and husband Richard Gregson, a writer, producer, and agent who resided in England, had Natasha.

When the interim marriages ended in divorce—Natalie's for a husband's infidelity, R.J.'s for listlessness—Natalie and R.J. felt like the two luckiest people on earth to have found each other again. They bought a house on Canon Drive in Beverly Hills. Natalie, this time around, wanted to be more of a traditional wife and, more importantly, a good mother. She took on domesticity with ease and devoted most of her time to making her new house a home—a beautiful and happy one.

Dedicated to making every aspect of their second marriage work, R.J. and Natalie trusted in togetherness in business too. They reestablished the production company they had previously formed, keeping the same name, RONA, an acronym for Robert and Natalie, but now calling it RONA II. The company's greatest success was its interest in the tremendously popular television series *Charlie's Angels*. Profits poured in, and Natalie and R.J.'s joint business venture added strength and financial security to their relationship.

But the sweetest, ultimate joy in their lives arrived on March 9, 1974, when their daughter, Courtney Brooke Wagner, publicized as "the most wanted baby," joined the family, completing R.J. and Natalie.

They had everything going for them, including world adoration. Their enchanting, charmed life took on new meaning. They devoted as much time as possible to their immediate family and made a pact that one or the other would always be there for the children, even if it meant turning down an acting role. They savored their private times aboard their new haven on the sea, *Splendour*.

Natalie devoted herself to motherhood and worked only if her schedule allowed her to spend time with her children on a daily basis. Natalie's studio work after motherhood—notable additions to her résumé but substandard accomplishments for her self-expectations—included *Meteor* with Sean Connery and *The Last Married Couple in America* with George Segal and Richard Benjamin. She also starred in two television specials—*The Cracker Factory* and a miniseries, the remake of *From Here to Eternity* with costar William Devane.

In 1979, the Hollywood Chamber of Commerce invited Robert Wagner and Natalie Wood to be the Grand Marshals of the annual Hollywood Christmas Parade. R.J. and Natalie, in the grand finale float, cruised with Santa down the boulevard. The stunning couple sat with their daughters and waved to the cheering crowd— *the perfect famous couple.*

Robert Wagner's individual fame soared to heights he had never before known. By the time *Hart to Hart* was in its second year, in 1980, he had come into his own. Suave and debonair, the Cary Grant of television, R.J. was, finally, a star, a popular heartthrob, and no one would mistake him for Redford, or Conrad, or Culp, or Goulet, or any other Robert again.

Writer Sidney Sheldon had presented the idea to ABC for a show called *Double Twist.* Leonard Goldberg, serving as head of programming for ABC, partner to Aaron Spelling, and behind the hit series *Charlie's Angels*, nixed the idea, but eight years later, he thought the public was ready for another "lighthearted murder" show. Goldberg went for it because *Charlie's Angels* had been tremendously successful. *Double Twist* was renamed *Hart to Hart*.

Screenwriter/director Tom Mankiewicz, son of Hollywood mogul Joseph L. Mankiewicz, was called in to write it. Goldberg was certain, after reading finished scripts, that only one actor could play the debonair, filthy-rich, charismatic character Jonathan Hart that Mankiewicz had created: Robert Wagner.

Wagner had just finished *Cat on a Hot Tin Roof* with Natalie and Olivier, had just made a high mark with his prominent and popular lead role in *Airport '79 Concorde*, and was filming *Pearl* in Hawaii when word came down that he was the *only* choice for the *Hart* lead. He returned to Los Angeles and talked business with the creators and developers, demanding a contractual provision for two separate projects for his and Natalie's Rona II. ABC not only approved the provision but acquired Robert Wagner as a partner. A shrewd negotiator, Wagner got 50 percent of the *Hart* series for Rona II and eventually became the popular show's executive producer.

The perfect costar was needed, and Wagner suggested Stefanie Powers for the part of his wife, Jennifer Hart. Mankiewicz had wanted Natalie Wood, but after the cast was established, with Powers landing the lead, Robert Wagner said, "I never thought of anyone else to play my wife other than Stefanie Powers. We worked previously in an episode of *It Takes a Thief* and I liked her a lot. Her style of acting is perfect for me. She's a terrific contributor and a total professional. I'm thoroughly comfortable doing the show with her."

R.J. convinced his colleagues that Powers was best. "You had the sense that she could get out of anything. If she had to run through reeds or swim up a river, she'd be there," he said.

R.J. told Natalie it would be difficult for the two of them to work in the same series on a daily basis, as there would be no time left for a home life. A series required working from six every morning until nine at night on a good day. Neither of them would be home with the girls for seven or eight months a season. A series can be the most demanding work any actor can undertake. Wagner claimed, "It's especially hard on a woman." His statement could easily have been considered chauvinistic, but Natalie realized that Stefanie Powers, a divorcee with no children, was better suited for a television series.

Sparks flew right into living rooms across the nation every Tuesday night when Stefanie Powers and Robert Wagner's onscreen, effervescent chemistry flared. Rumors of Natalie's jealousy circulated, but Natalie dismissed them. She could handle explaining to her children, while visiting the Hart set one day, why their daddy kissed another woman; she emphasized that it was only make-believe, their daddy's job—and their mommy's job, too, on occasion. The artist in Natalie wanted recognition for distinguished accomplishment. To achieve it through a show of Hart's simpler venue was not Natalie Wood. She often said that she preferred the big screen over television, but she wasn't opposed to good television. Natalie did not take roles for the sake of exposure or money. Wagner understood and accepted this about Natalie and continued to reaffirm that he was the lesser of the two when it came to big-screen acclaim. He sometimes even referred to himself as Mr. Natalie Wood or Natalie Wood's husband, but R.J., who professed privately and publicly that business smarts meant more than fame, was suddenly lapping up the fame. His studio film roles rarely drew big box-office money, but now his television popularity and business interests in his show provided the best financial draw of his career.

On a *Mike Douglas Show* shot in Hawaii, a year before Natalie's death, Robert Wagner was interviewed on an open-air set. Wagner surprised Douglas by bringing Natalie onto the stage. Douglas seemed in awe of Natalie's beauty and charm, and said, "You know, it's not all makeup, look at her, she's for real."

Audience questions included one from a man who asked R.J. if he thought of Natalie while kissing Stefanie Powers. That question took the conversation to Natalie's possible jealousy over Powers. Natalie said that all of the people involved with R.J.'s show were friends. A woman from the audience said that R.J. and Natalie have set a wonderful example for the world with their marriage.

Douglas claimed that everyone considered the Wagners the happiest couple in America, that there were articles about it everywhere. He asked the couple if they were boating enthusiasts, and Wagner explained that it was their hobby and was "really terrific." Later in the interview, Douglas talked to Wagner about snorkeling and then asked Natalie if she ever participated in water hobbies. She claimed, "No, I love being on and near the water, but not *in* the water."

Hart to Hart put Wagner and Powers on the map of fame, and Wagner reveled in it, a bit chauvinistically at times, but he still adored and loved his real-life wife, Natalie Wood. The Wagners' popularity as a happy, Tinseltown family flourished. They had defied the odds, and they seemed so much in love. Wagner had no qualms about showing his adoration for his wife. As cited in *Orange Coast* magazine in January 1980, when asked by Anthony Korba, "Where will you be in five years?" Robert Wagner answered:

"Oh, God. I don't have too many projections. I'd just like to stay where I am now. I want to watch my kids grow up. I'm very fortunate. I really am, because I'm in love, very much in love with my wife. She's just a terrific lady. And, I really realize how much I missed her when we weren't married. She is not only my lover, but she's my friend, and I'd rather be with her than anybody else in the whole world and that's no bullshit, that's straight out. The personal part of my life is being with my family. I want to be with my wife and I really enjoy that. When you came on the stage today, I was on the phone with her. She's out doing a film. We'll meet and have dinner tonight. Last night, we went out on a date all by ourselves. I picked her up and we went to a restaurant. I don't care about being around others sometimes, just her. You would think this guy would be out getting his head blown off. I've done all that. I've been around that track."

But he wanted his time too. He preferred Natalie as a stay-at-home mom. But that's not what Natalie had expected with their second marriage. She was dedicated to her daughters and her marriage, but she also wanted her career. The consummate competitor and actress, she itched to get back to serious work. She wanted another Academy Award nomination. The artist within her wanted to win the Oscar. She spent long afternoons upon her perch in *Splendour's* wheelhouse and long nights in her white-wicker bedroom office, scrutinizing scripts. Natalie wanted the script that would return the big-screen praises.

Dedicated to her profession, as always, she trusted her instincts. She had wanted the lead role in *Ordinary People*, Robert Redford's director debut film. Natalie asked for the part of Beth Jarrett, the mother who loses her oldest son to drowning in a boating accident, who then bitterly distances herself from her affluent husband and guilt-ridden younger son. Natalie recognized this role's potential but contacted Robert Redford too late, for he had already promised the part to Mary Tyler Moore, who was nominated for a Best Actress Oscar.

Anxious to explore the depths of her talents, Natalie looked forward to her scheduled 1982 stage debut as star of *Anastasia*, the mystery of Russian Tsar Nicholas Romanov's youngest daughter's fate after the Romanov family massacre. It was a story Natalie was partial to because it was that very historic tragedy that had driven Natalie's parents to America. She practiced her elocution aboard *Splendour*, exercising her voice and memorizing her lines along the side decks of the yacht, casting her voice to the deep, dark water she so feared. In mid-1981, Natalie flew to North Carolina to begin the filming of her role as Karen Brace in a sci-fi fantasy with special effects, directed by Douglas Trumball. Cast as leading man was handsome, playful, rising-star Christopher Walken, who had recently won a Best Supporting Actor Oscar for his portrayal of a suicidal Vietnam veteran in Michael Cimino's masterpiece *The Deer Hunter*. Costarring in the film with Natalie and Walken was Louise Fletcher, who had won a Best Actress Oscar for her famous role of Nurse Ratched in director Milios Forman's tremendously successful *One Flew Over the Cuckoo's Nest*. Natalie, no doubt, was in good company. Natalie's ties with the film would, in an ironic twist of fate, factor into her untimely death. What Natalie liked best about her new film was its leading man. The camaraderie she established with Walken, onscreen and off, would become one of the links in the chain of circumstances that led to her death. The film, her part unfinished, would be her last: *Brainstorm*.

Chapter 7

Accepting that Dennis needed to break from Robert Wagner's influence before I might learn more about Natalie's death, I asked Dennis questions about Wagner's demeanor after Natalie died.

"He worked long hours. I guess it got him through it. Then, we just drank," Dennis said.

"Who did he see socially?"

"Just me and Frank for a while. He was a recluse for about a year. After I broke up with my girlfriend, R.J. and I were together constantly. By my choice. I wasn't forced then."

"Forced?"

"After Natalie died, R.J. called the shots on my whereabouts. I was only allowed to see my girlfriend."

"Allowed?"

"That's the way it was."

"Did you ever tell your girlfriend anything about Natalie's death?"

"Never. She knew I wasn't right after Natalie died, but I never breathed a word to her. We broke up because I didn't trust her with the media."

"And R.J. gave up his boating friends?"

"He's socializing more, and he has been seeing Jill St. John for a while." Dennis became quiet, then added, "I thought R.J. was my friend, but he's ready to cast me aside. R.J.'s real friendly with his makeup artist, Frank Westmore."

"Does Frank know anything about that night?"

"He probably knows an argument occurred. His wife, Gloria, is nice, but Frank is obnoxious. I didn't like him from day one. Mart Crowley, Frank Westmore, and a *Hart* stuntman, Greg Barnette, came out on a fishing trip a few years back, and there was tension between Frank and Greg from the start. Frank got real drunk. Every other word out of his mouth was 'fuck.' He wanted the wheel, and R.J. told me to let Frank at it. I was pissed but followed orders. *Splendour* is too big for someone without experience, so I stayed close by. Well, we hit a fog bank and Frank panicked. Visibility was zero. I turned on the radar, then Greg wanted to see the screen, so he stepped in front of Frank.

"Frank yelled at Greg, 'Get the fuck out of my way, you fucking idiot.' Greg is huge. He could have pulverized Frank with one punch, but Greg just laughed. Frank threw a punch at Greg's face, but the punch landed on Greg's upper arm. R.J. finally told me to get the wheel, but Frank wasn't giving it up, saying he wouldn't trust anyone with his life in fog like that. R.J. ended up babying Frank through the whole thing and asked Frank if he wanted to play checkers. Frank ruined the day.

"Frank did help me to retrieve *Splendour* after Natalie died, and he defended me a few nights before the first anniversary of Natalie's death, when R.J. went nuts over something stupid, though."

"What happened that night?" I asked. "You were pretty uptight that first trip back to Jersey after she died."

* * *

Dennis sat on a barstool at Wagner's home bar, set for the night with a bottle of scotch. Thanksgiving was less than a week away—the first Thanksgiving since Natalie died—a year of pain and grief, loss and despair. R.J. and Dennis had suffered it, shared it, and battled it together.

In time, they had told each other, "We'll be okay."

If anything, time worked against Dennis, relentlessly tearing away the denial that had made living bearable. For him, time only embedded the reality and irreversibility of Natalie's death. He knew that he would never recover from the tragedy.

R.J. had insisted on paying for Dennis's professional therapy. Therapy had always been Natalie's answer to life's stress, and by her second marriage to R.J., she had convinced him of its value too. R.J. had taken Dennis along with him to talk to his doctor a few times. Then Dennis went alone for sessions.

Dennis would roll his eyes behind R.J.'s back after leaving the therapy sessions. Although Dennis derived a sense of relief from talking about his nightmares, he dared not reveal his secrets; hence, his therapy failed miserably.

Dennis hoped therapy would eliminate the frequent dreams in which he saw Natalie's smile, her beautiful eyes, her petite body walking down the dock or sitting in her wheelhouse perch. He would hear her laughter and her pleasant voice engaged in conversation. Then suddenly, he would be standing over her bruised body, and he would awaken in a cold sweat, trembling, frightened, and unable to distinguish between his waking life and dream state.

Most nights, Dennis and R.J. sat quietly at the bar, slowly tilting their glasses back and forth, staring at the bronze booze until bedtime. Then, the next morning, they would be off to the studio together.

When R.J. joined Dennis at the bar this night, Dennis mentioned that he couldn't believe a year had passed since Natalie's death, but R.J. wasn't up to talking about it. He never talked about it. Dennis was afraid the first anniversary would stir the media. R.J. had planned to take his daughters to Switzerland, where actor David Niven had offered his chalet for Wagner to escape the anniversary. R.J. insisted that Dennis leave California for the Thanksgiving weekend too—that he visit his family in New Jersey.

Dennis wanted to go with R.J. He thought they should stay together to hurdle this first juncture. R.J. argued that Dennis should go his own way. R.J. was beginning to build the wall that would eventually grow high enough to keep Dennis on the outskirts.

The telephone rang. It was Frank Westmore. He was coming over.

Frank Westmore's importance, as R.J.'s domineering makeup artist, did not end with powdering R.J.'s nose. Dennis did not understand why R.J. sought Frank's advice on nearly every aspect of *Hart to Hart*. Since Dennis started working as an extra on *Hart*, Frank loathed Dennis and R.J.'s closeness and constantly interfered by telling R.J. lies about Dennis. He accused Dennis of loafing on the set or of being late for work. Yet Dennis drove to work with R.J. every morning. If Dennis was showing up late, then R.J. was too.

A *Hart* crewmember had recently warned Dennis that he overheard Frank trying to convince R.J. of Dennis's disloyalty. "Dennis will turn on you; he's a waste to have around."

Dennis suspected Frank of stirring up rumors and blamed Frank for the recent tabloid paragraph, which headlined Dennis as the Death Yacht Captain who "mysteriously secured the job of permanent, general extra on *Hart to Hart*." The article noted that the decision to hire Dennis was not the official casting office's doing.

Now Dennis was spending an evening with Frank, but Frank surprised Dennis by siding with him when Dennis casually mentioned that he was thinking about shaving off his beard. R.J. sat there and threatened to fire Dennis from *Hart* if he shaved, but Frank intervened, claiming that without the beard, Dennis could get a lot more work on other shows. Dennis did not miss Frank's ulterior motive to separate Dennis and R.J., but liked that Frank, for once, was on his side.

R.J. and Frank went round for round. Frank maintained that men with beards stand out as extras on television and that casting agents avoid them. He angered R.J. by saying that R.J. had better make Dennis a regular on the show before viewers started asking why Dennis is the horse trainer one week, the plumber the next, and then the hospital assistant. Frank overdid it by accusing R.J. of underestimating his audience. "They're too keen to not find out that Dennis was your boat captain."

Slam! R.J.'s fist hit the bar hard. He yelled at Dennis, insisting he not cut his beard.

Frank's summation had stung, but Dennis agreed with Frank. Other studio work had been coming his way, and he was ready to branch out. If the beard would hinder him, he would shave it without a second thought.

Frank and R.J. argued as Dennis followed the verbal volley like a tennis match. Finally, Dennis burst out laughing and said he would settle the score by cutting off only half the beard.

R.J. and Frank looked at each other, then cracked up laughing.

After Frank left, R.J. asked Dennis's intentions about the beard. Dennis would not commit either way.

The following morning, Dennis's beard was still intact, mainly because there was a scene to finish shooting for *Hart to Hart*. R.J. and Dennis drove together to the studio. R.J. brought up getting away for the Thanksgiving weekend again, but Dennis insisted on staying with *Splendour*. "They'll be swarming all over that boat," Dennis told R.J.

R.J. insisted, "No, go home, Dennis. Forget the boat." He wrote Dennis two checks and instructed him to call for a flight reservation to New Jersey. One check covered the expenses for the trip, and the other was a thousand-dollar bonus should Dennis stay longer. That night, Dennis booked his flight.

Then he shaved off his beard.

Chapter 8

Receiving an early evening call from Dennis on September 30, 1983, surprised me, so I kiddingly asked, "To what do I owe this privilege of a call during normal waking hours?"

But it was a distress call.

"I'm calling from my new apartment in Reseda. It finally happened."

A few seconds passed.

"*Splendour* is gone," he announced flatly. "I've been with that boat for nine years."

"It's a big chunk of your life, Den, and sad it's over, but maybe you can use the commission to buy your own boat. Thirty-five thousand is a lot."

"I didn't get a commission," he interrupted, "R.J. donated the boat to the Sea Scouts, a boys club here in L.A."

This was going to be a hard conversation.

"I can't believe he couldn't wait a little longer," Dennis started. "We were planning to advertise in San Francisco next month, to get away from buyers here. I just wanted her to sell with dignity."

"He paid you to take care of the boat even though you lived there rent free?"

"R.J. gave me checks, a thousand here, two thousand there, but always I worked on the boat. My friend, P.G., warned me that it was hush money and that R.J. would dump me after dumping the boat. I think P.G. might be right."

"Do you consider it 'hush money'?"

"At first I didn't, and I always defended R.J. I still maintained the boat, and if R.J. was extra generous, I really didn't think anything of it. But who was I kidding? It was hush money. R.J. didn't even have the guts to tell me about *Splendour* himself. Bill, his accountant, called to break the news."

"Have you talked to R.J.?"

"He said he didn't want to waste more money in advertising. What's six hundred more dollars to a multimillionaire? The original owner of *Splendour* who lives on the East Coast sent a letter saying he would like to buy the boat back but that the price was too high. Instead of negotiating with the guy, R.J. up and gives her away? Any kind of deal would have been a dignified sale."

Dennis's anger centered on *Splendour's* having been reduced to a charity donation. *Splendour* was more than a boat to Dennis. She was home.

"Maybe the boat's reputation factored in, Den," I said. "You've even said it was a bad scene at the docks."

"I talked R.J. into letting me remove *Splendour's* name with a blow torch. This past year, people would cruise by and yell out 'killer boat,' 'bastard boat,' and things like 'who's being pushed overboard tonight?' I'd get dirty looks. Even a girl I used to live with and almost married called me a murderer just last night."

"That's just displaced anger. Why would anyone call you a murderer?"

"Because they can't call R.J. one. He hides in his house, and at the studios, or in Europe. He's protected by fame. I'm out on the docks, exposed. My friends don't believe Natalie just fell off a boat accidentally. People know what money can buy. R.J. bought my silence, even when he didn't have to, and friends say I'm crazy if I don't tell what I know before it becomes impossible."

"Isn't that a bit dramatic? You haven't even told me yet what really happened, but I know better than to call you a murderer. The taunting may never stop, with or without *Splendour*. Just try to go on, okay? But, honestly..." I hesitated before I finished the sentence, "it seems, with what you've hinted at to know—what authorities *don't* know—that there's incriminating evidence involved, which lends toward making you look guilty." I held my breath.

"I've kept quiet for R.J., and he has the nerve to have Bill call me?" Dennis could not see past his anger about the boat situation. "Why couldn't he call himself? He practically kept me prisoner in his house, Marti."

"Den, you've got to explain that one. *Prisoner*?"

"The alarm system would be set at night, and I wasn't allowed to open my bedroom door. I couldn't go downstairs...no phone calls, just walls. There'd be a bodyguard near the front door, and R.J. would have a driver escort me everywhere I went for months. When I suggested moving out of his house, he would go nuts on me, saying that couldn't happen until things died down."

I tried to get off the phone with Dennis because my family's dinner waited, but it was as if Dennis was incapable of hearing anything over his current frustration, so I stayed on the phone with him while he vented.

"R.J. stripped my life away, because what's a life, Marti, that you don't even have control over? I cleared *Splendour* of all his and Natalie's personal things. I stayed with him when he cried. I kept quiet for him. I needed his permission to see my girlfriend. Once, I tried to leave without telling anyone, and R.J.'s driver notified him immediately. Another night, at my girlfriend's place, I was muscled back into a waiting car by two of R.J.'s brutes. I wanted to stay past ten, and they wouldn't hear of it, so they banged on Yolanda's door, grabbed me, and dragged me down the sidewalk. Yolanda went nuts and screamed at them to leave me alone. R.J. was so fucking afraid that if I spent the night, Yolanda might get something out of me. Ten o'clock was my deadline! I was ordered to never talk to anyone about Natalie's death or there'd be legal consequences. And, stupidly, I did as I was told, and for what? This?"

"Den, it sure sounds like R.J. has something real offensive to protect. This is outrageous—bordering on unbelievable—but I wish everyone could just hear your voice right now to know you're not lying, and why you were afraid."

"Marti, afraid doesn't cut it. I was *petrified*."

"What was R.J. afraid you'd say out there?"

"Anything true. I'm not just telling you all this because I'm mad. I want you to know more, but not over the phone."

"Den, I'm getting just bits and pieces from you, and I want to help, and I believe you because even if you hadn't told me anything about Natalie's death, it still didn't make sense. But I'm becoming obsessed and neglecting my family and friends. And, by next week, you and R.J. might be buddies again. Did you think R.J. would give you the boat? How would that look? You've made a big mistake, maybe an irreversible one, but from what I gather, R.J.'s mistake is a hell of a lot worse. But you've hidden something too damn serious. R.J. has kept you under his thumb for his benefit—not for yours. Now he feels your weight. Being his burden is what should really scare you. I get scared talking to you sometimes."

"I haven't done anything to make him mistrust me. When I called you, blurting out things about that night, it wasn't to hurt R.J. The main reason I've kept quiet is to not hurt the family and Natalie's girls. But Natalie's flirting with Chris didn't warrant her death. If I had been questioned the right way, right away, maybe the detectives could have seen through my fear."

"It seems you're the only person who can offer answers and give her hope of justice."

"So can Chris, to a degree."

"What is Chris hiding?"

"Well, Chris sure knows that it wasn't a pleasant weekend like we told the authorities. He could at least admit that much."

"Would the truth hurt R.J. that bad? You forgave him. He has millions of fans. Could they forgive him?"

"They don't even know there's anything to forgive him for. I thought time would erase the guilt, but it's almost two years now, and it's worse."

"Den, flat out, did you take hush money?"

"No, but R.J. gave me permission to call his accountant any time. I could just pick up the phone and say, 'Hey, Bill, can you write me a check for a thousand or two? I'll be by in an hour.' But I didn't call unless I needed something for the boat. I worked for the money, and I do charters around the docks on top of working at the studios, but now I feel taken advantage of because of the amounts R.J. was *willing* to pay me. Does that make sick sense, or what?"

"Den, it sounds like hush money to me too. Please estimate for me how much, overall, Wagner gave you."

"Maybe ten thousand, or a little more. But it could have been any amount I wanted. That's what matters."

"No, Den, what matters is that you didn't take an astronomical amount. Ten grand over a two-year period as pay for a side job maintaining the boat isn't a whole lot. But I understand: it was the nature in which it was given—an unnecessary bonus that didn't seem right."

"Exactly. But R.J. started acting like the money was something else. Like he considered it hush money and was tired of giving it to me."

"A couple of months ago, you said I could ask you anything. I want to know: Did Natalie ever take the dinghy out alone?"

"Never."

"Is there any possible way, being drunk or mad, she would have taken the dinghy out the night she died?"

"No. Not without me. We left together the night before. And the light was out on the dinghy. We used a flashlight to get back to the boat from Doug's after dinner that night. But she wouldn't have gone out in that dinghy alone with a thousand spotlights on it—drunk, mad, insane with anger—no way."

"It was never reported that the light was out on the dinghy. Did the authorities ever ask about it?"

"Yeah, right," Dennis answered sarcastically.

"Den, we need to talk about the things the authorities should have been told. Everything. Soon, okay?"

"Okay. It's the good things that still keep me going, Marti."

"Well, get a grip and a perspective. You can always savor the good times."

Dennis obviously regretted the way he had handled himself since Natalie's death. I believed that until he unburdened himself, he would remain guilt-ridden. He needed to rebuild his self-confidence by acknowledging the years he had served as the "good captain." Then, the "death yacht captain" label would fade. I wasn't sure my personal opinions were safe to offer Dennis in dealing with such a heavy, tragic story, and I hoped I would never inadvertently hurt him. He deserved credit for the conscientious, dependable captain he had been. Sure, he had committed minor indiscretions throughout his *Splendour* tenure—having a girlfriend on board, throwing a small party when he shouldn't have—but the fact remained that Robert Wagner and Natalie Wood had kept Dennis in their employ from the start of their *Splendour* ownership to the day the boat was donated. They had placed their full trust and confidence in Dennis, and he had lived up to it.

Most precious to Natalie were her children, and she had allowed Dennis to care for them, to take them on outings, to change Courtney's diapers, to feed them, to play with them. Dennis had done something right to have deserved that kind of trust from Natalie. Natalie would not even allow her own mother to care for her children, Dennis had once told me.

My conversations with Dennis, as nerve wracking as they were for me, were therapeutic for him. When I told him that I felt like his therapist, it made him laugh despite his current anger. "You know, that's how Natalie and I were for the longest time," he said. "Our therapy sessions became a regular *Splendour* ritual. She would always tell me about her therapy, then she would give me advice."

"Was she that dependent on therapy?"

"Natalie knew she was a symbol of all that Hollywood represented, but Natalie was a regular person too. She always bragged about having gone to public schools. She loved public places. R.J. didn't. Natalie had a heart for real people. Talking to a therapist helped her, and she got a lot out of it. She always helped me with my problems, mostly with relationships. She made a lot of sense, too, even if it was all in fun, but sometimes it got serious. We would drink wine, pop a Valium, and tell each other our problems."

"Was she a recreational pill-popper?"

"Absolutely not. She took pills for motion sickness and sometimes Valium to calm herself down. She only took prescription pills. Natalie wasn't a real boater. She liked to socialize out there, and she forced herself to like boating for that reason, and for R.J. In our sessions, she constantly talked about drowning. She was afraid of flying, too, but she could get on an airplane. She never went into the ocean. She didn't even use her pool at home much, but it was being surrounded by dark water that scared her most. On our first cruise out, she was petrified because she had been in a storm with R.J. before. A storm hit *Splendour* once when Natalie and the girls were onboard. It was really big news out here and tore up the boat pretty bad. Natalie handled it, and R.J. almost died."

Losing *Splendour* would devastate Dennis, so I stayed on the phone with him late into the night. I asked Dennis to tell me about his first cruise with Natalie and R.J. and about the storm cruise. I wanted him to remember how important he had been to the Wagners.

* * *

Dennis said little to his new employers on their first *Splendour* cruise. Eager to make a good impression, he stayed completely alert and attentive to detail. The Wagners seemed to appreciate his experience and liked his casualness.

The cruise got off to a late start because Natalie had squandered the entire morning on a shopping spree for the trip. R.J. and Dennis swapped boat talk until she finally came up the dock, lugging shopping bags, and so frazzled that R.J. didn't complain about the late start.

"There are more bags in the trunk," she said, as she handed her keys to Dennis.

The threesome gathered in the wheelhouse as they finally, slowly cruised away from the dock. The afternoon sun was high and pale, and two or three boats were heading in from the ocean.

"People stared at me, the stores were crowded...now half the day is wasted," she complained. "Dennis, can you take over the shopping from now on?" she asked. Then, to justify giving him a chore she hated and that was beyond his job description, she added, "It makes more sense because you're here to see what's needed. If I have special requests, I'll call ahead. I'll give you a credit card to use exclusively for the boat, and we'll compensate your time."

"Fine with me," Dennis said, pleased that she trusted him.

R.J. asked endless questions about *Splendour* during the short day trip. Elated at owning a yacht, he boasted that ownership was far superior to chartering or having to wait for invitations. Now it was his time to host cruises and private fishing outings or to escape by himself whenever he chose.

Natalie poured forth dozens of decorating ideas and was eager to entertain aboard her new yacht. They enjoyed cheese and crackers and deli sandwiches in the wheelhouse, but when dusk began to settle around them, Natalie grew uneasy and insisted they head back to the marina. Her eyes stayed alert, her brows slightly furrowed, and she turned nervously at every sound. She asked Dennis if he had ever been in a storm at sea.

Dennis jumped at the opportunity to tell a good sea tale and went right into his roller-coaster ride through the Jamaican waters. He emphasized how the monstrous waves had engulfed the yacht and threatened to flip it over, and waited for Natalie's reaction, expecting her to be impressed. Instead, he could have kicked himself for his thoughtlessness. Her expression was not one of incredulity or admiration but of pure terror.

Dennis assured her that the likeliness of facing that kind of storm in the immediate area was slim. He turned on the radio to the weather station so Natalie could hear the monotonous but reliable voice that continuously reported the weather and forecast. "We'll hear small craft warnings if there's even the slightest chance of a storm around here," he told her. "*Splendour*'s a strong boat."

Her answering smile told him she believed him, and she had no one but herself to blame when a few months later a sudden, violent storm hit the Catalina coast and caught *Splendour*, with the Wagner family on board, in its path.

The cruise began on a brilliant summer Saturday morning. R.J. and Natalie's daughters, Katie and Natasha, had each brought along one of their girlfriends. Though Katie was a few years older than Natasha, they got along fabulously. Natalie told Dennis she hadn't brought two-year-old Courtney because the trip was intended for the older girls.

They crossed the channel to Emerald Bay, a good stop for sunning or hiking, but Natalie changed her mind and asked Dennis to cruise to Avalon, but *Splendour*'s generator went dead near the Isthmus. Dennis stayed aboard with mechanics as Natalie, R.J., and the girls dined on the island. They moored in the cove for the night. Early Sunday, Natalie cooked her special Mexican huevos rancheros breakfast, then it was off to Avalon for a shopping spree.

It was early evening when they returned, laden with shopping bags. Dennis helped carry in all the merchandise for a show and tell in the main salon. Natalie relaxed on the sofa with a glass of wine, radiating an innate joy as she watched the bubbly girls tear through bags, pulling out jewelry, clothes, games, and souvenirs. Because of the noisy fun, no one heard the strong winds picking up outside. By nine o'clock, the gusts were forceful.

The Harbor Patrol cruised the cove with warnings. "Do you intend to stay on board or want to be taken to the island now?" The loud, muffled voice came through a bullhorn and startled everyone. R.J. opened the main salon door leading to the side deck. Lightweight items started blowing all around the salon. A wicked gust of wind flattened R.J.'s hair.

"What's happening out there?" Natalie gasped.

"The winds are strong, Nat," R.J. yelled over the wind's roar, "What do you think? Want to take the girls to the island?"

"I think we should all go to the island." Dennis suggested, "or I'll stay with the boat. You all go, okay?" He ran to the wheelhouse to listen to reports that weren't good.

The girls cried to get off the boat, but Natalie decided to stay, so R.J. waved off the Harbor Patrol. Dennis ran back down and told everyone to leave, but R.J. said it was too late.

Quickly, the winds became violent, and the boat rocked furiously. Mooring cans smashed into smaller boats that sounded like a constant thunder. A threatening darkness approached and blackened the sky as the drop in temperature turned *Splendour* into a refrigerator. Natalie ran to her stateroom and grabbed warm clothing for the girls. She huddled with them for warmth on the sofa in the main salon.

An abrupt noise startled everyone. The girls screamed and tears ran down their cheeks. R.J. ran to the rear deck, looked up to the flying bridge, and yelled that the wind just blew the flying bridge cover away. Without a doubt, it was time to get Natalie and the girls ashore, but the dinghy would never make it on the ferocious sea.

As R.J. and Dennis discussed strategy in the wheelhouse, Natalie ran in, terrified. "What are we going to do?" she cried.

R.J. soothingly said, "We'll be all right," though he didn't believe it himself. "I'll radio for help, and Natalie, you go be strong for the girls."

Natalie went into a panic. "We're all going to drown," she shrieked. "Why didn't we leave when we had the chance? Dennis, you told me there are always warnings, and we didn't listen—"

R.J. hung up the phone and said, "Boaters are trapped all over the island. They're rescuing the most distressed first. We're on a long list."

Dennis was sure R.J.'s bulletin would send Natalie into another fit of panic. Instead, she took in a deep breath and said, "I'm going to go sit with the girls. We'll be all right. We're in a big boat. I just hope they can save the people trapped in the smaller boats."

"R.J., did you tell them who you are?" Dennis asked. "Did you tell them Natalie and the girls are here?"

"We don't expect special privileges, Dennis," R.J. said.

"No, we don't," Natalie agreed. "We had our chance to leave. Now others are in danger and we'll wait."

The Wagners' deference proved to Dennis what caring, considerate people he worked for. Some stars would have demanded immediate assistance because of their status, with no regard for others, but R.J. and Natalie were different. Dennis's respect for them grew.

Dennis knew of Natalie's fear of water, yet there she was, in the main salon, consoling her girls. "Thank God I left Courtney home," Natalie said to Dennis. He agreed and vowed to never question a mother's intuition.

It took nearly two hours before a patrol boat arrived through winds up to 70 miles per hour. Natalie and the girls made a shaky but safe transfer to the patrol boat. Although Natalie pleaded with R.J. and Dennis to leave, they stayed aboard *Splendour*, prepared to protect the yacht.

Right after Natalie left, a mooring line snapped, and the yacht swayed out of control. A new line needed to be fastened quickly or *Splendour* could break loose and smash into nearby boats.

"Dennis," R.J. yelled over the howling winds and pouring rain, "I'm going over the side of the boat to tie a new line. You'll have to hold me."

"No, Chief," Dennis, said, hardly audible over the pounding rain. Shaking his head, he insisted, "No, the winds are too strong. I won't be able to hold you!"

If another line snapped during R.J.'s plan, he could be killed by being slammed into the side of the boat and rendered unconscious. He might fall and be swallowed up before anyone could help. But R.J was already hanging headfirst over the side. "Come on, Dennis," R.J. ordered, "we don't have time to think about this. Hold my legs, now."

Dennis grabbed R.J.'s legs and held on with all the muscle and willpower he could muster, but R.J. started to slip from his grip. "Don't let go, now," R.J. yelled, "it's almost done."

A huge wave crashed into *Splendour's* side, completely covering R.J. "It's done, pull me back," he screamed, and he used his hands to help push himself back up to the deck. Completely drenched, temples pulsing and face flushed, R.J. held a glance with Dennis, then smiled from ear to ear.

"Man, this wasn't one of your scripts," Dennis scolded. "You could have been killed!"

Standing in the pouring rain, both of them smiling, R.J. and Dennis simultaneously reached out for a handshake. "Let's get the hell inside," R.J. said.

Natalie called to say she and the girls were safe on the island in a motel room. The storm continued to rage through the night, but subsided enough by morning to take the dinghy to the island to meet up with Natalie for breakfast.

When Natalie heard about R.J.'s mission from the night before, her eyes filled with tears. She promised to always listen to warnings, and to Dennis, in the future.

Chapter 9

As the second anniversary of Natalie Wood's death approached, Dennis continued working at the studios as a general extra. He called one night, late as usual, and surprised me with his upbeat mood.

"I played an orderly in a *Hart* scene today."

"You sound in good spirits," I said. "Tell me about the scene."

"It was nothing. I pushed a guy in a wheelchair down a corridor. That's it," he laughed. "Last show, I had an outside scene. Horses charged at me, and I lowered a red flag when they ran past."

"Isn't that dangerous? Isn't that more a stunt man's job?"

"The horses and stunt riders are so well trained that general extras can fill in for scenes like that. It costs less to pay an extra than a stunt. I get paid extra if a scene involves danger, like charging horses, or if I light a cigarette for a scene, because smoking is officially bad for you.

"I live right behind my new friend, P.V.—stands for Paul Vincent. We ride to work every day. He's been a general extra for years. His father, Paul Picerni, played Agent Lee Hobson on *The Untouchables* with Robert Stack in the early sixties. I'm still mostly working on the *Hart* set where it's back to normal now. No one ever mentions Natalie or Holden."

"It really bothers me that Noguchi was condemned for releasing information about Holden and Natalie," I said.

"Yeah, Mart, I'm sticking a steak in the oven here, so bear with me...."

I waited, knowing I had struck a chord—one presently out of tune. Considering Dennis's mood, I asked, "Whose idea was it for you to start acting?"

"Completely R.J.'s"

"What made him think you should become an actor? I mean, not that you wouldn't be good at it, but..."

"He could control me...keep an eye on me. I was a boat captain, now I'm an actor. Go figure."

"How are you getting along with R.J.?"

"Fine. He apologized about the boat. Said he didn't have the heart to tell me himself. He said he just couldn't bear keeping it...too much of a reminder."

I couldn't bite my tongue. "And how much longer before you're nothing but a reminder to be removed?"

Dennis didn't answer. I tried another question.

"Den, did Natalie's and Holden's deaths, happening so close together, affect R.J.'s and Stefanie's relationship?"

"There were a lot of rumors about them being involved, but they weren't. Stefanie is big on causes and can talk your ear off about them. R.J. listens—it's a diversion. Stefanie helped when he started buying Arabian horses. He boarded the horses until he moved to his new ranch a few months ago. He said he couldn't stay at Canon Drive. He and Stefanie collect western gear and shop at an expensive western store downtown where some boots sell for thousands and some saddles for over twenty thousand. They ordered custom-made, matching bridle chests there. R.J. really went out of character for a while. I guess horses replaced boating. At first, he would wear a western-style shirt with his usual jeans to work. Then he started wearing western boots. Soon enough, he was coming in looking like a cowboy," Dennis laughed. "Everyone on the set thought his new look was strange, but no one hinted they noticed a difference. People felt sorry for him."

"Do you think Natalie was ever jealous of Stefanie?"

"No, never. After she died, R.J. and Stefanie helped each other. They lunched a lot together, alone, in R.J.'s studio motor home, but after hours, they didn't see each other. I was always with R.J at nights, so I know. And, he started seeing Jill St. John soon after Natalie died. Too soon, in my opinion."

"Was Stefanie Powers ever aboard *Splendour*?"

"No. Not into boating. The boat was used once for a *Hart* scene, and she was there then, but that's it."

"How do you compare Stefanie to Natalie?" I asked.

"Natalie had it all over Stefanie. Natalie once told me that although Stefanie was one of R.J.'s most attractive leading ladies, the camera enhanced her beauty, and she was right. Stefanie is much prettier on screen than off. Makeup, camera angles, and lens filters can work wonders. Stefanie looked gorgeous on television, but in real life she has a blotchy complexion. She's pretty, but Natalie was stunningly gorgeous, on or off the set. And Natalie had a laugh that was like listening to a happy song. You know, Marti, there are so many good times I'd like to record, just so I don't forget about them."

"Den, that's what we've been doing."

I had suspected that once Dennis was over the donation of *Splendour*, he would renege on his original intention. He wasn't prepared to move forward.

"I'd rather tell her kids about the good times—let them remember their mom that way."

Sometimes Dennis could make me feel as if I had been the one coercing information that he had initially called in desperation to *offer* me. So I answered carefully. "Den, I think it's healthy to talk about your good times. When you finish telling the good things, and are still faced with the bad—you'll know it's time. Next year, next decade, whenever. You *were* a good captain."

"I was. And I always defended myself when Natalie would get pissed at me, but after a few times, that didn't happen much. I always still adored her."

"Tell me about a time she got mad at you."

The Wagner's entertained regularly aboard *Splendour* and treated friends and colleagues to dinner outings, harbor cruises, Catalina Island weekends, and fishing excursions. Natalie was a gracious and confident hostess. That's why, when she called to tell Dennis about a special overnight guest who would be visiting *Splendour* and asked that nothing be overlooked with the shopping, Dennis overreacted by purchasing every food, beverage, and miscellaneous item he could imagine being desired. From sardines to lobster, cold cuts to strip steaks, Soave Bolla to Dom Perignon, chips to macadamia nuts, toothpaste with and without fluoride, and countless other treats and supplies. Laden with his brimming shopping bags, he felt ready for the Queen of England. Dennis sighed with relief when he saw that the guest the Wagners arrived with was a man so profoundly admired that the Queen of England herself had anointed him Knight: Sir Laurence Olivier.

No wonder Natalie had been nervous. Dennis thought she would be pleased with his efforts to satisfy most any whim of this great man.

Although having Sir Laurence Olivier aboard was at first intimidating and overwhelming, Olivier quickly put Dennis at ease. He was an easy man, with quiet, gentle manners, yet was charismatic down to the soul. He was like royalty, a man who drew worldwide reverence, yet he was absolutely un-self-absorbed. Some of the minor stars Dennis had thus far met worked hard at their personalities, their words and actions designed to enhance a public image, even aboard a private yacht. Olivier, by contrast, was simply himself, a great man who did not have to work at being great. Dennis liked him, and Olivier voiced no qualms about allowing Dennis to take pictures to send home.

Olivier had brought along his nephew and son, and they all fished with R.J. after *Splendour* anchored. But after a mere hour, Olivier tired, so the better part of the afternoon was spent relaxing in lounge chairs on the back deck. Natalie was attentive to "Larry," and Olivier even asked Dennis to call him Larry. If ever Dennis felt star-struck, he did not reveal it, but enjoying the company of Laurence Olivier was a privilege Dennis would always appreciate.

R.J. and Natalie had recently worked with Olivier on *Cat on a Hot Tin Roof.* Natalie wondered aloud whether she had done her best with her role, not seeking a compliment but perhaps feeling a tad inferior next to the greatness of her lead. Olivier, famous for his unpretentious philosophy about acting, dismissed Natalie's doubts by telling her, "Dear, trust in your instincts as always and you'll be fine. Acting is a job, as simple as that."

His simplicity was brilliant, and he clearly appeared enthralled while listening to Natalie explain her confusion over method acting. She claimed she adored James Dean, a 100-percent method actor, but that she, who had learned to step to her mark and perform her lines, questioned the need for method acting in *every* scene, as James Dean had. She hated holding up production. The word action was once enough to get her going; now she was intrigued with method acting, but it stifled her instincts too. She confessed to Olivier that the demand for more reality acting was intimidating.

Olivier said that he worked with every kind of performer, and he told Natalie that she was one of the best he had ever shared the camera with. Larry raised his glass and toasted Natalie. She would not care what the critics would write about *Cat on a Hot Tin Roof*—she had received her genuine coverage from this profound actor sitting on her boat.

When Olivier asked apologetically to cut the cruise short, due to seasickness, R.J. asked Dennis to head back to the docks immediately. It was still daylight as Dennis secured *Splendour* at the pier, and Larry took the time to personally thank Dennis for a nice day. Natalie told Dennis he had done a great job, and R.J. shook his hand. A few weeks passed with no outings, but Dennis was aboard *Splendour* daily, doing odd jobs. With Natalie's permission, he had hired his cousin, Bay Givens, who had moved to California from New Jersey a year after Dennis. Bay kept *Splendour* sparkling clean and was well worth the part-time pay. Dennis constantly kept *Splendour* in shape by sanding and repainting, polishing, and checking all mechanics.

One afternoon, the phone rang aboard *Splendour*, and it was Natalie. She tore right into Dennis: "Dennis, are you taking food from *Splendour* for you and your girlfriend? Or is Bay stealing food? I won't tolerate it."

Dumbfounded, Dennis told himself to hold his temper, but he was about to lose it. Wanting to fight back, but intimidated by this other side of Natalie and wanting to keep his job, he got to the bottom of the problem fast.

"Natalie, I have no idea what you are talking about," he answered defensively.

"I just received the shopping invoice for the Olivier cruise, and it's over four hundred dollars! You couldn't have spent that much for food for one afternoon cruise. I trusted you with my credit card!"

Dennis fought back, job or no job. "Natalie, I overdid it because you told me to, and it was supposed to be an overnight cruise. How in the hell am I supposed to know if you planned to feed Larry steak or hot dogs? I wouldn't steal from you, and neither would Bay, and I resent the accusation. I'll return your credit card, but get your itemized bill ready, because we're going to go item for item—it's all stored away for the next cruise."

Natalie hung up. It was Dennis's first run-in with Natalie, and it upset him terribly. He hated for her to mistrust him and wished she realized how much he valued his job, that he would never jeopardize it by stealing food. Maybe others had taken advantage of her, but Dennis never would. He thought about taking off to her house but didn't. Instead, he left early and went home to the apartment he shared with his girlfriend. After venting his story, his angry girlfriend wanted to call Natalie, but Dennis wouldn't allow her.

By the next cruise, two weeks later, Dennis had not heard from Natalie, but when she and R.J. boarded *Splendour*, she first handed Dennis a lovely gift for him and his girlfriend. She was apologizing by gesture.

Although Natalie had been looking forward to a private weekend with R.J., before *Splendour* was untied to leave the pier, Dennis received an emergency phone call—his girlfriend was in the hospital. Natalie insisted that Dennis head straight to the emergency room. She said the cruise could wait for another day.

Dennis ran to the marina parking lot, jumped into his van, and turned the key to a clicking engine sound. While walking to their Mercedes, Natalie and R.J. saw Dennis's problem and offered him a ride. Dennis had expected to be dropped off at the hospital but instead was driven to the Wagner home, where Natalie handed him the keys to her prized, peach Mercedes and told him to use it until he could get his van fixed, no matter how long it took.

She trusted him.

Chapter 10

Dennis shared many fond memories of celebrity-studded weekends as we talked nightly. "Den, who was the most frequent boat guest?" I asked one night.

"Mart Crowley," Dennis answered without hesitation. "Natalie's associates and friends came on outings occasionally. Peggy Griffin, Delphine Mann, Liz Applegate, and Judy Scott-Fox were around a lot and on board for a small surprise party Natalie threw for R.J. on their fifth wedding anniversary. Natalie surprised R.J. with a replica model of *Splendour*, enclosed in a glass case. He loved it, and Natalie made a fuss over every gift they received. I gave them gold candlesticks, and she sent me a handwritten thank you."

"Was Peggy Natalie's social secretary?"

"Peggy helped Natalie with a lot of her correspondence, announcements, and calendar planning, things like that. She worked in Natalie's bedroom office. They were great friends, and so much alike. I would call Natalie and Peggy would answer, and I couldn't even tell their voices apart. Peggy walked like her, talked like her, and dressed like her."

"Why was Mart Crowley such a frequent guest?"

"He was with Natalie forever. She loved Mart. He saved her life when she took too many pills once."

"She told you something that personal?"

"She didn't get into it much, but yes, she often told me personal things. She always had a great time when Mart was on board. Mart had a secret salad recipe he kept taped inside a cabinet in the galley, so I guess it wasn't so secret. We always made his salad, whether Mart was on board or not, and we always kidded him that we would sell it to the owners of Natalie's favorite restaurant, La Scala, who Natalie sometimes invited for a cruise.

"Eddie Butterworth and Tommy Thompson, her makeup artists, were on board a lot too. I really liked Eddie. We hit it off.

"Let me explain about her two Tommys," Dennis continued. "Tommy Thompson the writer wasn't into yachting. Tommy Thompson the makeup artist was a frequent guest, but Natalie treated Tommy the writer to a few short cruises to the yacht clubs for dinner. Natalie considered him her personal writer. She would not agree to interviews with many others. Her daughter, Natasha, for some reason hated Tommy. One time, over dinner,

Natasha came right out and told Tommy that she didn't like him. It was the only time I ever saw Natalie scold Natasha. Natalie loved Tommy—adored Tommy—like family. It was kind of sad because Tommy loved her with passion. Natalie was furious when Natasha hurt his feelings. Natalie wouldn't go to Russia without Tommy."

"I remember reading about her visit in *T.V. Guide*," I said. "They were going to do a show about it, but it fell through. Did you like Tommy, the writer?"

"I really did, Marti, and Natalie liked me better for it."

"Did you ever meet Frank Sinatra?"

"He was never a guest on *Splendour*. Sinatra's around for the big things like black-tie parties, weddings, and funerals. Sinatra liked them enough to write that complaint letter about Noguchi announcing the argument aboard *Splendour*."

"Sinatra didn't know enough to write that letter."

"He just unconditionally believed Natalie's death was an accident."

"And just how well do celebrities really know one another? Keeping it light or sticking to shop talk and seeing each other only at affairs is no way to get to really know a friend. When we were younger, we talked about our deepest thoughts and aspirations. And when we didn't talk, we still understood each other because we *had* talked. Sinatra was protecting celebrity, not just a friend."

"Sinatra hated negative publicity, most celebrities do."

Did Natalie ever talk about stars like Marilyn Monroe, James Dean, Sal Mineo, or Elvis Presley?"

"Natalie said Marilyn was a victim of Hollywood. She felt sorry for her but blamed Marilyn for allowing herself to be manipulated. Natalie was a strong-willed woman who wouldn't let anyone get the best of her. Natalie could tear us up with her Monroe imitations. She would put her hands on her knees and push out her rear end. She had a pretty good sense of humor.

"She worshipped James Dean and said he would have been a megastar forever. She thought it was spooky how James Dean, Sal Mineo, and Nick Adams died before their time. She was afraid that the cast of *Rebel Without a Cause* was cursed. She was closest to Nick but said he was a troubled person. Her mother's gypsy stories got to her so much that she even contacted a personal astrologer, but she never wanted that public. She was always afraid of jinxing herself. She believed in destiny. That woman really saw herself dying in dark water. There were times that she would sit in the dinghy just shaking. Once or twice, she took the wheel for fun, but only when I was right beside her. Her superstitions controlled her sometimes.

"When Elvis died, Natalie said that he had brought it on himself, that you can't live the lifestyle he lived and expect to be around for long. But she loved knowing him. Natalie knew some of the biggest names in the world.

"Sean Connery and his wife, Micheline, came on board when Natalie made *Meteor* with him. She usually invited whoever she was doing a project with. Sean liked to be at *Splendour's* controls. He would hardly leave the wheelhouse because the technical aspects of boating fascinated him. Micheline would spend time chatting with Natalie in the main salon.

"Natalie loosened up with her closer friends. We would party late into the night, drinking, dancing, and singing. R.J. was the drinker, though, especially when Natalie was in a party mood. We would serve snacks around eight, turn on the music, and we'd sometimes dance. R.J. wasn't a dancer, so I was usually Natalie's partner."

"What's the funniest thing that ever happened on a cruise?"

Dennis laughed. "This isn't what you'd call funny, but we laughed our asses off when David Niven fell overboard. We were pulling back into the slip after having dinner at a yacht club, and David decided to jump onto the dock instead of waiting for a plank. It was about a two-yard leap. He plunged into the harbor. We ran to the side, scared to death he might've hit his head, but he was bobbing in the water and looked up at us, smiled, and said, 'Thought I could make it.' Niven was R.J.'s best friend."

"Who was your favorite guest?"

"George Segal. Natalie costarred with him and Richard Benjamin in *The Last Married Couple in America*, and they were both on board a lot then. Richard is married to Paula Prentiss. Those cruises were great fun because of George. Not only was he hilarious, but he always had the best weed."

"Did you smoke it?"

"When George was on board, I had no choice," Dennis laughed.

"Did Natalie and R.J. smoke?"

"No. George would act offended, kidding around, but R.J. still wouldn't touch it. The more George smoked, the funnier he got.

"One time, George fell in love with a stuffed teddy bear he found in Natasha's stateroom, and he wanted to take it home with him. He hugged and kissed the bear all night long, and we just cracked up every time we looked at him making out with the bear. He would bring his banjo and play for hours. He invited me to a bar, The Ginger Man, where he played on Sunday nights, and I started going every week to see him. We became buddies for a while. The only thing that ever bothered me about George was a comment he made about Sidney Poitier. Sidney was on board with his wife, and I can't begin to tell you what a distinguished man he is. And, so damn nice. When George was on board the week after Sidney, he noticed Sidney's name in the logbook and asked, 'So, Poitier was here recently? That's funny, I don't see any watermelon seeds scattered around the decks.'"

"Damn, Den, I always liked George Segal," I said. "You're ruining my image here."

"He meant it to be funny, but it sticks out in my mind because Sidney Poitier was stately and professional. I really did like George, though."

"So, did any of Natalie's female friends ever like you?"

"Just once—the daughter of the famous Haywards. She had just finished writing a book about her family, and Natalie invited her for a day cruise."

"That would be Brooke Hayward. She wrote *Haywire*."

"Yep. She flirted with me from start to finish of the cruise. I asked Natalie if she had noticed. She said I should have gone for it, but Natalie didn't tell me that until *after* the cruise." He laughed and continued, "I had to be captain too. Donna Mills was on board once, and I walked into the galley early one morning, and she was standing there in her skimpy nightie. Whew, what legs! But she was more interested in a two-day tan than in socializing."

"Who usually invited more guests, Natalie or R.J.?"

"Equal, except for fishing cruises. R.J. handled those. He invited Leigh Taylor-Young and her husband, Guy McElwaine, for pleasure cruises. Usually, R.J.'s guests were men, for fishing. Once, R.J.'s director and scriptwriter, Tom Mankiewicz, on a rainy day, stopped fishing to go inside and figured out a way to keep the pole in the water while he sat in main salon. He opened the side door about an inch and stuck his pole through it, and sat back with a beer. R.J. rode his ass all day, calling him a big baby, all in fun."

"How often did *Splendour* go out?"

"At first, about once a month, then gradually more. Summer was always more active, and if R.J. wasn't using her, he loaned her to friends or charters."

"Who handled the charters?"

"They wouldn't trust that yacht with anyone but me. I let my brother Paul handle a charter once, and Natalie was really upset. I really almost got fired."

* * *

When Dennis's brother Paul and their mother visited Los Angeles, R.J. provided studio passes for them and insisted they enjoy a *Splendour* cruise, courtesy of the Wagners. By the vacation's end, Paul was fascinated with Dennis's new life and chose to stay in California. Dennis had a chartering business, which he operated around the Wagners' schedule, so he hired Paul.

Dennis had promised to skipper a special cruise for a businessman that coincided with a weekend the Wagners offered a private cruise for Gregory Peck and his wife. Dennis explained his situation, but Natalie, as always, pulled weight, reminding Dennis to "remember his place." Dennis called to cancel the other charter, but the businessman pleaded with Dennis and offered extra payment, so Dennis came up with a solution. He skippered the outside charter and commissioned Paul, whom he had trained well and thoroughly trusted, to handle the Pecks' cruise. The Pecks will like Paul better, Dennis rationalized.

Paul, completely familiar with *Splendour*, skippered his first solo outing, handling the boat and the Pecks perfectly. After returning the Pecks from a two-day cruise to Catalina Island late Sunday afternoon, Dennis met the Pecks as *Splendour* was being docked. He had yet to see two more contented faces following a cruise.

"They must have liked you," Dennis told Paul after Mrs. Peck kissed Paul's cheek and strolled down the dock to the parking lot with her husband.

Paul showed Dennis the hundred-dollar bill they had tipped him. Then, he reached in his pocket and pulled out a check, "Look, Den," he said, "they didn't think one hundred was enough, so they wrote me a fifty-dollar check too!

"Mrs. Peck and I talked for hours last night while Mr. Peck slept," Paul told Dennis. "She was crying because her dog was just killed, and she's devastated. I consoled her after she told me the story. She left the house to go shopping, and saw her dog in her upstairs bedroom window. He kept barking then disappeared for a few seconds. She heard a loud shattering sound and looked up to see her dog flying from the window. He landed at her feet in a shower of glass shards."

"Paul, I'm glad you handled that one."

"Den, she would have gotten to you too. Overall, the trip was quiet. Gregory Peck read his *MacArthur* script most of the weekend while I kept Mrs. Peck company. They stayed in their pajamas the whole weekend, just lounging around. I cooked a few simple meals, and they raved over the food! They were thrilled with everything, I assure you."

Dennis thanked Paul for a job well done and paid him. Two days later, Natalie called. "How dare you have allowed Paul to charter the boat for the Pecks?" she hissed. "Dennis, this was Gregory and Veronique *Peck*! I can't believe you'd be so nonchalant about it and hand it over to Paul!"

Dennis defended his decision and praised Paul's work, but Dennis did understand her point and never missed a future *Splendour* outing. When the Wagners began using their yacht on a weekly basis, Dennis's charter business slowed and eventually ceased. R.J. realized what Dennis was losing with the charter business, but R.J. wanted to fish as often as possible, so he gave Dennis a substantial pay raise. R.J. trusted and liked Dennis.

After one morning of fishing with Dennis and Paul, R.J. invited the brothers back to his house for a barbecue. The Wagners' deep, narrow backyard, landscaped by lush shrubbery and flower beds, stretched behind a large inground pool surrounded by potted trees and flowers on a spacious brick patio. Natalie, wearing a one-piece, black bathing suit, a floppy-brimmed white sun hat, and large, dark sunglasses, immediately left her lounge chair and rushed to greet Dennis and Paul with a hug when they stepped onto the patio.

"Paul and Dennis, make yourselves at home," she said, "and you must try one of Paula's Bloody Marys! She makes the best—and the hottest—in town."

Dennis looked over to an umbrella-shaded table where actresses Paula Prentiss and Dyan Cannon sat and chatted. Three women, whom Dennis didn't recognize, sat by the edge of the pool with their feet in the water.

Natalie conducted introductions as she handed Dennis and Paul each a tall Bloody Mary. Dennis and Paul noticed they were the only men in attendance, other than R.J., and they felt awkward. R.J. suggested they take a dip in the pool and directed them to the guesthouse for swim trunks.

Paul and Dennis walked the flowered path to the guesthouse, passing a greenhouse filled with plants and flowers. Dozens of photographs, recounting R.J.'s and Natalie's many career accomplishments, covered the guesthouse walls. It was a virtual museum of Wagner's and Wood's histories. Natalie's three Academy Award nomination certificates hung in the front room.

Forget the party on the patio—Dennis and Paul would have preferred an afternoon alone in the guesthouse with the huge Jacuzzi, stocked bar, regulation-sized pool table in the recreation room, and large, personal gym filled with professional exercise equipment. A jungle of hanging and potted plants complemented the interior, and glass doors led to an attached pool house filled with rattan furniture and equipped with yet another bar. Upstairs, a warmly decorated apartment with sleeping quarters, kitchenette, and TV room left Paul commenting, "Den, this is just the guest house—I'd be thrilled if just this upstairs apartment were my main home!"

Paul and Dennis selected their swim trunks and rejoined Natalie's get-together. Mia Farrow had arrived and said hello to Dennis and Paul. Dennis went right into the pool from the shallow end, and Paul dove in from the diving board. Paul came up quickly with a frightened look plastered on his face. Urgently, he waved to Dennis, then summoned him, trying to not draw attention.

"What's wrong, Paul?" Dennis asked from across the pool.

"Shhhh!" Paul hissed loudly, "shhhh!"

Dennis swam over to Paul. "What's wrong?" he whispered.

"The trunks were way too big for me, and they fell off when I dove in. Hurry and get them for me, Den, before people notice. Dyan Cannon looks like she's on her way over here. Please, hurry!"

The yard filled with Dennis's laughter, and all the women looked into the pool.

Natalie's parties were the talk of the town, and Dennis was invited to many of them. Dennis recalled with special fondness the holiday parties. Ernie, a rough, retired police officer, played Santa Claus every Christmas Eve at Natalie's annual open house party. Natasha and Courtney and the invited guests loved having their pictures taken with Santa. Natasha caught on to Ernie, but Courtney was in awe that Santa came to her house. Natalie invited her friends and their children, and always had a gift for everyone. She loved having the house filled with children on Christmas Eve, and she decorated like a Christmas wonderland.

Natalie and R.J.'s black-tie New Year's Eve parties were the place to be to start a new year. Natalie made sure she spent time with every friend, and there wasn't a guest left untouched by Natalie's charm before the clock struck midnight.

Dennis's mother visited once or twice a year throughout Dennis's tenure, and one of her visits coincided with the private screening of Natalie's latest accomplishment, *The Cracker Factory*. Natalie told Dennis to bring his family and friends. Upon their arrival at Century City Studios, Dennis's party was directed to Studio B. The room was equipped with plush chairs, and coffee and pastries were served. Dennis and his guests first went to the front row to say hello to R.J. and Natalie, who sat next to the Pecks. Veronique Peck stood and kissed Paul on his cheek. William Devane, Natalie's costar in her current project, *From Here to Eternity*, sat behind Natalie. He nodded, acknowledging Dennis's family.

Dennis and his four guests took their seats behind Natalie's sister Lana Wood, who turned to introduce herself to Dennis's family. Paul and Lana chatted before the show started, but once the lights dimmed, everyone sat back quietly to watch Natalie on the screen.

When the lights came back on, Dennis's mother had tears in her eyes. She went directly to Natalie. "Natalie, you were wonderful. I couldn't help crying," Ruth Davern said.

"Thank you, Ruth," Natalie smiled graciously. "Your tears mean that I made my part believable. I thank you for them."

When Natalie and R.J. left town the day after the screening, they offered Dennis and his family the use of their home. Willie Mae made a big pot of chicken soup, and Dennis and his family watched movies all weekend at the Wagners' comfortable home.

Paul's work had slowed after Dennis was primarily back on *Splendour* duty, so Paul returned to New Jersey with his mother at the end of her vacation—after a year in California he would never forget.

Chapter 11

Dennis had taken the first step in recapturing his life, but it would be a gradual process. His trip down memory lane soothed his wounds, so I stuck to related questions. He was telling me more than he realized.

"Denny, how did you become so close to R.J. and Natalie?" I asked one night. "Were they as close to their other employees?"

"R.J. and Natalie were nice to everyone who worked for them, but because of the nature of my job, it brought me closer than if I'd been their landscaper or something like that. Bob Lang, a carpenter, worked for Natalie when she decorated houses. She was close to her hairdressers and makeup artists, too, but they were more a part of her business. Natalie adored a hairdresser named Ginger who never came on the boat. I wish I had talked more with her friends after she died, but I was too isolated with R.J."

"Was Natalie close to Willie Mae?" I asked.

"I was Natalie's sidekick aboard *Splendour* and the one who knew best how to maneuver that boat. My job was important. We became closer because of that. She trusted Willie Mae, too, but Willie Mae once told me she thought Natalie was cold toward her. Willie Mae said that when she used to take them breakfast in bed, R.J. would always greet her with a warm 'Good morning,' but Natalie sometimes wouldn't even acknowledge her. One day, Willie Mae came right out and told Natalie that she didn't like being ignored. After that, Willie Mae said Natalie never disregarded her again. Sometimes you just had to remind Natalie of who you were. She probably wasn't ignoring Willie Mae on purpose. She always told me how grateful she was to have found a wonderful nanny like Willie Mae.

"When Natalie got mad at me, it was for good reason. One time, I cruised R.J., Natalie, and the girls to a yacht club in Newport so the family could have dinner there. I had nothing to do, so called my girlfriend to meet me at the boat. I didn't think Natalie would find out, but they were sitting near a window having dinner, and they all saw Yolanda come aboard. When they left the restaurant, Natasha came running up to me, chanting 'You're gonna get fired. You're gonna get fired.' Natasha never spoke to me like that, so I knew Natalie must have been fuming. Natalie walked right up to me and asked, 'Dennis, what did you do while we were having dinner?' I told her I invited Yolanda to spend a little time with me. She said, 'Dennis, do you like working for us?' I said I did, and she said, 'Then don't ever do it again.' That was it."

"Would she have fired you?"

"Probably not, but she needed to be clear about rules. Sometimes her gripes were legitimate; sometimes they weren't. She didn't like Yolanda. Natalie liked having me available, and my personal life got in the way. When we had our sessions, she always told me to reevaluate my dating habits."

"And you welcomed that kind of advice from her?"

"I always listened. I dated nice girls, but I'd tell Natalie about my relationship problems, and she'd play the psychiatrist role by asking things like, 'If you stopped seeing this girl, how would you feel?' I'd answer that I'd feel sad, or set free, whatever applied, and she would take it from there. When she suggested I give up on Olivia, who I lived with, that was a hard choice. Three kids were involved, but Olivia and I argued constantly. When it came to my fiancée, Yolanda, Natalie recognized problems that took me longer to see."

"Did you end it with Yolanda?"

Dennis laughed. "No. As soon as the session ended, I took Natalie and her girls to shore in Avalon and went back to Yolanda, who was stowed away in my stateroom. I only did that a couple of times. When I lived with Olivia, I told Natalie that Olivia wanted me to quit my captain job to look for a job with regular hours. Olivia wanted me around on weekends. My weekends were devoted to the Wagners.

"Natalie liked when I took her girls to Knott's Berry Farm amusement park or to the movies. So when I asked for more weekends off, Natalie reminded me that my job *was* weekends, but she said, 'Okay, Dennis, take weekends off.'"

* * *

Although Dennis was given the nod for weekends off, his paycheck decreased, but Natalie sat him down for a "session" and offered him *Splendour* as a home. She knew Dennis would delight in living aboard the yacht and that it might help him to understand priorities. It, of course, benefited her, too, but Natalie genuinely seemed to care about Dennis's relationship problems. He moved out of his girlfriend's apartment and aboard *Splendour*, where he appreciated anew Natalie's decorating efforts.

While R.J. was content with *Splendour*'s original design and purpose as a sixty-foot sport fisherman's yacht—solid, seaworthy, and functional—Natalie had reveled in the challenge of turning the simply designed, rather macho *Splendour* into a luxurious boat that not only served its main purpose but also accommodated Natalie's desire to entertain with style. She had combined elegance, practicality, and hominess within a nautical theme.

The prevailing color scheme included varying hues of Natalie's favorite pelican blue. The stern's trim was painted pelican blue to match *Splendour*'s name on the back panel. The outside deck furniture consisted of two fishing chairs and two long benches, which opened for storage. Dennis designed a corner wet-bar that enclosed a washer and dryer beneath its counter. R.J. often complimented Dennis's innovation in hiding the bulky appliances in an attractive and useful unit, while keeping all the plumbing in one corner. It worked perfectly because the swim step was at the stern, which made it convenient after fishing or swimming to toss towels immediately into the washer. When partying on the rear deck, drinks were easily accessible from the wet bar. Otherwise, a trip through the master stateroom or along the side deck would be necessary to reach the main salon for refills.

The section between the back deck and the main salon was Natalie's and R.J.'s full-width master stateroom with a king-sized bed, built-in wall drawers, a standing vanity dresser, and a private head and shower. Natalie never minded that the master stateroom was used as a path from the back deck to the salon, as she liked her peach and autumn colors in there to be seen.

A few steps up from the master stateroom led to the dark blue–carpeted, spacious main salon. Four settees were done in blue and beige fabrics. A solid wood coffee table stood in front of the sofas. Sliding glass doors led to the slim side deck. A hatch door in the middle of the floor led to the engine room below. A floor-to-ceiling entertainment unit held flourishing plants, books, a stereo, a television, and a VCR. Birch walls with teakwood trim offered a distinct atmosphere of warmth. The birch and teakwood open galley took up a corner of the main salon. Its refrigerator was paneled in birch. A striking contrast in the galley, a small stretch of kitchen wall sparkled blue and white with tiles Natalie had imported from Spain.

Dennis had built a solid birch counter dividing the main salon and galley. Rows of round holes, which he had painstakingly cut into the salon side of the counter, created a beautiful wine rack.

The top of the counter served as a bar. Overhead cabinets enclosed varieties of liquors and spirits.

Stepping down a few steps, the main salon led to a forward guest stateroom, Courtney's and Natasha's cabin, and the captain's quarters at the very front of the yacht. Natalie chose a pale blue-and-white striped wallpaper in these rooms and all three bathrooms, accessible either from the hallway or from the individual rooms, were similarly decorated.

Above Dennis's quarters was the bow, a large open deck equipped with white, built-in cushioned seats. The dinghy, when not used, was stored on the bow top, tied to cleats.

Above the main salon was the wheelhouse, *Splendour's* control center. This solid and inviting room, which housed the wheel and the navigational equipment, was charged with energy and purpose. The white wheelhouse was carpeted in blue. The surrounding isenglass windows, framed in wood, welcomed sunlight and offered a view from any position in the room. A long, built-in bench with blue-gold-and-tan striped cushions crossed the wall behind the helm. A built-in corner settee, claimed by Natalie, was smothered with pillows, some that Natalie had designed herself. A large wood coffee table with navigation charts laminated over the top provided an instant conversation piece.

From the wheelhouse, a hinged ladder led to the all-white fly bridge directly above. It was easy to feel on top of the world when navigating *Splendour* from up there. A U-shaped, white vinyl booth surrounded the wheel.

Clocks, plaques, photographs, pillows, "yacht warming" gifts from the Wagners' friends, and various accessories warmly personalized *Splendour*.

Splendour fast became R.J.'s second home, and he was possessive of the boat, spending as much spare time as he could with it. He barely tolerated his former yacht club after owning *Splendour*. He felt that *Splendour* was too good for the stuffy yacht clubs. Soon into his ownership, visits to Newport got old, and R.J. chose Catalina Island as his retreat. He could not understand the other yacht owners who would fire up their engines to take a brief hour cruise to a yacht club for dinner, then brag about their journeys afterward.

R.J. had a special flag made for *Splendour*, which he proudly raised at the start of many cruises. The letters W.O.F.Y.C. were colorfully displayed across a white background. The acronym stood for Wagner's Own Fucking Yacht Club.

Natalie didn't like the familiarity of the marina area, so she kept having *Splendour* moved from marina to marina. Death threats, which she had received in her home mailbox and taped to her car, caused Natalie to be leery and fearful of public places. Although R.J. was able to beef up security at home with new deadbolts and iron bars on the windows, *Splendour* was public. Natalie felt vulnerable when visiting the boat.

A man had been following Natalie around, leaving notes. The notes said, "I want you, I've always wanted you, I will have you." Natalie called the police when she found a letter in her mailbox, and the stalker was caught and told to stay away from Natalie, and he did. R.J. approached the stalker when he once saw him outside and threatened, "If you ever come near enough to my wife to touch her, I'll kill you."

Once, at the marina, Natalie looked up to a nearby apartment building and noticed a man, from his apartment window, looking through a telescope aimed in her direction. That's when she insisted on moving the boat to a security-tight marina. At Tahiti Marina in Marina del Rey, Natalie finally felt comfortable and safe. Tahiti Marina became *Splendour*'s home and remained so until she was donated.

Dennis, now a permanent *Splendour* resident at Tahiti Marina, entertained his friends there, threw an occasional party, and with R.J.'s permission, hosted personal cruises. R.J. and Natalie were completely comfortable entrusting their yacht to Dennis. R.J. believed wholeheartedly in Dennis's reliability, and Natalie overlooked Dennis's shortcomings. They both accepted Dennis's occasional mischief in exchange for a top-notch captain.

However, every silver lining has a cloud, and Dorothy Metzler, the manager of Tahiti Marina, was a thunderhead. Short, fiftyish, with cropped silver-gray hair and rarely a smile to spare, Dorothy's pure drill-sergeant persona had her marching about her marina with an air of authority that could make the seagulls stand at attention. And Dennis was Dorothy's menace. It was not long before she had tolerated Dennis's shenanigans beyond her capacity.

One bright, breezy morning, as Dennis was refinishing some splintered wood, he heard an unfamiliar flapping sound. Curious, he followed it to the side deck where a nine-by-twelve-inch manila envelope clung to the boat by its last shred of adhesive tape. Dennis grabbed the envelope. Inside was a neatly typed two-page letter. His panic grew with every sentence he read (entire letter exactly as written):

August 27, 1979
Mr. Robert Wagner
603 North Canon Drive
Beverly Hills, Ca. 90213
Slip B-501/502

Dear Mr. Wagner,
No one likes Dennis better than I do, but we cannot continually stop
our lives to go out and resolve the problems he and his guests create.
Would you be kind enough to let him know how often he and his friends
can go on your boat, especially at night? It seems to be continual, and
obviously, he does not know the rules regardless of how many times I
tell him.

Problems are:
     1) Guests at night: no parking passes, banging of car doors,
loud talking, loud car motors (awoke our apartment tenants - tonight
8/27; dog in car barked for two hours consistently, and I had eighteen
calls. Dennis's guests left upon my request at 9:30 PM, and they were
nice, BUT - 3 cars here!)
     2) He does not give us guests NAMES; really, only BOAT
OWNERS have guests on property, except for Dennis. He seems to be
an exception to all our rules.
     3) He continually has his bike on finger despite a request by
us, the Harbor Patrol and Boat Fire Dept. to not leave it there. But it's
still there as of 8/27.
     4) Fire Dept., Harbor Patrol and Dept. of Small Craft Harbors
and ourselves have requested several times to not have your electrical
lines across headwalk - gangway (gone now), but have had to make this
request several times of Dennis.
If you have given him Carte Blanc on his personal use of your boat,
then he MUST let us know who, when. etc. his guests are and get passes
from us, like our other boat tenants do. Dennis is the only boat tenant
who isn't an owner!
I do not personally have the time to go out at nighttime to stop Dennis
from his wrong doings. I work all day and this is above and beyond the
call of duty for me, but I must protect and help my apartment and boat
tenants. Dennis is very nice, very sweet, and a charmer, but a constant
headache to me.

Thank God, my 240 other tenants do not take up as much of my time
as Dennis does.

Could we please get this cleared up once and for all?

Sincerely, Tahiti Marina
Dorothy Metzler, Manager

P.S. From what I hear, people were on boat all week with dog, and even
going to the bathroom with leg lifted on boat - per tenants (Apartment
and boat)

     Dennis, scared witless, rushed straight down to the marina
office with the letter, praying that Dorothy hadn't already sent it
to the Wagner home. Natalie would insist that R.J. fire him over
it. She could laugh away Dennis's minor indiscretions, but this—
the dog peeing on the boat—would be too much.

     Although Dennis was annoyed with how Dorothy had
portrayed him and his friends, he surrendered to her. It wasn't the
first time Dorothy had tried to blow the whistle on Dennis. She
once had the audacity to interrupt a commercial that was being
filmed aboard *Splendour*. The National Coast Guard had been all
set up and ready to shoot a piece about safe boat handling when
Dorothy stormed down the dock, screaming, "Dennis, I want to
talk to you! I know that an Oriental girl left here around six in the
morning, and we must discuss this matter now! I want you in my
office immediately!"

     All action came to an abrupt halt. Everyone heard her,
including R.J. However, R.J. was so angered by her inconsiderate
interruption that he forgot to reprimand Dennis. "And what in the
hell does the girl's nationality have to do with it?" R.J. later
commented, annoyed.

     This time Dennis was practically on his knees, promising
Dorothy he would behave. It took some doing, but Dennis finally
convinced her not to send the letter, and he offered her a cruise
aboard *Splendour* in appreciation for her compliance.

     When Dennis asked R.J. and Natalie if they would mind
his taking Dorothy and her guests out for an evening harbor cruise,
R.J. and Natalie praised Dennis's idea as an ideal thank-you to
Dorothy for all her hard work at the marina. Dennis told Dorothy
to invite whomever she wanted. Oddly, for a marina manager, she
insisted that Dennis keep *Splendour* in harbor waters where it
doesn't get too rough. "Just cocktailing, and no rocking," she had
said. She also insisted that Dennis buy nothing for the cruise when
he said it was the Wagners' treat. She would provide for her friends.

     Dorothy arrived early, carrying only a recycled jelly jar that
was half-filled with vodka. Dennis, amused by her provisions for

her friends, thought her even more an oddball than previously suspected. Ten of Dorothy's friends showed up. Luckily, despite Dorothy's previous objections, Dennis had stocked plenty of food and drink.

A week later, Dennis received a thoughtful thank-you note from Dorothy, along with a bottle of Chivas Regal. Dorothy and her friends had been thoroughly delighted with their moonlit cruise through the harbor, cocktailing with no rocking.

Chapter 12

Coinciding with the second anniversary of Natalie Wood's death, Dr. Thomas T. Noguchi's book *Coroner* was released in November 1983. I immediately purchased it, hoping for some new insight into Natalie's death. My questions, however, only multiplied after reading the chapter about Natalie Wood.

Noguchi stated that he was revealing for the first time the facts that recreated Natalie Wood's last moments. Those facts were uncovered in a report that Noguchi, to avoid "media indignation over too many details," decided not to previously release to the public.

Noguchi's information was based on a combination of Paul Miller's report and Marilyn Wayne's claim of having heard a woman's cry for help. Noguchi quoted his colleague, Paul Miller, saying that Natalie Wood had "died with class," fighting the currents that pulled her away from the yacht.

Noguchi asserted that Natalie Wood fell into the water wearing her nightgown, down jacket, and wool socks. She grabbed hold of the dinghy, knowing it would hold her up safely until she caught her breath. The wind began sweeping the dinghy out to the open sea. Within seconds, the dinghy was too far from the yacht for her to swim back to it. She began crying for help at this point, but she still felt safe because of the dinghy. She could crawl into it, start its engine, and be back on the yacht in minutes.

When she tried to climb into the dinghy, she found she could not do it. Using for leverage the metal frame that held the outboard motor in place, she tried again and again to hoist herself into the dinghy, but the weight of her saturated jacket dragged her back down into the water every time.

Finally, she decided to propel the dinghy back toward the shore of Catalina. Desperately, she started kicking her legs as hard as she could, paddling the water with her free arm. The heavy jacket pulled her down, and its weight sapped her strength, but she kept paddling.

She managed to swim, pulling the dinghy along with her, until she was less than two hundred yards from shore. Hypothermia then caused her to lose consciousness. She lost her grip on the boat, sank beneath the waves, and drowned.

Shaking my head in disbelief, I called Dennis. "I read Noguchi's new book. It doesn't even sound plausible to me how he explains Natalie's death."

Dennis answered, "I'm sure it doesn't, but tell me what it says."

"For one thing, Denny, he says, and I quote, 'Forensic evidence, such as the fingernail scratches on the side of the dinghy, the brush-type abrasion on her cheek, and the untouched algae on the swim step, seemed to indicate that she was trying to board the dinghy, not just adjust its rope, when the accident happened.' Then he says, 'Considering the wind funnel, when Natalie Wood, for whatever reason, untied the boat, the wind was strong and would have pushed it away from the yacht. And it is quite possible that, instead of trying to step into the dinghy, she might have been reaching for it and lost her balance.'"

"Marti, just forget his report. It has nothing to do with what happened. Natalie didn't untie the dinghy or try to make it stop banging. She didn't go anywhere near the dinghy."

"Then who did? Who untied it?"

"Well, it wasn't me. And Christopher was in his stateroom." He let out a long sigh. "I can't tell you over the phone. Tell me what else Noguchi said."

"Well, I could pick apart his entire report, but what good does it do if you won't answer my questions? He's completely ignoring the fact that those socks were on her feet when she was found. And his jacket information makes no sense. It supposedly dragged her back down every time she tried to climb into the dinghy, hindering her progress in paddling to shore, 'pulling her down' and 'sapping her strength.' Why didn't she just take it off?"

Natalie's oversight was explained by Noguchi: "The intoxication was one of the factors involved in the fact that she was not able to respond well to the emergency, after she was in the water."

Yet in a prior statement, Noguchi had said, "The point one four level of alcohol in the blood means she was only 'slightly intoxicated.' She apparently was having wine, champagne—perhaps seven or eight glasses. That would certainly not cause a person to be drunk."

"How drunk was she, Den?" I asked

He answered, "A little more than usual, but she never got flat-faced, falling down drunk, ever. She always had her wits about her."

"How could an investigation be closed so fast with so many unanswered questions? I want to know more."

"Not on the phone. I'll be in Jersey for Thanksgiving. We'll talk then."

I was caught up in Natalie's death and the mystery surrounding it. I had begun the project as Denny's friend and confidant—his unlicensed therapist. I wasn't motivated then by personal objectives. I had had no driving desire to explore Natalie Wood's death. I had accepted the tragedy as one might accept a movie with a disturbing ending, perhaps because all I had known of her was what I'd seen on screen. The real Natalie Wood had been as fictional to me as the characters she had portrayed. I had been a huge fan, but how ironic that the stardom that had made her name and face known across America and around the world could also take away the reality of her. But I lay awake nights now, obsessed with thoughts of the woman Natalie Wood had been, of the flesh-and-bone human being who had lived a life beyond the screen. She had experienced hope, fear, joy, sorrow, need, and desire. She had loved and married and been swept away by romance. She had given birth, changed messy diapers, encouraged first steps, and thrilled at first words. She had cuddled soft puppies, tasted snowflakes, and marveled at the same stars that shone outside my window. Because Dennis had brought me into the mystery of her death, it was now a personal matter to me. The little I knew of it tormented me with the constant need to know more. Furious with Noguchi's account, knowing what I knew— and tolerating Dennis's reluctance to tell more—was unbearably frustrating.

I took a deep breath, knowing that my conversation with Dennis would reveal little more, but I asked, "Denny, please tell me what her bruises looked liked when you identified her."

"She looked like she had been pulled from a boxing ring instead of from an ocean."

"Big fight with a dinghy?"

"No, that's Noguchi's convenient way to explain the bruises, but it's not how she got them. God, Marti, identifying her body was the hardest thing I ever had to do in my life."

"I think it's unforgivable that R.J. didn't identify his own wife."

"He couldn't, Marti. He just couldn't," Dennis said, with genuine pity in his voice.

* * *

Thanksgiving 1983, Dennis visited New Jersey. When I had Dennis to myself, Friday evening after the holiday, I reiterated that I wanted details. What Dennis said after numbed me.

"Marti, I'm going to tell R.J. that I want to write a book and that I asked for your help. I'll tell him that I'm tired of being hounded by reporters. Maybe I'll feel better if he knows what I'm doing instead of me going behind his back. Maybe I'll get his approval, and I can concentrate more on the good times."

I couldn't believe my ears. I said, "Den, if you want to write about your experiences with the Wagners, I'll gladly help, but I keep reliving your phone call a few months ago when you were completely shattered. That isn't going to just disappear now. Are you afraid of losing Wagner too?"

"I'm just afraid, period," he said.

I didn't push.

Dennis stayed in New Jersey for a week, and we accomplished nothing. His brother Paul, intending to join the Screen Actors Guild and try to build a career in general acting, accompanied Dennis back to California. Paul's acting career, however, never saw a start. After two weeks in Los Angeles, living with Dennis, Paul called me.

"It's obvious that you're your brother's brother," I joked. "It's three in the morning, Paul. Where's Den?"

"Passed out. Where else?"

"What's going on?"

"Marti, I need to get out of here, and I'm flat broke. Moving back here was the biggest mistake. When Den used to captain *Splendour*, it was a dream world out here. Now, it's pure nightmare. He's killing himself."

"Did you join the Guild?"

"No, and I want to leave here. Please, can you lend me the money? Den drinks constantly, and I don't know how he gets up every morning to go to work, but he does. He escaped a drunk driving charge by convincing the cop he's severely depressed, which he is. He hardly eats, and he's miserable. He's lost over sixty pounds. I can't watch this anymore."

"Have you seen Wagner?"

"Yeah, we went over his house the other night. He acted happy to see me, but it seemed like acting, and we weren't there long. Den was going to tell him he wanted to write a book, but he lost his nerve. I really don't care. He's not the Denny we all knew. He's aimless, completely torn apart. He wasn't even like this when our brother died!"

"Well, maybe a burden of guilt wasn't attached with your brother's death, just sorrow," I explained. "I'll wire you money, but I wish you didn't have to leave Den alone. He has to stop punishing himself. I'll wait for him to call me."

Two months later, on February 9, 1984, Dennis's call came early in the evening. He was sober. "Marti, a lot has happened since we last talked. I went to see R.J. last night to tell him about our plans."

I held my breath for what he next had to say.

* * *

When Dennis convinced himself that he should tell Robert Wagner of his intentions to recount his *Splendour* years' memories in a book, he had rationalized that he then wouldn't be going behind R.J.'s back. Despite another truth that ate away at him, he still felt a confusing loyalty to R.J. But just as Dennis had conjured the nerve to tell R.J., Dennis's ex-fiancée, Yolanda, whom Dennis had been engaged to at the time of Natalie's death and had broken up with soon after, phoned Dennis.

"Dennis, we broke up because of the change in you after Natalie died," she reminded him, "and I think the public deserves to know that I think you're hiding something, so I'm doing an interview with the *Star*."

"How much, Yolanda?"

"I'm not doing this for money, Dennis. This is to wake you up."

"Yolanda, please don't. You have no right. If I want things told about me, I'll tell them." Dennis trembled, imagining R.J.'s reaction, certain that R.J. would blame Dennis and think he was behind Yolanda's decision.

The article appeared in the January 17, 1984, edition of the *Star*.

Yolanda mentioned the tension aboard *Splendour* the night Natalie died. She told about an exchange of gifts between Natalie and R.J., about how loving R.J. had always been to Natalie the few times she had been in their company, about Natalie's mood swings, about the pressure Natalie was under while filming *Brainstorm*, and about how her own romance with Dennis had hit the rocks soon after Natalie's death.

The published information infuriated Dennis. He desperately wanted R.J. to believe that he had had nothing to do with it. He repeatedly called R.J. on the *Hart to Hart* set, but R.J. didn't return his calls. He phoned R.J. at home to no avail. Dennis went to the studio and knocked on R.J.'s motor home door.

"What do you want?" R.J. asked, perturbed, as Dennis stepped inside.

"I tried calling you, R.J., to tell you that Yolanda went public," Dennis spoke with the rapidity of a child hell-bent on getting out every excuse before punishment, "and she knows nothing, I swear. I never said *anything* to her. She's surmising it all, so don't worry. She's just getting even for our break-up, and I begged her not to do this when she called to warn me."

"Forget it, Dennis," R.J. interrupted.

"Do you believe me?" Dennis asked.

R.J. threw his hands in the air with exasperation. "Stop it! Just stop it, Dennis," he scowled. "I don't give a fuck anymore who says what! So, give it the fuck up, Dennis, okay? It's over!"

"Well, I just want to let you know that I had nothing to do with it," Dennis meekly explained.

"With what, Dennis? So fucking what, what that bitch had to say! I don't give a fuck if you sell out too. But, mark my words that *no one* will *ever* make a movie or publish a book about Natalie in *my* lifetime. Yeah, I *can* control that!"

Dennis left the trailer. Driving home, he recalled two separate incidents that had occurred years before that now helped him to understand his lack of surprise at R.J.'s reaction. R.J. had once told Dennis about a limousine driver who had written a book about his own former employer, and R.J. found it a deplorable stab in the back to the actor who had given the man a livelihood. Another incident now stood out. At the docks once, R.J. and Dennis passed a man who was genuinely happy to have bumped into R.J. The guy smiled, shook R.J.'s hand, and asked about Natalie and the girls. R.J., at first, looked as if he had seen a ghost, then he acted hurried, said he had no time to talk, and quickly dashed down the dock from the man. When Dennis asked who the man was, R.J. said that it was a former employee whose name he couldn't recall. But Dennis had noticed that R.J. had been too disturbed not to have recalled the man.

Dennis was now certain his friendship with R.J. neared an end. Knowing it and accepting it created a struggle. Dennis wanted to believe he had acquired something meaningful, a substantial relationship with R.J. over the past nine years, but apparently R.J. felt differently, and Dennis was now only more hurt, confused, and rejected. R.J.'s life did not involve playing cat and mouse with reporters, as Dennis's did.

Dennis had been a part of R.J.'s and Natalie's lives, but R.J. failed to understand that the reverse was just as true: the Wagner family had been an integral and vivid part of Dennis's life.

Dennis had every right to tell about his own life and experiences. Dennis's obsessive need to account for his life, and for a friend's death, gave him the courage to confront R.J. again.

February 8, 1984, Dennis drove to R.J.'s new ranch home, feeling every bit the stranger he tried to convince himself he wasn't. R.J. appeared at the door, annoyed with Dennis for having paid another uninvited visit. Dennis had always been welcomed, at any time of the day or night, at the former Wagner home on Canon Drive. Things had changed drastically.

Dennis wasn't invited past the foyer, so he started what he had to say right there. "R.J.," he nervously said, "I'm thinking about, you know, to get the reporters off my back, and to keep from...."

"Wait, Dennis," R.J. interrupted. R.J. disappeared into an adjoining room as Dennis stood awkwardly waiting by the front door. A few minutes later, R.J. returned, holding a check. "Here, Dennis," R.J. said as he shoved the check into Dennis's hand. "Take this as final payment for odd jobs and make it from here on your own."

Dennis, stunned, waited a few beats as a new reality shifted into place: R.J. was a man he did not know and probably never had known. Dennis turned his back, and R.J. slammed the door behind him.

Outside, Dennis looked at the check. Two thousand dollars. Odd jobs? Dennis hadn't even seen R.J. more than twice in the past few months. He considered shredding the check, but his days in Los Angeles were now numbered, and he could use the money to move away.

On February 8, 1984, the date written on Dennis's final check from Wagner, Dennis vowed to never see or speak to R.J. again.

Chapter 13

I had listened to Dennis's anecdotes; I had talked him through despair he could not bear alone; I had absorbed hints about a truth not yet told; I had altered my life to accommodate him; I had studied every published detail of Natalie's death and jotted volumes of notes for a story I did not know the ending to. The unanswered questions to Natalie Wood's death ate away at me constantly. What burning secret had turned my strong, upbeat, forthright friend into a frightened, intimidated drunkard? More than ever, I wanted to know. I figured my chances for answers now, since Robert Wagner was gone from Dennis's life, would be better.

But, I was wrong.

Dennis wasn't yet emotionally stable or brave enough to confront his story head on. His partial confession had released enough of his guilt and fear to postpone the entire truth. He still worked at the Hollywood studios. He was still confused over how truth might affect his life and the life of Natalie's loved ones. He would not venture out on a limb he felt too weak to support him. Limbs take years to strengthen. The truth came from Dennis in dribbles, not mouthfuls, but I didn't doubt for a moment that his information was true. I realized I was not going to coax, trick, or coerce one detail from him, so as difficult as it was to do, I bit my tongue.

Dennis concentrated on his acting career. He still lived in his apartment near P.V., and worked at various studios, away from the *Hart* set.

Almost a year to the date that Dennis had first called and asked for my help, he flew to New Jersey. I had drafted Dennis's *Splendour* years' memoirs and anecdotes and presented him with a rough draft when he stayed at my home for two weeks. At my dining room table, Dennis sat for hours, engrossed in his memories in manuscript form, but I told him that the material was for his eyes only. I said, "We haven't even touched on Natalie's death."

"Marti, I'm still not sure—"

"Okay, Den, whatever you want," I said, not hiding my aggravation.

"Marti, let me explain—"

"No, Den, let me explain," I interrupted. "Tell *all* or tell nothing. You were privy to her life at sea, which only a handful of people shared, and fans will appreciate reading about it—but they would never let you get away without mentioning that fateful weekend. You were *there*. And the way you're condemned for it, Den, don't you even want to clear your own name?"

He looked at me but said nothing, so I continued. "This is world-captivating information. Do you realize its value? And I don't mean money. It's a chance to right a piece of history that went down so wrong. Your experience does belong in a book, where it can be told right. But you have to *tell* it. Whether through me or someone else—just tell it! Now, either tell me what happened that weekend, or I don't ever want to talk about it again. I'd like to get back to *my* life. There's only one thing more I want to say."

I overemphasized my ending point, driving it directly in Dennis's eyes. "You slept with Natalie Wood in her final bed." I wanted to drop my shoulders, which had stiffened with my every word, but I remained upright, head high, because I was confident in my conviction.

Within seconds, looking straight into my eyes, Dennis said, "There was a big, horrible fight on board *Splendour* the night Natalie died."

I gasped. I could not believe I had finally heard those words. Dennis's truth. "Damn," I said, "So Noguchi hadn't been 'juicing it up'—the truth had almost been revealed from the start."

"I'll never lie to you, Marti. I may hold back, but only because I'm scared."

"Den, why didn't you tell the authorities, even if they didn't ask?"

"Because I did what I was told. And I was scared."

"For your life?"

"For my *life*."

"But you've deliberately withheld information pertaining to an investigation." I wanted Dennis to realize possible consequences down the road with what he now, finally, confessed.

"I was strictly ordered to say nothing. First by R.J. and then by attorneys. I was following my attorney's advice, and that is not illegal. The lawyers made the legal choices and wrote the history."

"What a vicious cycle. How bad was the fight?"

"Deadly."

"Would you consider talking to authorities now?"

"Marti, everyone lied. You think they would listen to me now? If they had asked more, or pushed me more, maybe I would have told more. I don't know."

"Well, detectives are supposed to detect, Den. It's not all your fault. Was the fight over jealousy?"

"It all went to her head. Natalie loved working with Chris on *Brainstorm*, and R.J. was afraid that Chris was the reason for her sudden new joy. I never thought that anything would tear them apart, but R.J. was insane with jealousy that night. *Brainstorm* meant so much to her. I won't ever watch *Brainstorm*. Have you seen it?"

"Yes, and it's such an eerie film to have made just before dying. When she's begging Walken's character back from death, it's chilling."

"Marti, are you ready for all this?"

"I am, Den. Tell me what happened that weekend. Start with how the trip was planned and don't stop. Just keep going for as long as you can; even tell me about retrieving *Splendour*."

"After I start, there's no turning back."

"I don't want to turn back, Den."

PART TWO

The Weekend and Funeral

While the make-up man's hands
Shut the eyes of the dead
Not to embarrass anyone.

—Bob Dylan ("Farewell Angelina")

Chapter 14

It drizzled when it wasn't raining throughout the greater L.A. area this unusually cold 1981 Thanksgiving Day. Dennis was living aboard *Splendour* at Tahiti Marina and expected to be docked until after the holiday season, but R.J. had called him a few days before Thanksgiving to plan a Catalina Island outing for Black Friday through Sunday.

On Thanksgiving Day, Dennis enjoyed a traditional meal with his two close friends, Phil Gorden and Sandy Dawson, at their home. He thanked them soon after the pumpkin pie, calling it an early evening, and returned to *Splendour*. The bleak weather matched his mood, for he had looked forward to having the holiday weekend off, and he hadn't heard back from R.J. so figured the outing was still a go. Why, for goodness sake, was beyond Dennis. The mere thought of cruise preparations for this off-season getaway irked him from the beginning.

Wrapped in a blanket in his wheelhouse chair late Thanksgiving night, Dennis sipped hot tea to offset the nipping iciness of the harbor air. He switched on the weather report and heard the forecast for more rain and cold. Unexplainable jitters upset his stomach. Hoping the dire weather prediction would change the Wagners' minds, he called them and spoke first with R.J., who maintained that the outing was still on but who didn't sound enthused about it. R.J.'s sentiments offered hope the trip might be canceled, but as soon as R.J. put Natalie on the phone, she started rattling off specifics for the outing's shopping list. Dennis cut her short, never insubordinate but hoping to change her mind.

"The weather sucks," he reminded her. "It's really kicking up down here, and it's going to be a bumpy, sloppy ride to the island. Think you want to postpone it, Natalie? You should," he quickly added.

After a short pause, she replied, "We've already made the plans, Dennis, so I think we may as well go ahead with them. We'll have a nice time."

"I'd better do some shopping then," Dennis said, unenthusiastically. "How many guests?"

"Just one. Christopher Walken. Others backed out."

"Well, do you want to wait until everyone can make it?" Dennis asked, still hoping to discourage her.

"Dennis, I've already invited Christopher, and I don't want to cancel now. Just get a few things—some steaks and the regular supplies. We'll see you around noon. And, I'll bring you some turkey and treats Willie Mae made, okay?"

A peace offering. She knew Dennis was making sense.

Early Friday morning, Dennis awakened to weather that had not improved, so he phoned the Wagners again, hopeful they had thought of a better way to amuse Christopher Walken for the weekend. R.J. answered the call and sounded as irritated as Dennis felt about the cruise. R.J. said that if it were up to him, he would call it off, but that Natalie still wanted to go. That the Wagners would brave the rain and cold for only one guest had already struck Dennis as peculiar.

What is so damn important about this cruise? And who is this Christopher Walken, anyway? All Dennis knew about him was that he was currently costarring with Natalie in *Brainstorm*— the Oscar winner. Natalie usually invited her costars for boat outings, but this scenario was different. Rumors of an affair between Walken and Wood had been whispered while the two actors filmed on location in North Carolina during the previous three months. Dennis, however, gave no substance to the alleged affair because R.J., after a weekend visit with Natalie in North Carolina, had returned casual enough to indicate he was satisfied that his wife was away acting, not having an affair.

The Wagners normally entertained no less than three guests per cruise, unless it was strictly a family outing. They had canceled previous trips for weather less severe.

Dennis hurriedly drove to Boy's Market, the marina area grocery store, to shop. He headed to the produce aisle for tomatoes, lettuce, green peppers, and celery. *Jingle Bells* played in the background: *Laughing all the way.* Dennis tried to smile, to change his mood. After all, this was Black Friday, the start of the Christmas season. He ordered strip steaks from the meat department, then rushed off to the dairy section for eggs and cheese. *Splendour* wasn't well stocked in the off season, so as he rushed to check out, he threw some extras into the shopping cart. While loading grocery bags into his car, shivering beneath his lightweight jacket, he became more aware of the chill. Off to the liquor store.

It took just minutes to purchase Soave Bolla, Pouilly-Fuissé, vodka, and scotch. Dom Perignon was already on board. On his way back to the boat, Dennis decided to make one last stop at Boat Owners Warehouse to buy extra space heaters because *Splendour* was currently equipped with only two. At B.O.W., as the store is known around the docks, Dennis complained to the clerk about his employers' poor choice to cross to the island. The clerk concurred.

Because she was one of the larger boats at the marina, *Splendour's* slip was at the end of the dock, and Dennis grudgingly walked the entire dock twice with his goods. As he transferred the bags from the dock to the boat deck, marina manager Dorothy Metzler approached. She sneered, in her usual abrupt and intimidating manner.

"What the hell are you doing? You're not going out, are you, Dennis? Do the Wagners know about this?" she accused before Dennis could even respond.

Dennis just smiled. This time, he had an ally in Dorothy. "Dorothy, you won't believe this," Dennis complained. "It's the Wagners insisting on this stupid trip! We're heading for Catalina, but it's not by *my* choice."

With all her marina managing experience, Dorothy understood better than anyone why the number of boaters willing to brave the rainy weather this weekend would be slight. "You're crazy, Dennis. This weather is going to get worse before it gets better. What's the matter with you? You can't take the Wagners out in this," Dorothy growled, gesturing to the sky.

"Look, Dorothy, I tried my best to talk them out of it," Dennis answered defensively.

"One day you'll learn to listen to your own better sense, kid. It's times like this ya gotta develop engine trouble. You know better than anyone, Dennis, how to get around something. If only you'd put that ability to work when it makes sense, we'd have a perfect Dennis," she smiled. "I'm surprised at you. You could have figured out a way to spare these people," she finished and walked off, shaking her head.

Dennis yelled out to Dorothy, as she headed up the dock, back to her office, "This is the first time in seven years they haven't taken my advice."

Several others around the dock approached Dennis and repeated most of what Dorothy had said.

The aroma of fresh brewed coffee greeted R.J., Natalie, and Christopher when they boarded *Splendour*, but they were more interested in a pitcher of Bloody Marys even though it was not quite noon. From the moment Natalie introduced Dennis to

Christopher, as R.J. busied himself with nothing in the background, Dennis recognized the tangible tension surrounding the party.

Everyone looked bundled up for a North Pole excursion. Christopher kept the collar of his dark pea-coat turned up, his hands stuffed deep into his pockets, as he bounced around on the outside deck to circulate body warmth. He complained, "It's cold out here, man; it's going right through me," then eagerly added, "but, I'm game, I'm ready, let's go!"

Natalie wore her red down jacket for warmth, and she radiated cheerfulness. The red in her jacket brought out the color in her cheekbones, and the damp weather moistened her face and turned back the clock on her complexion. Dennis had not seen Natalie for two months, and he thought she looked more beautiful than ever. She looked younger—more like Christopher's companion than R.J.'s, who appeared exceptionally older next to the two.

They headed for the galley, where Dennis pulled out the vodka and tomato juice. Natalie cut celery. With drinks in everyone's hands, R.J. suggested a boat tour. He showed Christopher his cabin, then guided him through the staterooms. They all stepped up to the wheelhouse, where R.J. started pointing out various instruments and equipment, purposely going over Christopher's head with tiresome technical jargon. Christopher made little effort to hide his disinterest, and Natalie continually interrupted R.J.'s condescending explanations.

"Christopher, come over here and see this," she would say, and Christopher's face would light with a smile and relief.

"Wait a minute," R.J. would counter with a challenge to his tone. "I want Chris to see the control panel, now."

Everyone stayed in the wheelhouse for the cross to the island, where the backbiting continued. Christopher and Natalie's sportive energy obviously angered R.J. He tried hard to imitate their mood, but his awkwardness was instantly apparent, and it seemed threatening. Dennis watched closely. R.J.'s eyes were subtly shadowed with self-doubt, pretense, and revenge, all out of character for him.

Never aboard *Splendour* had R.J. had a guest in whom he was not thoroughly delighted. Never aboard *Splendour* had R.J. had to monitor his behavior or pretend to enjoy himself. Never had he had to carry a script or worry about missing a cue. *Splendour* was R.J.'s haven, his escape from wearing a public face and getting his lines right. Now he seemed to be playing a role, badly, and trying too hard to hide his displeasure. It angered Dennis that Christopher Walken was allowed to intrude in R.J.'s and Natalie's personal lives this way and that Natalie appeared insensitive to R.J.'s position, but Dennis did not blame Christopher. If R.J. would lighten up, he would see that Christopher Walken was no threat to him and was not worth the energy it took to dislike him. He would see that Natalie's attention to Walken was just part of being a gracious hostess, as she was to all of their guests. But echoes of the rumored affair between Natalie and Christopher were now thickening the air, as dark and hovering as the clouds that spilled cold rain onto *Splendour's* deck.

R.J.'s twofold purpose of the cruise was suddenly clear to Dennis. R.J. seemed intent on proving to Natalie that he trusted her and could handle hearsay, that her young costar did not threaten him. If that had truly been the case, however, he would not have needed to prove to Walken that Natalie was his, as he was obviously trying to do. What better place to prove this point to Walken than aboard *Splendour*, where Natalie's and R.J.'s closeness had always been intensified?

Before *Brainstorm,* Natalie and R.J. had been virtually inseparable, and the time spent together on their yacht had been precious to them, bringing them even closer. R.J. seemed to want that oneness with Natalie now, for Christopher to witness. It was also apparent that R.J. wanted Christopher to know that he was equally as famous as his wife. R.J. always had subtly let those around him know that he was the man of the house, the breadwinner, the one who could afford a luxury yacht. But all he looked like on this day—next to his wife, who was eight years his junior, and her costar, an Oscar winner and twelve years his junior—was the older man on board. Christopher's Oscar, youth, and film success seemed to be eating away at R.J., despite his current *Hart to Hart* fame. R.J. was sensitive to Natalie's every word and action, and it struck Dennis that Natalie could have brought the situation under control with just a few right moves. Whether she was oblivious to R.J.'s distress or was calculating her actions in retaliation to it, she was now making some very wrong moves. When R.J. could not hold Natalie's attention, he vied for Walken's.

Dennis saw that Natalie was angry at R.J.'s disposition and knew she would not tolerate it. Dennis felt some sympathy for Christopher's position as the rope in R.J.'s and Natalie's tug-of-war, and he watched helplessly as Christopher fumbled his attention from R.J. to Natalie. Understandably, Christopher preferred Natalie's sincerity to R.J.'s pretense of congeniality.

Dennis believed that Natalie was overreacting to R.J.'s jealousy and poorly disguised animosity toward Christopher. She was offended by R.J.'s lack of faith in her and by his resultant mistreatment of their guest. She was overcompensating for R.J.'s coolness, which was probably far more flagrant to her than to Christopher. R.J.'s audacity fueled Natalie's desire to make Christopher comfortable, and Natalie's overattentiveness to Christopher fueled R.J.'s suppressed anger. Just an hour into the outing, Dennis wondered how the couple would break their deadlock and why they didn't just turn around and go home.

Dennis had witnessed R.J.'s and Natalie's minor disputes throughout the years and had always admired their ability to turn around a tense situation, to compromise with each other, and then to laugh it off. He had never seen them come this close to falling apart.

Natalie held defiance in her eyes, staring R.J. down with her conviction that her actions were justified. She was not going to back down. That made Dennis nervous. R.J.'s anger boiled beneath his facade of a smile, and that made Dennis damned nervous.

Dennis remembered that R.J. once decked a guy in the Polo Lounge for flirting with Natalie. The injured man sued R.J., but R.J. said he would not hesitate to do it again. Dennis saw it coming now, and he was not in the mood for a brawl at sea.

Christopher played along and remained polite to R.J. and friendly with Natalie. Walken could not have realized the volatility of the situation, or he would have backed off. Instead, he smiled when Natalie giggled or laughed at his every witty word. But what else could he do without hurting *her* feelings?

They each played their roles; Natalie out of injured pride, R.J. seemingly out of raw, jealous emotion, and Christopher because he was in an awkward situation and could only try to make the best of it. Christopher seemed quite aware of Natalie's charismatic charm, and Dennis saw the chemistry between the two that would surely be magnified on the big screen.

Any of the three—Natalie, R.J., or Christopher—could have defused the tension, but no one gave in. Dennis tried to divert Natalie's attention with small talk, then turned his attention to R.J. to ramble on about fishing and general topics. R.J. and Natalie appreciated Dennis's efforts, but neither paid attention to him.

Dennis ran out of conversation and waited for the blowout—expecting it to happen even before they reached Catalina. *What a shitty cruise.*

Then Dennis thought of another diversion. It was a stupid idea, wrong, and he had no idea how it would go over, but he needed to calm these people down, so he brought it up.

"Hey, Natalie, I've got some Quaaludes. What do you think?"

Dennis guessed that Christopher would be interested. He wasn't sure about R.J. He hoped Natalie would comprehend his mission, which is why he had addressed her, while averting R.J.'s eyes.

Splendour's medicine cabinet was checkered with a variety of Natalie's prescription pills. Natalie dealt with tremendous stress and found prescription drugs a handy remedy for all the pull and drag. A glass of wine and a Valium, along with the lay psychology she practiced on Dennis during cruises, had always relaxed her. Natalie's therapy had taught her to listen well. Dennis had always admired her ability to remain objective and analytical, yet compassionate. She intuitively knew what made people tick, and she could generally see beyond words and actions to the motivations behind conduct. Dennis wished that she would take an analytical look at the situation now facing her. Or take a pill.

"Great, Dennis. I'll exchange a few Valiums next week," Natalie told him.

Dennis and Natalie both looked to R.J., the onboard father figure, for his reaction. R.J. was generally reluctant to take unnecessary pills. Yet he understood that pills were necessary for Natalie's seasickness, nerves, and rest.

"What do Quaaludes do to you?" R.J. asked.

Natalie and Christopher giggled, but R.J.'s cold glance shut them up.

"Oh, come on, R.J., let's just have some fun this weekend. I'm laughing because everyone knows what Quaaludes are known for. I've never taken one, but I know why people do take them," Natalie said.

Dennis jumped in to continue answering R.J.'s legitimate question.

"All they do, R.J., is relax you. They calm your nerves. You start feeling good about things, and everything seems to go in slow motion."

On any other outing with any other guests, R.J. would never have considered a Quaalude. Today, he did not intend to allow his wife and Walken to share a pleasure in which he was not a part, and perhaps he did want to calm down.

He smiled, and with his big grin, everyone expelled a breath: R.J. smiled—there might be hope for this cruise!

R.J. asked, "How slow do these things make you?"

"Sometimes they impair your speech a little," Dennis explained, "but these aren't that strong. People like to take them before sex, R.J. They're known as the sex drug. The pleasure lingers, and everything is slower and better."

"Where did you get them?" R.J. wanted to know.

"They're from a doctor," Dennis said, omitting that it was not his prescription. Dennis's friend had given him the pills.

Natalie and Christopher smiled.

R.J. grinned again and attempted to lighten things up. "You mean, if I take a Quaalude," he cupped and rubbed his chin, "and have sex...then right before I come, I'll say, real slow, 'Ooooohhhh, aaaahhhh, I'mmm mmmm comm-mming?'"

Natalie belted out a loud laugh, and Christopher and Dennis followed. It was obvious that Natalie appreciated R.J.'s attempt to lift the tense mood. She truly found R.J.'s dry humor hilarious, and R.J. appreciated that she had.

Dennis saw Natalie and R.J.'s closeness shine through— he saw them exchange their glance that spoke volumes. He suddenly was relieved he had mentioned the Quaaludes.

Everyone continued to roar with genuine laughter that somehow seemed to dispel the underlying tension. It was a start.

They each swallowed a Quaalude.

Chapter 15

Christopher felt seasick, so he went to his quarters. Natalie sat in her perch as R.J. and Dennis stayed at the wheel. Everything seemed fine. About three in the afternoon, as they neared the island, Dennis asked, "Has anyone decided where we're heading?"

As with most cruises with guests on board, Avalon was the designated stop. R.J. almost always preferred Isthmus Cove or Emerald Bay, primarily for the privacy there, and his preference had not changed for this visit, but Natalie wanted Avalon, for its entertainment.

"Isthmus," said R.J.

"Avalon," said Natalie.

"Let's have the privacy of Isthmus, Natalie," R.J. persuaded.

"Come on, R.J., what are we going to do on the boat all day at Isthmus? I want Avalon for some early Christmas shopping," Natalie argued.

They anchored at Avalon. Dennis was relieved Natalie had won that small debate. Natalie liked to give everyone a sense of comfort, as she did not lose herself to haughty fame. The famous persona emerged when necessary, but on this day, she was looking for nothing more than a fun trip to the island. Dennis recalled Natalie telling him about when she had won the year's worst actress award in 1966 from the *Harvard Lampoon*. Natalie good-naturedly accepted the award in person: the first elected actor to ever do so. R.J. worried too much about appearances, allowing his status to somehow dehumanize him. Natalie was better at keeping things real and sensible. Avalon's appeal might quell the tension. R.J.'s choice was flat-out stupid in Dennis's opinion. At least Natalie was thinking. Dennis did not even want to imagine what it would be like at the Isthmus, just the four of them, stuck on the boat in the nasty weather.

Christopher joined the party again as R.J. and Dennis anchored *Splendour*. Natalie, eager to go ashore, went to the master stateroom to change her outfit. Dennis removed the motorized dinghy, *Valiant*, from the front of the boat, where it was normally stored when *Splendour* was docked.

Natalie, R.J., and Christopher boarded *Valiant* from the swim step at the stern. Dennis stayed on deck.

"Dennis, come on," Natalie said.

"No, I think I'll pass. I'm pretty tired. What time will you be back? I'll have dinner ready."

"Sounds great, Dennis," Natalie said. "We'll see you around nine. Thank you."

"See you then," Dennis said, avoiding eye contact with R.J. He felt as if he were deserting R.J., leaving him to deal with, ironically, being the third wheel of the group. But Dennis was relieved to be left alone on board. He went to the galley and cleaned up the afternoon cocktail glasses. Natalie had drunk a glass of wine, R.J. some scotch, and Bloody Marys all around, but Dennis had not felt like partaking. He had already sensed he might need to be in full control of this cruise, and he emptied his hardly touched Bloody Mary into the sink.

He tossed a salad, pulled four steaks from the freezer, and then went to his quarters for a nap. His bunk felt like the best part of the day thus far. His last thought before his eyelids closed was like a prayer: *Please let them work things out on the island so we can salvage this horrible cruise.*

Dennis slept peacefully for about three hours, then reluctantly got up to go start a barbecue on deck, which he would leave for R.J. to finish when the group returned.

R.J., Natalie, and Christopher seemed pleasant enough as they transferred their shopping bags from *Valiant* to *Splendour*, and Dennis was relieved that the tension seemed to have eased up.

"So, what did you do on the island?" Dennis asked.

"We ate Mexican earlier, then shopped and had a few drinks at the El Galleon, and Chris bought some artwork," Natalie answered. "And, I bought you an early Christmas present, Dennis," she said, "but you can't have it until after dinner."

Natalie and Christopher went to their rooms. Dennis stayed with R.J. on deck. R.J. seemed in better spirits, "You know, Dennis," he said, "I don't feel anything from that Quaalude."

"They're not strong, R.J.," Dennis told him. "But do you feel more relaxed?"

"Maybe," he answered indecisively.

As the steaks came off the grill, R.J. mentioned his idea to move the boat to the Isthmus, about twelve miles up the coast. Dennis ignored the suggestion. R.J. can't be serious, he thought. It's almost ten o'clock.

Things seemed cozy and comfortable as everyone sipped cocktails in the main salon, with steaks and salad waiting on the galley table. Then R.J. asked Natalie if she liked the necklace he had bought for her on the island. Natalie assured him she did.

It was habitual for R.J. to lavish expensive gifts upon Natalie. The costly gift impressed her, yet Natalie's show of appreciation lacked her customary exuberance. Perhaps she had picked up on something Dennis definitely sensed. The gift was an elaborate show not only of love but also of money and power, of what R.J. could presently provide in comparison to Christopher Walken, an Oscar winner but still not a famous actor. The jewelry seemed an overdone gift for the occasion. It was more a personal, Christmas-morning type of gift. Natalie's near-indifference to the gift irritated R.J.

Natalie turned to Dennis. With a mildness and sincerity to her voice he had never before heard, she handed Dennis a dark velvet box and said, "A little early, but Merry Christmas, Dennis."

When Dennis saw what was inside the box, he could not hide his surprise. "This is great!" he exclaimed as he gazed in astonishment at a roughcast chunk of fourteen karat gold. The piece was chisel designed, attached to a gold chain.

"It's called pieces-of-eight, or pirate's gold," Natalie explained. "I bought matching earrings for myself. See?" Natalie opened a tiny box and displayed the petite replicas of Dennis's gift. "I hope you like it, Dennis," she said sincerely.

Like it? He cherished it. He truly was speechless. Natalie had never given him anything to write home about. He ran a quick mental comparison of some of her previous gifts.

There was the parrot, Max. Natalie had purchased the exotic bird for her family, but his constant loud screeching and babbling drove her crazy. Natasha and Courtney cried when Natalie gave Max to Dennis as a birthday gift. But Dennis told the girls they could still visit the bird. Dennis eventually found a new home for Max for the same reason Natalie had unloaded him.

Natalie once gave Dennis a Cartier watch for Christmas. After about six months, the gold began to wear. He took the watch back to the store name that was printed on the box it had come in, only to be told that they had never carried Cartier watches. Perplexed, Dennis phoned Natalie's secretary to see about getting the watch repaired. Embarrassed, Peggy Griffin explained that Natalie hadn't purchased the watch at the Beverly Hills shop named on the box, but instead had sent for a dozen of them through mail order. Most of her employees had received the same token gift. Dennis rationalized that at least he had received a gift, as it had been his first year working for the Wagners.

This pirates' gold sure made a new statement. As Dennis latched the chain around his neck, it was his proof that he had grown to a new status in Natalie's world. He would treasure the gift of friendship forever.

It was early for the Christmas spirit, but Natalie's gift to Dennis and R.J.'s gift to her had indeed set a more positive mood. Dennis was determined to milk it, as was R.J. It was suddenly a whole new foursome—of pleasant conversation and laughter—and R.J. seemed to have reached a comfort zone.

Dennis's relief, however, was soon challenged when Natalie let out a long sigh and said, "I wish *Brainstorm* could be released sooner than they expect." She looked at Christopher. Her comment totally changed the dynamics of the short-lived comfort zone. R.J. and Dennis might as well have been sitting below deck in the engine room as Natalie and Christopher exchanged *Brainstorm* anecdotes.

"Christopher, despite the problems with *Brainstorm* on the set, you have to admit it's a unique film," she said.

Brainstorm had experienced directional problems, and the studios had brought in outside help when things got behind schedule and ran over budget. Natalie explained some of the problems, like weak scenes, but said that all should turn out well, mentioning how Christopher's input helped to "save the show."

Dennis did not mind listening to Natalie, but R.J. tired of it. Cut her a break, Dennis thought. Natalie's enjoying her new work. She's proud of herself and wants to impress you, too, R.J., probably because she wants you to be proud of her. If you would share her enthusiasm, she would include you more.

Natalie obviously had been rejuvenated, even physically. She actually looked younger as she sat there sipping her wine, smiling with sparkling eyes at Christopher's contribution to the conversation. Her new aura of youthfulness, however, brought with it a truculence common of rebellious youth. Her undivided attention to Christopher emitted defiance to R.J.'s presence, the way a child might purposely ignore an authoritative figure to prove independence. When Natalie did decide to let one of the two bystanders in on her and Chris's tête-à-tête, Dennis wished it had been R.J. She instead included Dennis.

"Dennis," Natalie said, "the special effects in this film are amazing. You won't believe what that department has done! It's good science fiction, even if some of the lines need work."

"I like science fiction," Dennis said, for lack of anything better to say.

"Well then, you'll like *Brainstorm*," she insisted. "And wait until you see Louise Fletcher's heart attack," she boasted of her other costar. "You see, she has a heart attack and records her death on a machine that she, Michael—that's Christopher's character—and my character invented. The machine records sounds and colors and emotions."

"And another person can experience anything this machine has recorded," Christopher added, "by hooking up to it with a headset. The military wants the machine, and Cliff Robertson's character betrays those of us who invented it by selling out to the military."

"Christopher hooks up to the machine and experiences Louise's heart attack," Natalie added. "Dennis, why don't you come to MGM next week for a preview? I can arrange it for you," she invited.

"I won't be busy next Wednesday," Dennis said.

"Wednesday would be perfect, Dennis. Please come. You'll have fun," Natalie said.

Dennis nodded.

"Good. Next Wednesday," Natalie confirmed, then continued on. "You'll love the bubble scene. It took hours for a special machine they brought in to make foam and bubbles to fill the *Brainstorm* control room. The stuff just turned us all into kids. We couldn't resist playing in it."

R.J. seethed.

"*Everyone* played in the foam and bubbles," Natalie giggled.

Ordinarily, Dennis would have loved seeing Natalie so relaxed and animated, but the contrast between her and Christopher's gleefulness and R.J.'s silent, dour expression was enough to take away any humor Dennis might have found in Natalie's foam and bubbles. He sat as silently as R.J., waiting for Natalie to change the subject.

Christopher finally caught a glimpse of R.J. He stopped laughing and straightened out his face and announced he would turn in early. He went to his cabin. Natalie called it a night too.

R.J.'s tolerance snapped.

He stood up abruptly and said, "I'm moving the boat to the Isthmus. Now!"

Natalie looked like she'd been slapped. "What on earth for, R.J.? I don't understand."

"You don't have to understand," he shot back, mimicking her tone. "I feel like moving the boat, so I'm moving the fucking boat."

"R.J., don't be crazy. It's almost eleven. It's cold and dark. I'll leave the boat and go to the island before I'll go to the Isthmus tonight. Stop acting crazy!" Natalie demanded. "You're not going to move the boat tonight!"

"Watch me!" R.J. stormed off to the wheelhouse, leaving a stunned Natalie and Dennis in the main salon.

Dennis sided with Natalie on this one. It was a ridiculous idea to move the boat. Isthmus was an hour away. The weather was dreary, and it was just plain stupid to try to maneuver the boat around the island in the dark. They were all feeling the liquor, too, and R.J.'s daylong consumption hadn't mixed well with his disposition. But they heard R.J. messing with the anchor. Here, in Avalon, the boat was not moored with outside lines, it was anchored, and R.J. seemed to be setting them free. *Splendour's* engine soon started.

"Dennis, please go do something," Natalie pleaded. "Stop him. I just don't understand. This is outrageous, and I want to go to the island. I won't stay on this boat if he wants to move it."

The engine gunned louder.

Natalie headed to her stateroom.

Dennis, fed up, rushed to the wheelhouse. R.J.'s face was beet red. "R.J., what in the fuck do you think you're doing? Natalie wants to leave, you know."

"Then leave with her!" R.J. yelled. His face flushed and sweat beaded his forehead as he ran his hand through his hair.

Dennis rushed to Christopher's cabin, to see if he was sleeping yet. Christopher raised his eyebrows when Dennis asked if he had heard the engine and explained that R.J. was thinking about moving the boat and that Natalie was upset about it. "Want to help out here?" Dennis asked.

Christopher declined, advising Dennis to not get involved in any husband and wife dispute, ever.

That was easier said than done in the situation now facing Dennis. It was time to be the real captain. The possible danger of cruising at night with an angry, drunken boat owner at the wheel of a 60-foot yacht called for it.

Dennis returned to R.J. in the wheelhouse. "R.J.," Dennis changed his tone to one of concern. "What's going on here? This isn't like you."

R.J. lowered his head and turned off *Splendour's* engine.

"Dennis, I'm sorry. I'm really sorry," he apologized.

"It's okay, R.J.," Dennis told him. "Maybe you should go talk to Natalie, though."

"No, go take her to the island. I think it might be better if she does get off the boat tonight. Go stay with her, and keep an eye over her. Don't tell her I changed my mind. Just go."

Dennis would rather R.J. have done whatever possible to apologize to Natalie and to resolve the situation immediately. Separating for the night was drastic, but Dennis saw the positive side too: that separating for the night just might end the entire fiasco of a cruise, so he agreed to leave the boat with Natalie.

Dennis met Natalie at the back deck. "I'm taking you to the island," he informed her.

"Of course you are. I've been waiting." She held a small duffel bag filled with clothes and toiletries. She wore her red jacket over her jeans and blouse. Dennis asked her to wait a few minutes while he grabbed a change of clothes, but Natalie insisted they get into the dinghy that very minute. She was hell bent to get away from R.J. She looked scared, bewildered, and plain sad.

"R.J. is really sorry," Dennis tried.

"Of course he is," she sneered. "I don't want to hear about R.J. Let's go!"

Within two hours of returning from Avalon to the boat, Natalie was on her way back to the island, this time with Dennis. They cruised silently to shore, and Dennis tied *Valiant* at the dinghy dock. They walked a couple of blocks to the El Galleon Restaurant, Dennis carrying Natalie's bag. Natalie was aggravated, and her evening wine intensified her mood.

Inside the restaurant, Natalie found manager Paul Reynolds to ask when the next boat would leave for the mainland.

"Don't you have a boat?" Reynolds asked, confused.

Natalie explained that she needed to cut her trip short, but she did not elaborate. That she was standing in the restaurant with Dennis by her side left no room for doubt that something with the *Splendour* party had gone awry. Reynolds let her know that she would have to wait until ten in the morning to catch a boat back to the mainland. By the look on his face, he obviously wanted to ask more about why Natalie Wood needed to know the public transportation schedule. Natalie asked about private seaplanes, but Reynolds, again, said she would have to wait until morning. Natalie then asked Reynolds if he would help to secure two rooms for her. Reynolds looked at Dennis, then went to check into Natalie's request. Natalie suggested they wait at the bar. Dennis pulled a barstool out, and Natalie sat down, prepared to order a drink like any other bar patron of the evening. Dennis sat on a stool next to her.

They were a strange sight for curious eyes, Natalie and Dennis, sitting there sipping wine across from customers who could not help but stare. It would be the ultimate intrusion to ask for an autograph. No one did.

"Dennis, I think that man over there is staring at me," Natalie whispered.

"Well, come on, Natalie, what do you expect? Let's get out of here."

"No, I want another glass of wine. Call the bartender."

Paul Reynolds approached and told Natalie that two rooms were waiting for her and her companion at the Pavilion Lodge, a few doors down the road. Get out of here, his eyes said.

During the walk to the modest Pavilion Lodge, Dennis and Natalie stepped inside a small shorefront store to purchase a bottle of wine. Dennis put the bottle in Natalie's bag, and they continued on to the lodge.

As they walked, Dennis noticed that Natalie was breathing deeply, her chin held higher than usual, as if inhaling the freedom of the moment along with the island air. The show business industry might be only as distant as the mainland, twenty-two miles away, but Natalie had never seemed further away from it in all of the years Dennis had known her. Tonight, she had escaped. Her boat skipper was by her side if she needed protection or companionship, but in this moment, she had no image to maintain—Dennis saw only Natalie Wood, the person. She looked especially beautiful in this freeze-frame.

Nonetheless, Dennis realized what a complicated situation this was for Natalie. She had left her costar behind with her angry husband on the boat, and she was obviously planning to abort the weekend outing, so there would soon be apologies, disappointment, a marital spat, and probably publicity to deal with.

It was after eleven when they stood at the reception desk in the Pavilion Lodge lobby. Natalie handed her American Express card to the night desk clerk, who barely took her eyes from the odd duo standing in front of her. Rooms 126 and 219 were booked and paid for in Natalie's name.

Natalie asked for ice, and the clerk walked them to the ice machine. They took a bucketful to room 126, Natalie's room. One king-sized bed, an end table, a chest of drawers, a chair, and a small television crowded the standard-sized motel room. It was not Natalie's usual style, but she seemed relieved to be a regular person in a regular room in a regular world. She was concerned about security, however, because her room faced a central courtyard next to the main street.

"Dennis, you don't think anyone would try anything here tonight, do you?" she asked. "People saw us come here. What if someone followed us and tries to break into my room?"

"I'm here with you, Natalie."

"What if you don't hear me screaming? Your room isn't near mine."

Her fear was valid.

"Do you want me to stay with you? I could sleep on the floor."

"I'd feel a lot safer if you would. Did you see the way that guy gawked at me back at the bar?"

"Everyone gawks at you, Natalie."

The room was cold. Dennis checked the heater and could not get it to work. He asked Natalie if she wanted to move to his room, but she felt that a complaint was in order.

"No, Dennis," she insisted. "Why should we move?"

"Well, it's not like we're settled in here, and we have a key to another room, which probably has a working heater. Why draw more attention to ourselves?"

"Call."

Dennis called the desk for service. He sat on the floor, fidgeting with the heater knobs as Natalie let in a boyish-looking attendant, who made a few quick adjustments to the heater, fixed it, and left.

"Natalie," Dennis said, "this doesn't look good—the two of us together in this room. That guy knows who you are."

"It doesn't matter," she responded. "I'll be out of here first thing in the morning. Let's open the wine, Dennis."

Dennis poured wine, then sat at the foot of the bed. Natalie sipped from her hotel glass. Dennis sensed she drank to calm her nerves and anger.

She propped two pillows at the headboard and leaned back against them. Taking a pill box from her bag, she told Dennis, "I'll take this now, but it won't work for about half an hour. I need to sleep soon so I can get up by eight."

Dennis watched as Natalie swallowed a sleeping pill. He felt tired too. It was not the best time to talk, but Dennis had a few things to say. He wanted to be sure Natalie left the island in the morning. He brought up the situation with R.J.

"R.J. felt left out tonight."

"I'll call in the morning for a boat off the island, Dennis. Or I'll see about catching a seaplane."

Dennis smiled. Those were the best words he had heard so far on this miserable outing. He could return early to *Splendour*, cruise back to the marina with R.J. and Christopher, and this disaster of a weekend would be over and done with. His relief was obvious.

"I see you like my idea," Natalie smiled.

"Well, no sense in carrying on an unpleasant experience."

"Exactly. And what a shame, because this really could have been a nice weekend. We were having a nice time, weren't we, Dennis?"

"Well, I started to—"

"Exactly! Before he went crazy on us, right?"

Dennis was not ready to verbally turn on R.J., although he already had turned on him privately after R.J.'s choice to move the boat, so he ignored her question. "Did you ask Christopher to leave with you tonight? I saw you go to his room."

"Are you crazy too?" she asked, astonished. "I didn't do anything wrong tonight, Dennis. I just asked Christopher if he would talk to R.J. I thought maybe a man-to-man conversation would calm R.J. down. R.J. has no legitimate gripe with me or Christopher, and he knows it!"

Dennis saw both sides. R.J. would not have liked it if Natalie had been rude to his guests, but he was jealous of Natalie's guest. Natalie was so angry at R.J.'s jealousy that she behaved in defiance of his attitude. But it would all end by tomorrow, so Dennis was not too concerned with who was right or who was wrong. He just wanted it to end. This was a minor butting of heads, he believed, yet R.J. was beginning to scare him too. "Natalie, tomorrow night we'll all be where we should be."

"I'm still mad, though," Natalie added. "You have no idea."

"Yes, I do. I've never seen you or R.J. like this before. You're here with me for the night, and R.J.'s on the boat with Christopher."

"Well, he had no right to embarrass me that way in front of Christopher. I just wanted to show Christopher a good time the way R.J. always shows his guests a good time. I was really enjoying myself, and he ruined it."

Dennis understood that the whole fiasco was as simple as Natalie's explanation. Christopher Walken was a *Splendour* guest, invited by Natalie, and she tried to be a warm, friendly, and gracious hostess. She was simply entertaining a guest, and R.J. was blowing it all out of proportion, reading all kinds of things into it that just were not there.

"He lost it, Natalie, but he's sorry." Dennis didn't know if he believed his own words, but he wanted to calm the situation.

"Christopher is a good guy, Dennis. I learned a lot from him, doing this film. He reminds me of James Dean. Oh, I don't mean he looks like him, or even acts like Jimmy. But he's got that something special. Christopher will be a great force in the industry, mark my words. Chris and I mostly talk *shop*. R.J. infuriates me."

She saw in Christopher Walken a talent she had not seen for a long time—he was a maverick, in a class all his own. Dennis wondered what R.J. saw in Christopher—the kind of actor he had always wanted to be? The kind his wife had always admired?

"Natalie, he was just jealous of Christopher. Maybe he thinks you want to leave him for someone like Christopher. I had no idea you two could have problems like this."

"You always see us when we're ready to escape work and have some fun. But every married couple has problems at one point or another. Especially Hollywood couples. There's always so much pressure, and it's so hard to be yourself. I have a professional relationship with Christopher, and R.J. needs to respect that. I respect his relationship with Stefanie. I marry Christopher in a film, not in real life!" Natalie said defiantly. "What's R.J.'s problem? I don't go crazy over his costar. It's his *job*."

"When you're done filming, he'll be glad you're back home."

"How one-sided, Dennis. I'm an actress. I don't think this project will seriously matter, but it has me thinking about the next. It's not a bad project." She was obviously proud of the film despite its possible grim future. "They made me look younger for a flashback wedding scene. I wore a long wig and tons of pancake makeup that was supposed to make me look like I was wearing none! The scene came out okay. I know I can't go back in time, but I think I pulled it off." She paused with a little uncertainty, then went on with conviction. "Yes, I am pleased with that scene."

"Natalie, you are beautiful, even off screen. And I know you are an actress, but I mostly see you as a wife and mother, and you're the best at that too. That's all I meant."

Natalie smiled. "You're sweet, Dennis. But I'll tell you a secret. I was surprised to get this part opposite Chris. I was afraid I was—I don't know—Christopher Walken is the hottest new star in town. Everybody wants to sign him. He's handsome and...and young. It's thrilling to have the part of his wife. You've seen me read tons of scripts, and this isn't a bad one. Production is killing it, and Chris saw that. I just wanted to celebrate tonight that we're so close to wrapping up."

"I understand, Natalie," Dennis said. "It's the start of the holiday season, and everyone is getting in the mood, and Christmas is around the corner. You just wanted to have a good time. I heard *Jingle Bells* at the grocery store, and it almost—almost—put me in a mood for the outing."

Natalie smiled.

"I really like this pieces-of-eight, Natalie. Thank you again."

"You deserve it, Dennis. You're welcome. Let's toast Christmas."

Dennis poured more wine. "What can I get the girls this year?" Dennis asked.

"Why don't you take them to Knott's Berry Farm again, or something like that, Dennis? They'll get so many toys and gifts, so why don't you show them a good time at the park? You know it's hard for us to take them there, and they love it."

"That's a good idea. But how do I wrap it?"

Natalie laughed, but Dennis was serious. He liked to give the girls presents they could unwrap. Natalie suggested he purchase gift certificates or get a picture of the Amusement Park to put inside a small box with a written promise to take them there included. Then she told Dennis about how upset Natasha had been Thanksgiving night.

"Natasha did not want me leaving her for this cruise this weekend. I almost brought her along, she was so upset about it, but because of the weather, I decided not to. Good thing. This trip obviously wasn't for the girls."

"Forget the weather. I'm glad she wasn't around to see what we just saw," Dennis agreed.

"I can't tolerate this kind of nonsense from R.J.," Natalie continued complaining.

"But, Natalie, just cut him a break."

"I'm too old for breaks at this stage in my life."

Dennis, a perceptive man, even if it did not always show, could not verbalize his scrambled thoughts, but he wished he could have, for Dennis wanted to tell Natalie that he saw a woman looking toward midlife and getting scared witless. He saw her overlooking her talents, her goodness, her essence. Natalie was so much more than beautiful. She was the most spectacular and professional woman Dennis could ever have hoped to meet. Still, he understood that her doubts and fears, as unfounded as they might seem to others, were real. And in the midst of them, she was cast as the wife of a hot new star. She was elated and had regained her confidence. Her renewed confidence was too much for R.J. to handle, and in spite of his television success, he felt overshadowed by Natalie's rekindled career and insecure about her devotion to him. It was all that plain and simple, but Natalie could not get past her anger at R.J.

"I feel tired now," Natalie said, sliding beneath the covers, still dressed in her jeans and blouse. "Drinking too much isn't good. And I want R.J. to stop drinking so much. He obviously can't handle it anymore."

"It's been a rough night. None of us have been ourselves, and we all drank too much," Dennis said.

"Dennis, I know why R.J. came to North Carolina. He thought I was up to something. For the record, I wasn't. Why on earth would I invite Christopher to share a weekend with us if I were?"

Dennis realized she made sense, but repeated, "We just weren't ourselves."

"You mean R.J. wasn't himself. Why couldn't he let me be happy tonight? I'll tell you one thing, Dennis," she added with intent, "come Monday, R.J. will face the music on this. And he knows it!"

"What do you mean?" Dennis asked.

"I mean that I'll do something about this. I won't tolerate this kind of nonsense. It's getting old. R.J.'s jealousy gets the best of him. This isn't the first time he's gone crazy over my costar. It's insane. He can't do this to me again! It's the drinking, Dennis. He's out of control, and I blame the booze. I'll see a lawyer if I have to. Maybe that will send the message loud and clear."

Dennis was taken aback by talk of seeing a lawyer. He never suspected it had gone that far. He knew of R.J.'s jealous streak but had never considered the damage it could do to their marriage. He sided with Natalie but said, "Don't you see how threatened he felt? You have to admit that you seemed to be flirting with Christopher, kind of flaunting your movie. Don't get mad. It's the truth."

"You really see R.J.'s side in this, don't you?"

"Yes, I do. But I see your side even more. And I'm pissed off at him too. You don't take the boat up the coast near midnight. But I'm trying to reason with someone here. Just to get past it all."

They were silent for a while. Natalie leaned back and closed her eyes. Dennis thought she had fallen asleep, but then she said, with her eyes closed, "What infuriates me the most is that he doesn't trust me. If he did, he wouldn't behave like this. I mean, I know where to draw the line."

"Well, I've never seen you act like this, ignoring R.J. the way you did. You took him by surprise, and he doesn't know how to react."

"Dennis, think about it for a minute," Natalie was suddenly wide eyed to make her point. "When Mart is on board, don't I always give all my attention to him? Or anybody?"

"Well, R.J. doesn't care if you ignore him for Mart."

"Why, because Mart wouldn't want to sleep with me?" Natalie said, mocking R.J.'s double standard. "Mart is a close friend, Dennis. Christopher is just my costar, whom I really like."

Dennis reminded her of the promise she had once made to him. "Natalie, remember that storm years ago when I told you to leave the boat with the girls? But you didn't, and the Harbor Patrol finally came to rescue you? You said you would listen to me, always. Well, I'm telling you, for your own good, for everyone's sake: don't go back to the boat tomorrow."

Natalie stayed silent.

"I'm serious, Natalie. R.J. is wacky this weekend."

She sat up. "Is there any wine left?"

Dennis poured a little more wine into her glass.

"I don't have to explain anything to R.J.," Natalie added defiantly.

"Natalie, do you know what R.J. said to me when a beautiful girl walked by us on the dock one day? He said, 'She catches my eye, but Natalie takes my breath away.'"

"Really?" asked Natalie. "He toasted me last New Year's Eve with those same words. But to say it when I'm not around..."

"He means it too, Natalie."

They fell silent again.

"You were right, Dennis. The weather sucks."

"It would have been a better weekend for kicking back at home," Dennis agreed. "What in the hell are we doing here?"

Natalie wasn't ready to take responsibility for the failed outing. R.J.'s wrath, besides angering her, had also scared her. Otherwise, she would have remained on board *Splendour*. She remembered the night in the Polo Lounge and brought it up. She had a good sense of R.J.'s capabilities and fleeing to the island had been a good move.

"I hope R.J. doesn't take this out on Christopher. He doesn't deserve this."

"He won't," Dennis assured her.

"We'll order a big breakfast in the morning, Dennis, and then I'll leave here. Let's get some sleep."

To Dennis, that seemed like a fantastic plan. He stood up to unbutton his shirt.

"Oh, no, no, no, Dennis," Natalie said, smiling and wagging her finger back and forth like a windshield wiper. "The clothes stay on."

"I'm only taking my shirt off, Natalie. I'll leave the jeans on."

"Leave all your clothes on."

There was no arguing with her tone. "Okay. Toss me a pillow and the bedspread. I'll sleep on the floor like a dog—an uncomfortable dog with clothes on."

She giggled and pulled back the bedspread. "Here. Get in. I'll sleep under the lower covers and you sleep under the bedspread."

Dennis kicked off his shoes and socks and climbed into bed with Natalie.

They settled down in the dark. Natalie interrupted the stillness. "Dennis, thank you for being with me tonight. I'm glad you're here. And thanks for letting me let off steam."

"You're welcome, Natalie. Good night." Dennis clutched his pieces-of-eight, overwhelmed again by it.

"Good night."

Dennis's eyes closed heavily. He was nearly asleep when Natalie added, "Dennis, I can't wait to fly my body out of here tomorrow."

Her voice sounded so forlorn, so alone in the dark, that Dennis turned and put his arm over her blanket. He comforted the fearful child in Natalie, the child she kept hidden from the public, from almost everyone, the child who did not want to sleep alone. She was so strong, so professional, but a scared little girl lived inside her too. The child in her did not object to having her boat captain's arm protect her from the dark of night and soothe away the day's events.

"Go to sleep," he whispered.

Her words repeated themselves in his head. They brought him relief tonight—this terrible cruise was done—but they would haunt him forevermore: *I can't wait to fly my body out of here tomorrow.*

Dennis fell asleep, unaware that he was about to spend the last sleep of Natalie Wood's life with her, beside her, in her final bed.

Chapter 16

The worst scenario Dennis could imagine—being alone at the Isthmus with the foursome with nothing to do—was manifesting before he awakened on the ominous Saturday morning of November 28. He woke up alone in the motel bed. The slight beats of a hangover told him to keep his eyes closed. He heard water running in the bathroom, and after a few minutes, Natalie quietly slipped out of the room. Dennis slept a short while longer until she returned.

"Did you get a plane? A boat?" he sat up and asked when she entered the room.

"No. Get up. We're going back to *Splendour*."

No way, Dennis thought. He jumped out of bed, straightened out his shirt, and reached for his socks. "Don't worry. I'll get you a plane," he said frantically as he hustled on his socks and shoes. He did not want the cruise to continue.

"There are no planes available, Dennis. We're going back to *Splendour*."

"But that's crazy," he protested. "I'll get you a boat."

"Dennis," Natalie insisted, and he didn't like her inarguable tone, "I thought of that already. I tried to call Lana and Peggy to meet me at the marina, but I can't reach anyone, and I'm not going home without someone waiting at the marina to pick me up. We're going back to *Splendour*. Anyway, I've been thinking, and I feel bad about leaving Christopher alone with R.J. It's bad enough what he had to put up with last night."

Dennis fell back onto his pillow, exasperated. "Natalie, I hardly got any sleep. Why don't we hang out here a while? Maybe in an hour or so, we'll be able to get you a plane."

"I want to go back now," she said, then softened her tone. "Come on, Dennis. I'll cook breakfast when we get back to the boat."

"I don't want breakfast," Dennis retorted, like an angry child. Normally, Dennis enjoyed Natalie's special huevos ranchero. Not this day.

Natalie said, "I'll meet you at the dock in twenty minutes. Hurry." Then she left the room.

Dennis stood in the hot water, face lifted toward the shower's nozzle for as long as he could push Natalie's twenty-minute demand. He brushed his teeth with his finger, then reluctantly ran to the dock, where Natalie stood waiting near the dinghy. They cruised back to *Splendour* in silence. Dennis was angry, and Natalie knew it.

Christopher was still in his cabin when they entered the galley, where R.J. stood with a cup of coffee in hand. R.J. offered a feeble hello, and Natalie said she was going to change clothes, then make breakfast. She went to her stateroom. Dennis poured a cup of coffee and joined R.J. at the galley table.

"Chief, why don't we cut this weekend short and go back to the marina this morning?" Dennis suggested.

"Nope. Natalie wants a pleasure cruise with her guest, and who am I to interfere with that?" R.J. said sarcastically.

"This isn't a pleasure cruise. It's a cruise from hell," Dennis said. "Let's just bring in the dinghy and go back."

"Dennis, we're not going back. After breakfast, we'll make a bridle, and we'll tow the dinghy to Isthmus so we don't have to bring it in. Natalie's cruise will go on as planned."

Yes, boss.

Dennis was furious. He was not about to help R.J. make a bridle. He always trusted R.J. to make rational decisions, but his insistence upon continuing this farce of a cruise made no sense whatsoever. It would have been so simple, so logical, and so easy to just go home. But, so far, no one could be reasoned with.

Natalie came into the galley wearing a tee shirt and tight jeans. "Good morning, R.J.," she said in a plastic tone.

"Good morning, Natalie," R.J. responded.

They didn't look at each other.

"I'm going to make breakfast," she announced. "Dennis and I are starving."

"I'm not hungry," Dennis hissed.

Christopher joined the group as Natalie stood over her aluminum bowl, whipping eggs. Chris greeted everyone with a pleasant good morning, and light and airy conversation started up as if nothing had transpired the night before.

Appalled, and insubordinate or not, Dennis stormed out of the galley.

Dennis rested in his quarters until breakfast was over. Now his anger with R.J. grew. He had tried to persuade Natalie the night before to understand R.J., but perhaps R.J. didn't deserve understanding. When he was sure his anger was in check, he rejoined the group. These three professional actors on board had poorly cultivated a lightheartedness so brittle Dennis thought it would shatter with a breeze. The entire scene sickened Dennis, but he reluctantly accepted that his only option was to join the pretense.

That R.J. stuck to his original plan to go to Isthmus Cove outraged Dennis even further. The dinghy had been bridled up, the breakfast table cleared, and the excursion from hell was about to carry over to the Isthmus, to Two Harbors—the quiet part of the island.

The ride along the island's coast was a bit bumpy, but no one seemed to mind. There were smiles, small talk, and gaiety, which in some weird way was scarier than the argument that had transpired the night before.

When they moored at Two Harbors, Dennis foresaw nothing but more trouble. There were no distractions on this part of the island. There was a restaurant, Doug's Harbor Reef, and that was it. The four would have to entertain themselves, and Dennis had witnessed the trouble that had caused the night before. When they were alone outside, tying the moorings, Dennis attempted another appeal to R.J.

"R.J., why are we mooring here?" he asked, not really expecting an answer, but the one he got startled him.

"Because Natalie wants a weekend with Christopher Walken, and Natalie will get more than what she came for. *That's* why."

Further attempts to change R.J.'s mind would be worthless, so Dennis decided to just ride out the weekend by going along with the program. If this was what R.J. and Natalie wanted, who was Dennis to interfere? He had done all he could to prevent the continuation of the cruise.

Natalie wanted to go ashore, and she wanted to go with only Christopher. "R.J., you wanted the peace and quiet of the boat this weekend," Natalie said sweetly, "but Christopher is anxious to see the island. I'd like to take him ashore, if you don't mind. You're welcome to come along."

Between her lines, the message was apparent: R.J., you're the one who wanted Isthmus, so have Isthmus all to yourself.

R.J. either didn't get it, or he got it and felt guilty.

"Sure," R.J. agreed with amplified pleasantry. "You two go and have fun. Dennis and I will join you later for dinner."

Between R.J.'s lines, his anger was clear to Dennis.

Dennis asked himself, "Am I the only person listening to what's really going on here?"

R.J. waved Natalie and Chris farewell when they boarded a ship-to-shore taxi boat. He may have felt guilty for his behavior the evening before and wanted to make up for it, but now his guilt seemed overpowered by fresh doubts and disappointments. He had been pleasant to Natalie, even though it was forced, but his effort had obviously meant nothing to her. She was off with Christopher and on her way to a public bar. R.J. stood still on the back deck, his face drawn, watching his captivating wife cruise away with her handsome costar. R.J. turned quickly and was startled to see Dennis standing on the side deck. Dennis had watched them leave too.

R.J. said, "Let's go over some details for winterizing the boat." It was R.J.'s way of telling Dennis to not dare mention the obvious.

There wasn't a whole lot to say about winterizing *Splendour*, but R.J. stretched it out until Dennis's yawns begged for release. "R.J., I think I need a nap. How about you?"

Dennis went to his room but couldn't sleep. He wondered if he should have allowed R.J. to go on talking about the boat to help keep his mind off Natalie, but then Dennis got angry all over again. He had begged R.J. to return to the mainland, and R.J. had refused.

Near four o'clock that afternoon, R.J. and Dennis were in the galley with a cocktail when R.J. decided he had given Natalie enough time alone with Christopher. Dennis expected to have left *Splendour* hours sooner. The afternoon had dragged on at an agonizingly slow pace.

R.J. and Dennis boarded *Valiant* and cruised to the island and headed straight for Doug's Harbor Reef. The buoyant charm of Doug's did not serve as a shock absorber to the sight of Natalie and Christopher huddled together at the end of the bar, so totally engrossed in conversation that they had not even noticed R.J. and Dennis approach. Darts shot from R.J.'s eyes.

Surely Natalie had expected R.J.'s arrival, but she was not "on guard" for him as she might have been for someone whose behavior or intention was inappropriate. Obviously, Natalie believed she was doing nothing wrong. R.J.'s smoldering look indicated a different opinion of Natalie's behavior.

She and Christopher, who had been facing and leaning toward each other, smiling and talking, continued to do so after R.J. stood behind them.

"Take a seat," Natalie said to R.J.

Dennis and R.J. took seats near Natalie. Christopher appeared a bit nervous when R.J. sat down.

R.J. sat calmly, waiting to order a drink. Although R.J. had lost his temper within the privacy of his boat the night before, here in public, Dennis could tell he tried hard to keep his anger in check. Natalie pleasantly greeted Dennis.

Dennis noticed she was wearing her pieces-of-eight earrings. He and R.J. ordered scotch. Natalie sipped wine. Conversation slowed.

R.J. downed his drink, then ordered another.

"Let's move to a table," R.J. suggested.

"Relax. Have a few drinks first, R.J.," Natalie said. "It's a little crowded now. Let's wait."

R.J. beckoned a waitress and made the dining room reservation for seven o'clock.

The situation exasperated Dennis. To hell with trying to figure out R.J., Natalie, Chris, or the purpose of the crummy outing. Monday morning could not come fast enough.

When the waitress informed the group their table was ready, all patrons' eyes studied the foursome's move to the dining area. Dennis felt protective of Natalie and wanted to tell everyone to stop staring. Dennis had never cared before that people stared at the Wagners. He held no pride in his employers this night.

But Natalie suddenly seemed extra friendly. After seating herself, she chatted with a teenage boy sitting next to their table, she pleasantly waved to a couple sitting two tables away, and she smiled for and obliged a young girl who approached and asked for her autograph. Then Natalie called the waitress over to their table and complained about the bright lighting. The waitress explained that she could dim it only by covering it, but when she placed a cloth napkin over the basket hanging shade, Natalie complained that it was too dark.

Other patrons watched.

"I don't like anything on this wine list," R.J. complained.

"The wines are fine, R.J.," Natalie disagreed.

"R.J.," Dennis interrupted, "I can get wine from the boat if you want. I'll get some Soave Bolla."

"I'll go with you," Christopher offered quickly, not surprising Dennis. Although the two had not talked much during the outing, perhaps Christopher preferred Dennis's company to being left alone with R.J. and Natalie. Suddenly, Dennis was Christopher's refuge.

"How do you find your way from the shore to the boat?" Christopher asked as they cruised in *Valiant* back to *Splendour*.

"There are rows of mooring cans forming passageways. The rows are numbered. And you get to know your way around too," Dennis explained. "Besides, we're usually one of the biggest boats out here, which makes *Splendour* easy to see."

Aboard *Splendour*, Christopher sat at the galley table as Dennis pulled two bottles from the wine rack.

"I don't think we'll need two bottles," Christopher said. "I hope dinner doesn't last that long."

Perhaps Christopher felt as Dennis did. Why prolong any part of this weekend?

"Well, I'll take two bottles and leave one in the dinghy just in case."

"Do you want to smoke?" Christopher asked.

"Sure."

Christopher pulled a joint from his pocket. Perhaps he wanted to relax, or perhaps he wanted to befriend Dennis. Dennis wondered if Natalie had smoked with Christopher and almost asked. He changed his mind because he did not believe she had.

Back at Doug's, Dennis knew that things must have been tense between R.J. and Natalie during the half hour it took for him and Christopher to fetch the wine, but that tension was carefully concealed.

The group drank champagne while they waited for their seafood and steak dinners. When their meals arrived, Natalie picked at her seafood. She was not pleased, so she ate only a few bites. The waitress offered to have the kitchen recook Natalie's entrée, but Natalie said, "Never mind, I'm fine." R.J. fumed.

Conversation slowed as the men ate, and Natalie chatted with fellow diners as she sipped wine. An accordion player came by and played *Laura's Theme*. R.J. tried to smile but appeared irritated. Natalie complimented the serenade.

As the waitress cleared away plates, Natalie ordered after-dinner cocktails. R.J. asked to leave but gave in and ordered cognac. Dennis dittoed R.J.'s order. When Natalie went for a second round of drinks, R.J. tried to take control.

"Natalie, we can go back to the boat for drinks. Let's not stay here," he said. He glanced around the room, then rolled his eyes, so much to say that it was demeaning to display their partying in a public place full of common people.

"No, R.J., I want to stay. I want another drink. Here...see, this is empty," she said, holding up her glass.

"Natalie," R.J. hissed, "let's go now!"

"Oh, let's stay," Natalie giggled. "I'm having fun."

R.J. stood up and Dennis thought he was going to lose it, but he walked off to the men's room. Natalie ordered another round of drinks.

Christopher stayed silent.

"Come on, Natalie, I want to get out of here," R.J. insisted when he returned. He threw cold looks around the table. Dennis ignored the ones directed at him. He wanted to remain neutral, and he would rather drink at the restaurant than back on the boat. He agreed with Natalie. A public domain simply felt safer. R.J. was getting angrier, like a time bomb ticking louder and louder. But Natalie finally gave in.

Dennis felt his booze but knew that his companions had drunk a lot more than he had. He noticed R.J. stagger. R.J. put his coat over Natalie's shoulders, as if to shield her from the paparazzi, although the only people left in the restaurant were those Natalie had chatted with throughout the evening.

At the dock, they all climbed into the dinghy, and Dennis navigated slowly back to *Splendour* in the dark, using a flashlight to spot mooring cans because the dinghy's headlight was out. They made their transfer from the dinghy to *Splendour* in a night extraordinarily damp and cold, but there was hardly any wind. Dennis tied the dinghy up for the night to the cleats on the transom and joined the trio in the main salon.

"I'd like wine, Dennis," Natalie said as she lit her beeswax candles on the coffee table.

Dennis uncorked a bottle of her favorite Pouilly-Fuissé. Natalie was well aware of R.J.'s wrath, yet she sat on the settee with Christopher. She looked lovely in the candlelight. Wearing a simple outfit of jeans and a golden pullover, she looked sexy. Her eyes sparkled, enhancing her aura of sensuality and youthfulness. She chatted and giggled with Christopher as R.J. and Dennis stood a few feet aside. R.J. rubbed the back of his neck. His eyes vigilantly watched Natalie as she entertained Christopher.

At one point, R.J. interrupted with his dissatisfaction with how much *Brainstorm* had taken Natalie away from their home, and Christopher responded that such is to be expected in the world of acting, especially for big stars.

R.J.'s face flushed red. He took one deep breath after another. His restlessness bothered Dennis, but Dennis had given up. He just didn't know how to distract R.J.

Natalie's mesmeric attention to Christopher Walken and their movie filled the room. Every sound and move she made seemed panoramic and in slow motion.

Finally, R.J. burst and shouted at Christopher. "So, what do you want to do to my wife?" he thundered with spine-chilling challenge. "Do you want to fuck my wife? Is that what you want?"

There wasn't enough time to absorb the shock of R.J.'s outburst before R.J. grabbed the opened, half-filled wine bottle by the neck, pulled it up and back behind his shoulder for force, then brought it down fast and hard, crashing it against the coffee table.

Instinctively, Natalie, Christopher, and Dennis threw their arms to their faces to shield against the shattering glass piercing through the main salon. After the glass settled—small, sharp pieces everywhere—and all was quiet, no one spoke or moved a muscle. The standstill seemed an eternity.

R.J. turned his back to the group.

Dennis could tell Christopher was afraid. He saw Christopher's hands start to shake. Then Christopher slowly and carefully stood. Shaking his head, he took a few steps to the side door and stepped outside. He stood in the cold air and drizzle for a few moments, then reentered to go directly to his cabin without a word. Once there, he closed his door.

Natalie stayed seated and looked mortified. When she heard Christopher's stateroom door close shut, she stood, faced R.J., and broke the painful silence.

"I won't stand for this, R.J.," she hissed. "This is outrageous, and I promise you, I will not tolerate it!" She stomped off to their stateroom and slammed the door behind her.

The death feud had begun.

Chapter 17

Dennis had remained oddly detached as he sat at my dining room table recounting the Friday and Saturday details of the 1981 holiday cruise, as if reliving a surreal experience. When he described R.J. smashing the wine bottle, Dennis had demonstrated by grabbing an empty wine bottle on our table. He stood up from his chair, raised the bottle, simulated slamming it forward, imitating R.J.'s facial expressions and repeating R.J.'s words. Dennis screamed, "So what do you want? Do you want to *fuck* my wife? Is that what you *want*?"

Dennis's reenactment was so compelling, I threw my hands up to protect my face, but Dennis, of course, had stopped short of the table with the bottle. I stared at him, shaken and speechless. His eyes were wide, and his hands trembled.

"God, Denny," was all I could say, as though I had just watched an intense scene from a movie—a scene I needed to review. I rewound the account through my mind to assimilate each word and action for its implications. This story was light years from Wagner's official statement, released by his attorney, that it had been a pleasant weekend, and he didn't know what had happened.

Dennis and I sat in silence for several minutes.

Finally I asked. "How did the authorities get wind of an argument?"

"We all stuck with the same statement that it had been a pleasant weekend, but maybe Chris mentioned a spat with R.J. And some of the weekend was pleasant, so it wasn't necessarily a lie—it just wasn't near the whole truth."

"Rationalize it all you want, but the authorities should have been given more information, Den."

"That was up to the lawyers. Believe me, it made me sick."

"Did you tell your attorney about the bottle?"

"I only answered what I was asked. I mentioned the seas were rough on Friday night. R.J. and I had talked about using that excuse for Natalie and me staying on the island Friday night. R.J. told me to say nothing more, and I obeyed. The lawyer asked basic questions."

"What happened after R.J. smashed the bottle?"

"After Natalie went to her stateroom," he continued, "I made her tea but I didn't expect her to come up for it. R.J. and I waited for her. R.J. was real edgy and then went below to go apologize to Natalie."

"When you say 'below'—how far of a distance is it?"

"Just a few steps from the main salon to their master stateroom." Dennis lowered his eyes and remained silent for several minutes. He started to speak, looked up, and hesitated. Finally, in a flat voice, as if some major detail were still impossible to tell, he said, "R.J. returned about a half hour later and told me Natalie was missing. He said he searched everywhere. I wanted to turn on the searchlight and look for her in the water, but R.J. asked me to help search the boat again."

"But, Denny, didn't you see R.J. looking for her?"

Dennis stared into my eyes, and he held the chilling gaze until I shifted my eyes uncomfortably. "No," he answered, vindictively, "I didn't."

I couldn't ignore his tone. "Why did you answer with such malice, Denny?"

Dennis's eyes pierced mine as he answered, "Because this is a malicious story."

Again, I shuddered. "I know it is," I said. "Go on."

"R.J. went out back. I checked the front. When I looked inside Chris's room, he was sound asleep. I was surprised Chris hadn't locked his door. R.J. and I met back in the wheelhouse. He said that Natalie must have gone ashore and that she would probably be back in a while. By this point, I somehow knew Natalie was in danger, but I told R.J. to have faith, but I *knew* Natalie was not out for a midnight dinghy ride."

"Did you see or hear anything during the half hour that R.J. searched the boat for Natalie?"

Again, Dennis did not answer. He just looked at me without flinching or blinking. I was certain that his silent and lengthy eye contact were an indication of details he still was unprepared to talk about.

"I remember asking R.J. if he wanted me to clean up the broken glass but he said, 'No, leave it there!'"

"Why? Wasn't it a blaring indication of trouble? If he didn't want bad publicity, it would have seemed smart to clean it up."

"R.J. decided it was best to not touch the glass."

"I'm utterly amazed that you talked about it," I said. "Did you talk about what else you would tell the authorities?"

"Of course we did, Marti. R.J. was scared to death of bad publicity so, of course, we discussed what we would say."

"I can't imagine in the midst of this horrible crisis that R.J. would gather his wits to make sure you had your stories straight. That's repulsive, Denny."

"It was hell, and I didn't have any wits to gather. I'd been drinking, and I was scared. And, he was pouring me more booze. I just went along with him."

"Was R.J. specific about what he wanted to tell the authorities?"

"He said to insist we had had a pleasant weekend. He didn't want them to hear about anything that might sound suspicious. We figured that Chris wouldn't say anything about the broken glass because he wouldn't want bad publicity either—with his movie just about to wrap up. He wouldn't jeopardize his career. 'And I can't jeopardize mine, either,' R.J. told me. I wanted to say, 'You fucking asshole, you're worried about your fucking career while your wife is missing somewhere out there in the cold, dark ocean.' But I didn't. I hated him, loved him, and pitied him all at the same time."

"So why not just clean up the glass anyway, since he was so sure Chris wouldn't talk?"

"If the slightest chance existed that Chris might say something about the smashing of the wine bottle, R.J. didn't want it to look like we were trying to cover up anything. He would deal with explaining the broken glass only if Chris mentioned how it got there."

"Well, what if the detectives had asked about it? What did R.J. plan to say?"

"If they had asked, and if we were sure Chris hadn't talked, we were going to say a bottle fell. But they never really thought anything about the glass because R.J. said the sea was rolling. Lots of good questions weren't asked. It was unreal. I couldn't believe how they treated R.J.—there wasn't any suspicion—the boat was a mess, but it was all overlooked."

"But, Den, you have to accept the responsibility of not being cooperative with them. You didn't offer the truth, either."

"When the authorities found the bottle of Soave Bolla that I left in the dinghy, they assumed Natalie put it there for her midnight voyage," Dennis shook his head. "Like she was some kind of lush who was too plastered to think about getting dressed but hadn't forgotten to pack her booze. Reports were published saying it looked like Natalie did plan to take wine on a midnight dinghy ride—'to gaze at the stars, like she always did.' Natalie never took out the dinghy."

"Exactly where was that bottle inside the dinghy, Denny?"

"On the floor. Up front. Why?"

"Well, if the authorities thought Natalie put the wine in the dinghy, you'd think they would have questioned how the wine ended up safely tucked away in the dinghy while Natalie ended up in the water. What about the banging-dinghy theory? If she'd fallen while untying the dinghy to tighten it, how does the bottle of wine factor into that scenario? I'm just rolling off questions I think the authorities should have asked after finding that bottle of Soave Bolla—if they believed it factored into her leaving *Splendour*."

"We braced ourselves for all kinds of questions like that. We really thought the authorities would put us through the wringer and make us account for every single second. I was totally dumbfounded when that never happened."

"Would you have told them the truth about how the wine bottle got in the dinghy if they had asked?"

"Of course I would have. There was no sense in lying about that, but after I left *Splendour*, I was told to direct all questions and answers through the attorney, Mark Beck's office, and to not mention one word to the authorities."

"So you were instructed to not cooperate with the authorities?"

"The last day I was in my lawyer's office, Rasure came to see me there. We saw him walk up the sidewalk to the door, and Mark Beck said, 'Here he comes, let's make him wait. Let's let him sit a bit and stew'—like Rasure was the enemy or something. Mark made him wait over ten minutes, then insisted I say no more than a few words. We laughed and snickered at making Rasure wait. Does that sound like cooperating with the authorities?"

"No, and it certainly sounds like no one, including R.J., wanted to understand what happened to Natalie."

"R.J. already knew what had happened to Natalie. He didn't need any answers. He just needed to be covered."

"Good point, Den. R.J. didn't need answers. And since you were told to not answer any questions or offer any information, you couldn't even correct the authorities' assumption of why the wine bottle was in the dinghy."

"What's worse," Dennis continued, "is that the bottle of wine I could've logically accounted for if anyone had been interested swayed suspicion from R.J. The authorities assumed that Natalie had been acting crazy. Know what?"

"What, Denny?"

He stared at me intently. "They suspected the wrong person of acting crazy for that weekend."

"It must have been hell for you to sit there with R.J., getting your stories straight, while Natalie was in God knows what kind of danger."

"We did the same thing with our attorneys afterwards— we got our stories straight. That's what Natalie's death was about—getting our fucking stories straight. It wasn't about, 'Oh my God, how are we going to tell her girls?' or 'This will destroy Natalie's mother', or even 'This poor, young woman—her life is over.' It was about getting our fucking bullshit stories straight, right up until the afternoon she was buried. Then it was about never changing those stories we had so fucking straight!"

"And you stayed for months at R.J.'s house after Natalie died." It was a statement.

"I went back and forth from his house to the boat, but mostly I stayed at R.J.'s. People were in and out of his house for at least two weeks. The only place I went to was Yolanda's when I left R.J.'s. I was watched *all* the time."

"Why did you go along with that, Denny?"

"R.J. said it was for my own protection, and I believed him. Reporters swarmed his place for weeks. R.J. didn't want me to get cornered by them. I was a mess. After a couple of weeks though, I felt like I was in prison. I wanted to get the hell out of there. R.J. and the girls were always crying. People came by constantly, and it was so depressing. After ten at night, everything was locked down. Nothing seemed real. What a living nightmare.

"Telegrams and letters poured in daily from people I hadn't seen or heard from in years. But R.J. asked me to wait before contacting anyone or returning any messages, even to my own mother. He wanted things to cool off. I knew, even then, that things would never cool off. I expected to hear from you, and you're the only one who didn't try to contact me. Thanks," he said genuinely.

"You're welcome. Who did contact you?" I asked.

"About every person I'd ever met who knew that I was the *Splendour* captain. Almost every girl I ever dated tried to contact me. I even got a message from that girl I invited on the boat when Phil Bloom and I docked at San Diego—the one I met at the Alley Cat seven years earlier."

"What did the messages say?"

"Sympathies mostly, but some gave their numbers or mentioned dates they would be at a certain place if I wanted to talk or needed a shoulder to cry on."

"Well, I admit, I thought about calling you," I confessed. "Not for information, but just to say I was sorry. So maybe some of the condolences were genuine. Mine would have been."

"People wanted to be a part of it all. Who would want to be a part of this?"

"I'm not so sure I would have asked to be a part of this, Den, but I'm glad I am. I'm learning a lot about the ways of the world that I just don't understand."

"From the day Natalie died, you never once brought up the subject. You'll never know how much I appreciated that."

"I knew you would tell me when you were ready. A part of me sensed I would be this involved one day."

"How did you hear about Natalie's death?" Dennis asked me.

"I was cleaning up the kitchen after dinner. It had been a real peaceful kind of Sunday. I wasn't thinking about much else but the holiday season starting. About six the phone rang. It was my brother Dave. He asked, 'Marti, have you heard about Natalie Wood? She drowned last night.' It was such shocking news, Den, I felt like someone had punched me in the gut. I kept asking, 'Are you sure? Are you sure?' He told me to put on the TV, and I did. Within minutes I saw the vague report and was afraid there might have been a boating accident and that you might be dead too. I wanted to call, but knew better to wait to hear from you. Ironically, my phone rang off the wall that night. Every person who knows we're friends called and asked what happened—like I would know!"

"People called my mom too."

"Den? Please tell me, really, why you've involved me."

"Trust. And I know you'll somehow make sense of all this, and that you'll be fair. I know I fucked up, but I know you won't turn on me for it. There are things I don't even understand about all that went down, but I think you'll see through some things and help me."

"This story is impossible to make sense of, but I do understand, even though I think you should have handled things differently. I don't blame Natalie. I blame R.J. Whether Natalie was flirting or not, he shouldn't have humiliated her in front of Walken. She deserved better than that."

"Jealousy got the best of him. I wish I could go back and change things."

"I want to help you to set the story straight."

It was a pure, innocent, and naive belief I clung to, that I could help Dennis to tell his story. But the Natalie Wood legend would begin to take on a life of its own, a life that could not be controlled. That's what legends do.

I thought back on my first conversation with Dennis after Natalie died. I happened to have caught him on his very first night back aboard *Splendour* since the tragedy. It had been a chance call—I hadn't expected to reach him and had planned the message I intended to leave, but he answered the phone.

"Everything seems beyond coincidence, Den—even from the first moment I spoke with you after Natalie died," I reminded him.

"When you finally called, Marti, your timing was perfect. It was my first night back on the boat, and I was spooked. I don't believe in ghosts, but you know what they say about people who die unexpectedly haunting the place where it happened? I was so creeped out that night. Then, you called, said you were sorry, and you talked about other things. You brought reality back into my life. If I never thanked you for that night, I'm thanking you now."

"I remember how jittery you were."

"I couldn't stand being at R.J.'s every night, so I'd sleep on the boat every now and then. And now I'm glad for the time I had with *Splendour* before R.J. got rid of her. Maybe it's silly, but I feel like the boat is another victim of this tragedy. But that first night back on *Splendour*, I couldn't stop thinking about identifying Natalie. That was more painful than anything else."

"Den, can you tell me about it and her funeral?"

He obliged.

* * *

A man Dennis didn't know led him to Natalie. Her body lay in a cold decompression chamber, on a metal table in the small building near Doug's Harbor Reef; the building was used by the local divers after deep-sea excursions.

About six unfamiliar people guarded her body, inside and outside the building. One woman stood near the body and jotted notes on a clipboard. Dennis approached with his eyes lowered. He caught a glimpse of Natalie's red jacket placed across her chest.

Dennis, unable to bring his eyes to focus on her, choked out, "It's her."

"You'll have to look at her, Mr. Davern," he was told.

His breath was shallow. He wanted to scream and run, knowing that once he looked, the lifeless image of his beautiful friend would forever haunt him. Dennis trembled as he forced himself to move his eyes from Natalie's torso to her face. Her arms were exposed, and he saw the bruises. The fronts of her legs also showed bruises, far too many. Dennis wondered why her nightgown had not been pulled down to cover her exposed legs. He caught his breath when he saw that her eyes were still open. Her face appeared swollen, but not deformed, a bit greenish white in color, and her mouth had gone limp. She looks at peace, though, he tried to convince himself.

He dropped his eyes and whispered, "Yes, it's Natalie Wood."

Someone took hold of Dennis's elbow to lead him away, but he pulled back and looked again at Natalie. He scanned his eyes across her body and concentrated on her legs and arms, noticing even more bruises. He started to count. One, two, four, seven...ten...he had seen enough, but there were more, including a scrape on her left cheek.

Dennis said quickly, "I want to get off the island, now."

But Detective Duane Rasure, who had been assigned the case, was waiting for Dennis. Mutual discord existed from the start of the interview. Rasure asked for Dennis's input, but Dennis offered little. Pleasure cruise...dinner...Natalie missing...She's gone, just gone....

When Rasure asked Dennis about Friday evening, Dennis lied and said that the four had spent the night on the boat. Quickly realizing from Rasure's expression that the detective already knew Natalie had not slept on the boat, Dennis said, "Okay, I spent the night on the island with her, but if you check, you'll see that two rooms were booked. Before I say anything more, I want to talk with R.J. or see my attorney. Right now, I just want to get off this island."

A movie star was dead, and her boat skipper had just lied to him, yet Rasure dismissed Dennis.

Dennis boarded a passenger speedboat departing for the mainland. The transport boat filled with people going about a normal day, people smiling and chatting, unaware of Dennis's tragic weekend. Dennis avoided eye contact, took a seat, and closed his eyes. He felt the weight of fatigue and realized his dire need for sleep, for it had been since the motel with Natalie, Friday night, that he had last slept.

The limousine waiting for Dennis at the marina took him directly to R.J.'s home where Natalie's mourners and the media had already assembled. The limo passed reporters holding video cameras and microphones. News vans lined a quarter-mile stretch approaching R.J.'s house on North Canon Drive.

"All kinds of people are swarming the place," the driver told Dennis. "I heard that the FBI and the CIA are watching the place too. Can you believe it?"

Dennis did not respond. He found the information far-fetched, but he didn't doubt it. They reached the gates of Wagner's house where security guards guided them through a path of lingering reporters, whom the guards constantly reminded to "stand back." One reporter ran past a guard, but the guard caught him by the back of his shirt, halting his entrance onto the Wagner grounds. Other reporters surrounded the limousine. One even pressed his face to the tinted window, desperate to see who was inside. Dennis noted the disappointment on the man's face at seeing no one recognizable.

Cars were parked bumper to bumper on each side of R.J.'s circular driveway. Up the narrow lane the limousine crept to the Wagners' front door. Dennis's back passenger door was immediately opened by two bodyguards who escorted Dennis inside the home.

Dennis stepped into the entry hall where another unfamiliar guard, without saying a word, took Dennis by the arm and led him through the living room. Dennis noticed all the people, but faces were a blur. He was taken directly to Paul Ziffren, R.J.'s attorney, who stood alone near the bar. The guard walked away. Ziffren led Dennis up the stairway to R.J.'s room. With every upward step, Dennis's knees felt as if they would bend and fold him to the floor.

Paul tapped on R.J.'s bedroom door and opened it. R.J.'s feeble voice granted them permission to enter the elegant master bedroom that had been Natalie's pride and joy.

It was all too much for Dennis. He had not slept in over thirty-four hours. He had just identified Natalie's body, and that morbid task alone had been enough to separate him from coherence. Now, he knew that the next "let's-get-our-stories-straight" session was about to begin.

R.J. sat on the edge of the bed and still cried. He looked horrible.

Dennis asked to use R.J.'s bathroom. He splashed handfuls of cold water onto his face and fiercely rubbed it into his pores as if he could force it to the core of his brain and wash away the vivid mental picture of Natalie's body. However, the cold water revived him only for the moment.

R.J. had composed himself when Dennis returned to his bedside. Paul Ziffren got down to business. "Dennis, I can't represent both you and R.J. in this matter," he explained. "However, it is imperative that you have an attorney. We've hired Mark Beck, who will talk to you tomorrow. In the meantime, do not speak to anyone concerning any details of this entire incident."

"I understand," Dennis answered. He did not blame Ziffren for doing his job, and he knew how close Natalie and R.J. were to Paul. He could see the grief in Paul's eyes. Paul was hurting, too, for Paul was more than an attorney. He had been in Natalie's life for years.

"Dennis, why don't you go downstairs for a bit? Just don't say anything," R.J. said.

Dennis was infuriated that R.J. was so damned concerned that he would talk. He did not need R.J.'s lawyer or anyone else reminding him to keep his mouth shut. He did not even want to see the crowd downstairs.

"R.J., would it be okay if I just went to one of the guest rooms up here?" Dennis asked.

Ziffren explained that Wagner was going to see no one other than family this day and hinted that they did not want it to appear as if Dennis were hiding from any one.

Propriety was Dennis's last concern, but he hadn't the energy to object.

"I won't be going to the funeral, but I want you to go, Dennis," R.J. mumbled.

Paul raised his eyebrows. "We have to talk, R.J."

Dennis was certain that R.J.'s attorney would insist R.J. make an appearance at the funeral. Dennis understood Wagner's reluctance, but Paul couldn't. Dennis numbly went downstairs.

The crowd had grown considerably, and it continued to grow. People consoled one another; tears were abundant; grief touched every face. Dennis headed for the bar. Natalie's sister, Lana Wood, stood behind the bar. Dennis took a seat opposite her. She looked at him with tear-brimmed eyes and seemed about to speak, but a sob caught her throat, and she remained silent.

A hand squeezed Dennis's shoulder. He turned around, and there stood Willie Mae. She hugged Dennis as they exchanged tear-filled remorse.

It was getting late. Voices rang in his ears. Faces swirled before his eyes. Next thing he realized, he was leaning against the wall outside R.J.'s bedroom. Had he planned to say something to R.J. before retiring?

R.J.'s ex-wife, Marion Marshall, tearfully exited R.J.'s bedroom. She didn't recognize Dennis and gave him an odd look. Dennis heard Natalie's children crying from inside R.J.'s room. Their weeping shattered his heart. He tottered his way down the hall.

When he closed the guest bedroom door, he closed off the world. The solitude was such a relief that he did not even break open the scotch Willie Mae had put in the room. He fell onto the bed, fully clothed, and closed his eyes.

Dennis remained in a zombie-like state. Other than his room, the Wagner bar was the only place he visited. Breakfast consisted of double screwdrivers, and at noon, scotch became the main course of the day. R.J. stayed in his bedroom with his daughters. Late Monday afternoon, R.J. summoned Dennis to his room.

"Dennis, sit down," R.J. said.

Dennis took a good look at R.J. They were less than 48 hours removed from Natalie's death, and R.J. already looked aged with sunken eyes and new, deep lines creasing his face. Dennis sat on the sofa facing the glass coffee table covered with family photographs. What a living hell.

"As you know, Paul has secured legal counsel for you," R.J. said, "and we'd like you to contact Mark Beck today."

"I'll call right away," Dennis said. He got up to leave.

"Wait," R.J. said. "I've hired a driver for you. Anywhere you want to go, let me know. All I ask is that you check with me first. And Dennis, use my credit card for anything you need or ask for cash."

A guard approached Dennis as he left R.J.'s bedroom. "There's a girl outside demanding to see you," the guard said. "She claims she's your fiancée, Yolanda. She's not listed, so we can't let her in."

Dennis went to the front lawn, as far as Yolanda had been allowed access. She threw her arms around Dennis and cried.

"Dennis, you're coming with me! Right now!" she demanded. "You don't belong here."

"Yolanda, I can't leave," Dennis explained. "There are legal matters I have to take care of for R.J. He needs me to stay. He's hired a driver for me, so I'll see you in a few days when things cool off."

Yolanda stepped back in anger, obviously prepared to argue. Two security guards carefully watched and moved in closer. When she noticed that her every word and action was being monitored, she calmed down and left.

Dennis then called Mark Beck. They talked briefly, and Beck assured Dennis that the official statement would be prepared and wrapped up by Wednesday, before Natalie's burial.

Dennis was driven to Beck's office the morning of Wednesday, December 2, to sign his official statement. Mark read words to Dennis that went in one ear and out the other. Dennis did as he was told and signed the statement.

Dennis's assigned driver then took him to the chapel and cemetery on Wilshire Boulevard. He stepped inside the chapel as young Courtney was asking to see her mother one last time. Someone reopened the casket. Dennis turned his back as R.J. stood near the casket with Natasha. Dennis could not look at Natalie, dead, again.

Over one hundred mourners solemnly exited the chapel into the bright sun and strode to Natalie's nearby plot, where her casket was placed over her grave. Dennis stayed just a few feet behind R.J. Those who carried the casket walked with tears: Howard Jeffrey, Mart Crowley, Peter Donen, Josh Donen, John Foreman, Guy McElwaine, Tom Mankiewicz, Paul Ziffren, and Bob Lang. Dennis stayed close to R.J. at the gravesite. Honorary pallbearers included Sir Laurence Olivier, Fred Astaire, Gregory Peck, Gene Kelly, and Frank Sinatra.

A Russian Orthodox priest blessed Natalie, then *Midnight in Moscow* was played on a balalaika, a Russian stringed instrument.

Hope Lange spoke to the grieving crowd. "Natalie, you put us to a very severe test today," she said. "It's difficult to feel joy and laughter when you're not here to share it."

R.J.'s face streaked with tears. His sobbing daughters clung to him.

Thomas Thompson, Natalie's writer friend, who had been in love with Natalie since interviewing her for *Life* magazine years before, shared his brief, tearful farewell. Tommy could barely choke out his departing words.

Then Roddy McDowall said, "She found not only a way to put life into her art, but art into her life."

Darling, you are an artist, Dennis recalled at that moment. He wanted to say something. He wanted to shout at the top of his lungs that Natalie shouldn't be dead. She shouldn't be dead! He choked back his tears.

R.J. picked up several of the gardenias—Natalie's favorite—that lay near the casket. He handed them to his daughters to say goodbye with. Dennis had always placed a fresh gardenia in a bowl of water on Natalie's stateroom dressing table before the start of each cruise. Natalie had told him that she smiled each time she was greeted by the floating flower. The gardenias today seemed inadequate, but they reminded Dennis of Natalie's smile. Dennis picked up his own gardenia, going through the motions. He held the flower tightly, knowing the death of Natalie would be the death of his world too. He would trade anything to be able to turn the clock back to last Saturday night.

The priest gave a final blessing, and R.J. bent to kiss the casket. He and his daughters placed their gardenias on top of Natalie's casket, then walked to a waiting limousine as they clung to each other in despair.

The funeral procession followed the limousine to R.J.'s home where an elaborate, catered buffet and open bar was offered. The house was bursting at the seams with all of the people who had known and loved Natalie.

Dennis saw Christopher Walken briefly at the wake. Seeing Walken reminded Dennis that today, Wednesday, was the day Dennis was to have visited Natalie at the studio for a private preview of *Brainstorm*. Walken seemed ill at ease. Dennis figured he would never see Christopher again. Walken departed the viewing within an hour.

At Wagner's house, visitors came and went throughout the day. Only a few saw R.J. in his bedroom, where he stayed secluded all day.

Natalie's mother, Maria Gurdin, stood at the front door to bid appreciation and farewell to the mourners as they departed. She had not spoken a word to Dennis all afternoon but had thrown plenty of contemptuous looks his way. She kept repeating to everyone, "Aren't we blessed to have had her?"

As a favor to Natalie, about a month before, Dennis had sanded the hardwood floors in Mrs. Gurdin's condo, and even then, the woman had behaved coldly toward him.

After the crowd thinned, a small group gathered in the kitchen. Dennis stood apart from the family members, eager to escape to his room, but had carried some food trays to the kitchen to help out Willie Mae. Mrs. Gurdin walked in and busied herself at the sink. Abruptly she turned and snapped at Dennis, "How could you have allowed this to happen? You are the *captain*, and you should have prevented this! This is all your fault! My daughter's dead because of *you*!"

Blood rushed to Dennis's temples. Although he realized Mrs. Gurdin may not like him and was certainly devastated over losing her daughter, he had never expected her to hurt and humiliate him in such a manner. He had tried to prevent it. Yet he knew not to defend himself. He walked away quietly and went to his room. He closed the door behind him, slid down to the floor and stared at the far wall. That's where he awoke the next morning.

Chapter 18

On the next Wednesday, December 10, Dennis returned to Mark Beck's office for another interview with Detective Rasure. Beck and Davern saw Rasure strolling up the walkway, and Mark Beck shook his head and laughed at Rasure. When the secretary announced that Rasure had arrived, Beck said to Dennis, "Let's have him wait and stew a little. Do *you* have any questions, Dennis?"

Dennis thought it an odd question. Shouldn't everyone have the questions for him?

Duane Rasure had a few. In Beck's office, he asked Dennis again about the Friday evening stay on the island with Natalie. "Yes, I stayed with her there," Dennis answered, "because of rough seas."

Rasure asked about the tone of the cruise. "Fine," Dennis answered.

Rasure asked if Dennis had anything he could add that might shed light on why or how Natalie disappeared from *Splendour*.

Dennis's every answer was a glance to Mark Beck's eyes. Mark would nod, Dennis would say, "No." Rasure departed, perhaps not satisfied but willing to close the case, which he did that very day.

Splendour remained moored off Isthmus Cove for over a week after Natalie's funeral. The authorities had her sealed with official yellow tape, but the boat was simply left floating alone. A week after Natalie's burial, an official called R.J. to give permission to retrieve *Splendour*.

Too devastating a task for R.J. to handle, as was identifying his wife, he again called upon Dennis to return *Splendour* to her homeport. Sensing it also was a tough job for Dennis, R.J. arranged for three trusted friends, makeup artists Frank Westmore, Eddie Butterworth, and Tommy Thompson, to help with the mission.

Frank, Eddie, and Tommy offered unconditional support for R.J. and were willing to help in any way possible in the dark days sure to linger long after Natalie's funeral. Dennis was doubly grateful for their support, for their help meant that Dennis wouldn't have to retrieve *Splendour* alone.

"I'll never be able to board that boat again," R.J. told Dennis from his bed.

"You'll never have to. I'll take care of everything," Dennis assured him.

Frank, Eddie, Tommy, and Dennis boarded a chartered helicopter on the mainland and flew to Catalina. Looking from the skies over Isthmus Cove, Dennis's heart sank at his first glimpse of *Splendour* since the tragedy.

The irritating sound of the chopper's rotors cutting against the wind worked Dennis's nerves. Landing on the island, Dennis shivered uncontrollably as he tried to reassure himself he could handle the task at hand.

The four men boarded a Harbor Patrol boat to reach *Splendour*. Nearing the yacht, Dennis wished someone else had been commissioned for the job, yet he understood that no one else could be trusted. He felt an obligation to *Splendour*. She was a part of Dennis's heart, which now skipped beats at the sight of her.

Dennis easily set aside his dislike for Frank this day. Frank, Eddie, and Tommy had been frequent guests aboard *Splendour*, and each had adored Natalie. This task overwhelmed them too.

About fifty yards from *Splendour*, Dennis took a long, sickened look. There she sat, floating and swaying, deserted and dejected as though being blamed and punished for the deplorable tragedy. *Splendour's* windows were sealed off with yellow tape, and the harsh sight proved that *Splendour* might forever remain maligned. The demoralizing sight ravaged Dennis.

Eddie Butterworth noticed Dennis's flushed face and heavy breathing as the patrol boat inched its way near *Splendour's* swim step. Eddie rested his hand on Dennis's shoulder as they made their transfer from the patrol boat to *Splendour's* deck.

"It'll be okay, Dennis," Eddie comforted. "We're here for you."

Scenes from the night Natalie died raced through Dennis's anguished mind. He saw R.J.'s terrified face again and heard his wretched voice. *She's gone, she's gone, she's gone.* He saw Natalie's dead eyes. Still in the denial stage of grief, this task was the rude awakening he was not yet ready for. If not for the presence of his three companions, he might have broken down.

The group passed through the tossed-up master stateroom. Frank asked why the pillows and blankets were all over the place. Dennis did not answer. Frank admitted he had been forewarned by R.J. that the boat would be a mess and that R.J. confessed there had been an argument. Dennis still did not answer, as he was sure R.J. had downplayed the argument's severity.

The sight of the once cozy main salon, now dank with ghostly remnants of the final party aboard *Splendour*, raised a collective gasp from Frank, Eddie, and Tommy. The shattered glass was most telling. Questioning eyes turned to Dennis.

Frank broke the shock. "My God! It looks like someone came in and trashed the place. What the hell went on here?"

It was a *bad* argument. Dennis thought about saying it but refrained.

Splendour seemed to whisper indignantly: Look at this! We know what happened, Dennis. We know what really happened.

Dennis looked away from the men to hide his tears. What could he say? There was no whitewashing this scene, no apologizing for it. It spoke for itself.

Although it occurred to Dennis to allay suspicions, he thought with defiance that he was not responsible for what they witnessed, and he felt vaguely relieved that his companions saw this evidence of trouble the authorities had so quickly and willingly dismissed.

Saltwater had sprayed the entire boat, and the sea mist left the familiar ocean stickiness upon everything the men touched. Empty wineglasses stuck to the coffee table. A thick, moist ring of clear grape residue had turned to a glue-like substance inside Natalie's wine glass. And there on the counter sat Natalie's untouched cup of tea. The tea was pitch black. Death black, Dennis thought.

Depressingly fitting, *Splendour's* batteries had gone dead. Dennis had figured she would not be ready to go at the push of the buttons. He called the Harbor Patrol for a battery charge, and the wait seemed an eternity.

Dennis could not clean up. His companions sympathized when Dennis explained his helplessness. In the bedroom, Dennis watched as Frank Westmore found Natalie's earring—the one that matched Dennis's pieces-of-eight medallion—on the floor in the corner of the master stateroom. Frank picked up the earring and looked at Dennis.

"How did this earring get in the corner over here, Dennis? Was there a fight?" Frank asked.

Dennis shrugged his shoulders.

Frank stared at his palm, pondering the earring.

The guys wiped down and straightened up every room as Dennis navigated *Splendour* back to the marina. During the painfully quiet cruise across the ocean, there wasn't one dry eye among the four men. Dennis understood that each man missed Natalie in his own way. A life of splendor was truly over for so many people who had shared life with Natalie.

Fearful that *Splendour* would become a public exhibit at Tahiti Marina, Dennis docked the boat outside the Harbor Patrol station and was promised that she would be watched over carefully.

When Dennis visited R.J. in his bedroom, R.J. asked Dennis to secure a broker's license so *Splendour's* commissioned sale would be legal. R.J. also assigned Dennis the responsibility of clearing *Splendour* of all belongings. Everything was to be stored in R.J.'s guesthouse to be dealt with at a later date.

After avoiding the boat for over a week, but calling to check on her daily, Dennis left R.J.'s house every afternoon for boat inventory and clearance. Filled with sadness, he boxed, labeled, and listed each item he removed from his home, Splendour.

Next, Dennis listed over 25 pieces of equipment that would be sold along with her, including the Wesmar Sonar. Dozens of "extras" were listed to stay on board as part of the sale, including inflatable seats for the dinghy, spare propellers, telescopes, the galley's deep fryer, wastebaskets, serving trays, boat flags (not including the WOFYC flag), and other boat equipment that any new owner would appreciate as a bonus, as these items had been owned by Robert Wagner and Natalie Wood.

The personal items Dennis removed especially reminded him of the great times aboard *Splendour*. Natalie's needle-crafted pillows took him right back to their wheelhouse afternoons when she had warmly included him as part of her family. He set aside the small beeswax candles that Natalie had lit just before her retreat to the stateroom. Dennis had blown them out when R.J. told him Natalie was missing. Dennis wanted to keep the candles. Then Dennis removed the coffee table from the main salon and walked it to the dock. On a mindless mission, he kept walking toward the parking lot. At his van, he opened the back door and placed the table inside. He planned on telling R.J. he was going to keep the table. R.J. would have no problem with that. It was the table R.J. would never want to see again. It was the table R.J. had smashed the bottle of wine on. It was the table Dennis needed to keep, for unexplainable reasons.

Then he returned to the yacht to pack up Natalie's handmade pillows. His tears poured as they had when he was a young boy, moving from the beach near Atlantic City, when he had to leave his boat and his cousin Jimmy behind.

The logbook went directly to R.J.'s house. That logbook included the names of all the guests who had enjoyed *Splendour* throughout the Wagner ownership. It was filled with notes and names of fun-filled outings and adventures, but the last name entered—Christopher Walken—closed that book forever.

PART THREE

Interviews, Authorities, and Lines

Oh, ev'ry thought that's strung a knot in my mind,
I might go insane if it couldn't be sprung...

—Bob Dylan ("Restless Farewell")

Chapter 19

I knew Dennis told the truth, but I also knew it wasn't the *whole* truth. Dark secrets showed in his eyes and mannerisms. His nightmares continued.

Perhaps a publisher's interest would prompt him to reveal more information, so I queried an editor, David Sanford, of Holt, Reinhart & Winston in New York City, who had rejected my prior, unrelated manuscript. Sanford was intrigued and agreed to meet with us.

In my family room, the night before our meeting, Dennis and I talked with Chuck Esser, who had volunteered to drive with us to New York.

"I've got a suggestion for your title," Chuck said. "Den is saying goodbye to both Natalie and *Splendour*, and actually to a life of splendor. Why not call it *Goodbye Natalie, Goodbye Splendour*?"

Chuck had been a well-respected homicide detective in Burlington County, New Jersey. A few years into his career, however, he had been the first responder to a brutal murder scene involving the stabbing of a teenage girl. On the heels of that case, a bomb exploded outside a residential garage in Willingboro, killing a baby. Chuck could not wrap his head around the senseless violence, and he suffered what today would be diagnosed as posttraumatic stress disorder. He soon divorced and left police work for a construction job where a job-site accident permanently damaged his foot.

Given his history in homicide investigation, I thought Chuck could give us some insight into how a death such as Wood's should have been treated by the police. "What would you have done at Natalie's death scene?" I asked.

"Detective class 101," he answered. "Wagner doesn't take off in a helicopter. The first twenty-four hours involving a body are crucial. No one leaves. You grill, then grill some more. Fact-finding flew away in that chopper with Wagner, especially in a high-profile case where people lawyer up fast."

Chuck described a homicide detective's duties and responsibilities: "The first officer gathers all possible witnesses. If it's not a crime scene, the truth will unfold. But, here we had a famous dead body with bruises, pulled from the ocean in her night clothes. Den, Walken, and Wagner would have been taken into custody—even taken to headquarters. They would have been checked for bruises too. Attorneys could have been contacted from the station. But sometimes being at the station gets a person talking, especially the innocent or scared ones who wish they could talk." Chuck glanced at Dennis, who had closed his eyes. "Wagner, Walken, and Den should have been separated and questioned thoroughly. The scene should have been protected from any possible disturbance while the event is reconstructed and a timeline framed."

"Small-town newspaper reporters I know might have done more," I said.

Chuck explained, "A detective should act like a reporter. The who, what, where, when, why, and most importantly, how, should all be answered before a case is closed. When a couple argues and it gets physical, usually both end up with some kind of evidence on their bodies. Critical things were overlooked."

"Everything was ignored, Chuck," Dennis opened his eyes and interjected.

Chuck answered, "Celebrity got in the way here."

"Can't blame detectives for three witnesses lying," I added.

"Still, they should have seen through that."

"I think you would have, Chuck," I said.

Early the next morning, my husband offered to skip work to chauffeur us to New York. George always believed Dennis's words, and he supported me as I sacrificed time from my marriage, my kids, and my friends. I devoted every spare hour, and took time late at night, to help Dennis cope with his problem, and sometimes George took Dennis's late calls doing his best to console our inconsolable friend. Driving us into the city was just one more example of George's steady support, but Chuck and Dennis rested their eyes in the backseat of our Buick Regal for the entire ninety-minute ride, rebuffing any attempt I might have made to discuss our expectations—and perhaps more importantly, Mr. Sanford's expectation—and now I felt slightly panic-stricken.

George parked near the Fifth Avenue publishing house, then he and Chuck went for breakfast. After announcing ourselves, Dennis seemed in no mood to be forthcoming. We talked through the morning in the editor's small office, filled with papers and books, then ate turkey sandwiches for lunch. By one in the afternoon, Dennis still hadn't passed the bottle smashing.

A courtesy letter from Mr. Sanford after our unproductive meeting said, "If Wagner's smashing the wine bottle is the extent of Dennis's account then it's a story meant only for those involved rather than for the ears of the world."

Because Dennis had withheld information concerning a death shrouded in mystery, David Sanford suggested we tell all or tell nothing. I agreed.

Dennis returned to Los Angeles. He called a month later in the middle of the night. "Marti, I'm so confused," he started, then mumbled on.

"Den, you need help," I sighed.

"Marti, I tried to prevent it all weekend. I said, over and over, 'Turn around, Natalie. Turn around, R.J.'"

"I know, Den." His turmoil seemed beyond my capacity to help. "Denny, you didn't do anything wrong, but let's do the right thing now, okay?"

"I knew we shouldn't have gone out," Dennis muttered. "It was stupid and crazy. There was gonna be trouble from the minute I started the engines...."

Suddenly I felt angry. "Stop blaming yourself, damn it!"

"Marti, I may as well die." He took in a deep breath. "I'm sorry."

"Denny, is this any way to live? Keeping this god-awful story inside of you is worse than eating a quick bullet."

"Marti, if I had a gun, I might do just that."

"Denny, no you *won't*. How dare you feel this way while Robert Wagner is off at some Hollywood event, or filming in Switzerland, staying at David Niven's fucking chalet. See your own doctor. Tell it! *All of it*."

"The truth is...the truth is...it's a mess." Again, Dennis worked himself up to the point that it all might have come spilling out, before managing to regain control of himself.

"Okay, at least tell me what it is you're afraid of."

"R.J.," he answered without hesitation.

"Is the truth that bad, Den?"

"Marti, foul play was involved," he blurted out.

I shouldn't have been so surprised, but I gasped and declared it was time for an attorney. Dennis agreed and flew to New Jersey. In Philadelphia, we met with an attorney, Paul Rovner, who came highly recommended by Dennis's father, who lived in the Main Line district and had met Rovner at church.

In Rovner's high-rise office, Dennis told the attorney everything I thus far knew. Then Dennis and Rovner spent a private hour together. The attorney brought up questions and aspects we hadn't considered, and Dennis felt secure with valuable legal counsel.

Dennis returned to Los Angeles. I refrained from asking specifically what foul play meant, and Dennis didn't bring it up again. Perhaps Rovner had advised him to not tell me everything, but without details, I was suspended in the middle of a mystery with a half-told truth taunting me. I had been transferred to a marketing position at a printing company owned by the newspaper corporation where I worked, and I had difficulty adjusting. I was consumed with Natalie. I wondered if the emerging generation would even remember her. It seemed Natalie had been buried twice: first her body, then her legacy.

I had read a brief news release that mentioned a planned Natalie Wood biography. Wagner had told Denny that no one would ever make a movie or write a book about Natalie while he was alive. Why would a grieving husband be so vehemently opposed to memorializing his legendary wife's life? It seemed a convenient way—the less she's remembered—to keep her death from being analyzed.

Through Dennis, I sometimes felt like Natalie's last chance for justice. It wasn't pompous thinking. It was the unlikely fact that her legend had crossed the path of this "nobody" from New Jersey. I naively believed truth could overpower any amount of money or power. Legends find their own way, but I wanted the world to know that a "pleasant weekend" had not surrounded her mysterious death. She deserved that much.

I told myself, tried to convince myself, that sometimes it takes just a nobody.

Chapter 20

Dennis said excitedly when he called about a month later, "A dentist needed his yacht refurbished and hired me as a resident worker. I'm living on a yacht again. I'll miss driving to the studios with P.V., but my brother Paul is flying out to live here again." I remembered Paul's last disaster move to L.A., but said nothing.

Dennis's lighthearted calls were rare, so I made a concentrated effort to not disturb his mood. "Now you have the best of two worlds—the marina and the studios." I asked, "Are you doing movies?"

"Movies, television, commercials. I just had a speaking part on *The A-Team*, and that's unusual for general extras. But I'm getting a hell of a lot less work than P.V. and other extras. They're called in daily, but I get about one part a week. P.V. says it's like I'm blacklisted."

Dennis was registered with Central Casting Corporation and with RichMar Casting, Inc. He belonged to the Screen Actors' Guild and paid his own dues. He had worked for Warner Brothers, MGM, Twentieth Century Fox, Columbia Pictures, and for television networks ABC, CBS, and NBC.

"Tell me about some of the parts you've played," I asked.

"Well, in *Bay City Blues*, a camera panned the bleachers for a baseball game scene, hometown side and a visitors' side. The camera closed in where we all gathered close to make the bleachers look full. Then, to film the visitors' side, about four hundred extras exchanged what we were wearing while tearing across the field to the other side. I ended up with a girl's sweater," he laughed. "In *Hill Street Blues* I play a cop in briefing room, and played a homeless bum in a winter scene. I wore an old, beat-up overcoat in the hundred-degree sun, pretending to be freezing. The stunt guys on all these shows are so trained and professional—especially on *MacGyver*. Richard Dean Anderson is a cool guy."

"Den, as a kid, I remember Sammy Davis Jr. washing his rented car at a gas station in front of the hotel I used to swim at, and people talked about how *real* that was for a celebrity. What could be *not* real about washing a car?"

"These big stars are just people. Some have tremendous egos, but on the set, it's nothing but business. Every second costs money. I wish you had been able to visit me when I worked for the Wagners."

"Den, ironically, we were planning it for the summer of eighty-two. I missed meeting Natalie by a matter of months." To stay off course, I asked, "So, what other shows have you been on?"

"Let's see, I've played in *Trauma Center, Trapper John, Hotel, T.J. Hooker, Hardcastle and McCormick*, and I did a Wells Fargo Bank commercial we filmed in the mountains. I'm in a McDonald's commercial filmed in a gymnasium, an Old Milwaukee Beer, and a Wranglers Jeans spot."

"And you say you aren't busy?"

"Nowhere near as busy as P.V. and other extras."

"Are commercials easier and faster than television scenes?"

"It's all hard. You get up at five in the morning, sometimes wait around for hours for direction, work all day, and most likely don't get home until midnight. That's just general acting. The big stars have many assistants, and everything is set up before they're called for their scenes."

"What major films have you done?"

"*Masquerade, National Lampoon Vacation, No Small Affair, Rhinestone*. I met Dolly Parton, who's the sweetest person ever."

"Are you ever near the *Hart to Hart* set?"

"Never. It was canceled. R.J.'s filming mostly in Europe now."

"Tell me about a favorite part you've played."

"*Goodnight Beantown* because of Bill Bixby. In a bar scene he directed, the male extras sat at background tables with pretty women and Bixby practically commanded us to get hard-ons while we silently pretended to hold conversations, because the boom will pick up even a whisper. Bill was a one-man band. The crew gave him a three-visor baseball cap that said actor, director, and producer."

"I caught a glimpse of you in *Splash*, Den—when Madison leaves the building and is doused with water and transforms back into a mermaid."

"Ron Howard was a great director—pure perfectionist. Took three days for that scene, and Ron never changed his clothes! We all felt sorry for him. Everyone loved Tom Hanks, a real nice guy. I like working at the studios, but I'm just not getting the calls now. I never planned to be an actor. People wait years to get the kind of work I got within days. It's who I knew that made the difference."

"It's good you recognize that, Den. I hate to say this, but maybe Frank Westmore had a point about your being on *Hart to Hart*. Maybe he would have appreciated you more if R.J. hadn't arranged everything."

I ended the conversation with hope for Dennis—that he might be able to outlive the repercussions of the high-profile tragedy that had altered the course of his life. No, Dennis had not chosen to be an actor. Neither had he chosen to be the forever-followed witness to a tragedy.

It was enough for me that my friend was happy again. I didn't expect to hear from him for a while. But I would. He was still being followed.

Chapter 21

On October 16, 1984, Dennis and his brother Paul called on extension lines from the dentist's yacht where they resided at Marina del Rey.

"Marti, you have to fly out here tomorrow," Dennis insisted. "The *National Enquirer* has always wanted a story from me, and I've agreed."

"Are you crazy?" was my instant response.

"Marti," Paul interrupted, "I met the two reporters—they're okay."

Dennis said, "The publisher didn't work out. You told me to 'tell it.'"

"Not to the *Enquirer*!"

"Marti, they're talking $150,000—our story, if you'll fly here."

"Is this about money now, Den?"

"No, it's about getting this behind me, telling the truth, then moving on."

I refused to be a part of it and ended the conversation, but my phone rang again within minutes.

"Hi, Marti? This is Rick Taylor with the *National Enquirer*. I'm on conference call with Dennis. We want to promote your book, and we'll be fair. We'll cover the cost of your trip down to chewing gum, if you chew gum, that is," he chuckled. "Please, fly out here, under no obligation, and just meet us."

I answered, "Rick, I don't want to participate, so I would only be wasting your publication's money."

"Then waste it," he replied. "We'll handle this story with care."

Against all better judgment, the next afternoon I was seated on the TWA wide-body about to take off from Philadelphia International Airport as I rationalized that seeing Marina del Rey and Los Angeles would enhance my understanding of Dennis's world.

Near midnight, Dennis and Paul met me at the gate as I walked into the L.A. terminal. Dennis stood behind Paul, who sat in a wheelchair.

"What happened?" I asked, stunned.

"My lung was punctured in a car accident last week. Let's get out of here, and I'll explain later," Paul said, edgy.

We drove to their home on the bay, to the yacht that resembled *Splendour*. Dennis described the boat as we toured it, comparing it to *Splendour's* layout. I wondered how someone could just fall from a boat this size.

We sat at a table on the rear deck. The warm, breezy air carried a refreshing scent to complement the spectacular view overlooking Fisherman's Village, a group of restaurants and novelty shops, all lit up in white lights across the harbor. I stepped to the stern and looked down to the dark water. A shiver ran up my spine as dark thoughts went through my mind.

By two in the morning, I had checked in at the Marina del Rey Hotel with a prearranged open tab. I called Rick Taylor, per his request, to schedule for the next day at noon, then fell into a sound, jet-lagged sleep.

I ordered eggs for breakfast, then drew open the draperies at the sliding glass door that led to a ground-level patio and opened the patio door a few inches. A mild breeze warmed me as I glanced over the *L.A. Times* delivered to my door. Momentarily, I ignored the purpose of my visit. Intuition had told me to not bring written material. When Dennis arrived, I again voiced my reservations.

Dennis called his answering service and announced with concern that he had a call from George Kirvey, R.J.'s publicist.

"Do you think they know about this?" I asked.

"I'll find out." I stood close to Dennis, my ear near the receiver so I could hear Kirvey's voice.

"Dennis, we know what you're up to, and I called to tell you to stop while you're ahead," said Kirvey.

"What are you talking about, George?" Dennis asked.

"Dennis, we know. So, just don't—Don't. Do. This," he said very slowly and intensely. "Don't hurt R.J.'s kids."

That statement made me think that R.J. knew how much Dennis adored Natalie's daughters and that this probably was not the first time her daughters were used as leverage to help keep Dennis quiet. It seemed dramatic how Dennis sometimes used "hurting the girls" as a reason to keep his secrets, and although I had never questioned that reason's authenticity, I had not previously connected it as one of Wagner's possible tactics.

"What makes you think that what I have to say will hurt them, George?" Dennis asked challengingly.

A lot can happen if you go ahead with this, Dennis," Kirvey warned.

"Like what?"

"It could really hurt you at the studios, for one thing."

"That really doesn't bother me, George, And I think that's already happened at the studios," Dennis retorted.

"Dennis, listen to me carefully. Other things can happen if you proceed. Think about it."

"I don't know what you're getting at, George. What can happen?"

"Other things, Dennis. You'll be sorry. Don't do it."

Dennis slammed the receiver down. Kirvey's concern clearly confirmed that R.J., at least, acknowledged Dennis as a bearer of damaging truth. Why would R.J. want to stop something if there was nothing incriminating to stop? Why would R.J. continually follow Dennis's moves?

"Denny, that sounded like a threat. Please let's not do this interview."

There was a knock at the door. Thirtyish Rick Taylor and fiftyish Tony Brenna entered. Introductions were pleasant, and as much as I hated admitting it to myself, I felt comfortable. To remember their names, Rick and Tony, I used association, as I often did in business, and made a mental note of the pasta rigatoni. I told them so, which they condescendingly found hilarious.

Although they were patronizing in order to gain information, Rick and Tony seemed reasonable. I had expected two ruthless reporters who would try to badger us, but they appeared professional, courteous, and interested. I had worked with many reputable newspaper reporters over the past decade, and Rick and Tony seemed no different. However, I wanted Dennis's story told by the book.

Dennis asked me to talk, but Tony said, "We need to hear this story from *you*, Dennis."

I preferred it that way too. As when we had visited Mr. Sanford in New York, I was hoping to learn something new. The interview began. Dennis took it to the bottle smashing.

Finally, Rick asked the pertinent question, "Who untied the dinghy?"

Even I turned expectant eyes to Dennis—who didn't answer.

"I'm getting tired now," Dennis said. "Can we take a short break?"

Rick and Tony left the room.

"Den, are you going to tell them who untied it? No money is worth this."

"I don't care about the money. The tabloids won't leave me alone. If I talk, they might stay away. Will my next girlfriend be a tabloid spy? That's why I want to get this over with."

Rick knocked on the door, and Dennis opened it. Rick immediately asked, "Dennis, can we use the word murder in our headline?"

"I'd prefer not," Dennis answered.

"Well, we've just talked to our home office, and we'll have to drop the amount we've offered unless we can use the word murder," he explained.

A series of phone calls to the tabloid's home office resulted in a final $35,000 offer for Dennis's story without his permission for the word murder; $150,000 stood with Dennis's permission. Dennis could easily have said, "Use whatever you want," and made a lot of money. But that was not his purpose.

This was the moment I first realized the significance of this story to the media—just one word meant big money. More than a word was at stake. A life had been cut short, a family grieved, and a mystery remained unsolved. Yet, here we were, down to one expensive word. I didn't know if Natalie Wood had been murdered. I didn't even know if Dennis knew.

"I don't want to continue at all," Dennis said flatly.

Rick and Tony fawned all over Dennis, saying things like, "Don't worry, we'll protect you; we'll do this story right; we'll help you through it all."

Paul Davern arrived, and the five of us dined in the hotel restaurant, the Crystal Fountain. Rick ordered Dom Pérignon to toast our project—what they hoped would be murder. I wanted to go home. The dinner tab totaled over six hundred dollars, and I could not help thinking how that much money could fill my home freezer with meals for a month. They wanted this story badly.

We scheduled to resume talking at noon the next day. After Rick and Tony left, Dennis, Paul, and I drove through Beverly Hills, then went to Boy's Market. I returned to my room and went to bed early.

At eleven-thirty the next morning, Dennis and Paul arrived, but Dennis called Tony Brenna's Studio City apartment and rescheduled to meet at eight that evening at Tony's apartment.

Before we left my hotel room, I brushed my hair at the dresser mirror and opened a drawer to put the hairbrush away. I half-seriously commented, "If they come looking for material, they'll be disappointed to find only this hairbrush."

We lunched at the Crab Shell in Venice Beach, overlooking the Pacific, then walked out to a nearby dock where the misty image of Catalina Island, far off in the distance, dampened Dennis's mood. I asked if he might ever return to the island.

"I doubt it," he said.

We toured past the breathtaking estates of Bel Air and Malibu, then went to Tahiti Marina where *Splendour* had docked. The marina was more beautiful than I had imagined. Palm trees surrounded clean, teak-colored buildings, and boats glistened in the sunlight. To see where the Wagners had parked their cars, to see the dock they had walked so many times, to see *Splendour's* slip at the end of that dock, offered a sad tangibility to all that Dennis had experienced and lost.

Dennis, Paul, and I again ordered dinner at the Crystal Fountain, courtesy of the *National Enquirer*. Our tab totaled much less than the previous night, but by this time, we had been stewing over the *Enquirer's* offer that was now contingent upon a dangerous word. It was not the drop in dollars that was so disturbing—it was the weaseling for a murder headline on Dennis's signature.

Upon entering my room after dinner, we all noticed an unfamiliar blue jacket on the dresser. The dresser top had been clear when we left. The jacket's pockets were empty. Had I relocked the sliding doors since yesterday? I called security at the front desk and asked if anyone had been allowed access to my room. I was assured that no one had been, but they were not sure about the sliding glass door being locked. I asked if a ground-level room had been specified when my room had been booked. The security representative I spoke with did not know. My personal belongings were intact, but I could not tell if anything had been disturbed. We decided to say nothing to the hotel staff or police.

Frightened and bewildered, I wondered how long had someone been in my room to remove and forget a jacket? Would an intruder be looking for a manuscript? Was this intrusion random, something connected with the *Enquirer,* or worse? Was this story that important?

Dennis called Tony Brenna to cancel our evening interview and insisted on not leaving me alone in the room. He was shaken. To calm down, he ordered a few beers and downed them, and then ordered more. I tried to explain that we would be better off sober, but by seven, Dennis was passed out across my bed.

"Well, he's not going to be any kind of a bodyguard tonight," I told Paul, "and you can barely walk. But I'm glad you're sober."

"My car accident, Marti," Paul said flatly. "This is too strange. Den's this scared because weird things have been happening."

"Tell me, Paul," I demanded.

"I'm not sure it's related, but Den and I stopped in a bar over at Fisherman's Village last week after work. A couple, way in the back of the outside line, kept staring. We got a table, then the couple showed up right next to us, way too fast, and bought us a drink. Why? The guy asked a lot of questions: where we lived, what we did for a living, and stuff like that. Maybe they were just being friendly, so we drank up, then left. I was driving and talking about the couple, that I thought they were following us. Den said he felt 'funny.' Then, out of nowhere, I got dizzy, and the next thing I knew, I woke up in the hospital. They told me I smashed into a brick wall.

"I think the guy slipped something into our drinks. My alcohol level was way below the legal limit, but they didn't test for anything else. No charges were pressed. They chalked it up that I fell asleep behind the wheel. I *didn't*. I think we were drugged. Den couldn't remember driving home, either. Thank God he wasn't hurt. I wondered if it has something to do with him getting ready to talk about Natalie."

"Paul, wasn't this a red flag for you guys? You guys should have told me about this. I have kids. And now, someone came into my room—would they have come in even if I had been sleeping?"

I grabbed the phone and called the airport, but no flights were available before my booked flight the next night. I felt trapped, no matter how hard I tried to convince myself that I was overreacting to Paul's story and the strange jacket.

"I'm really afraid, Paul," I said. "This is surreal to us, but Denny knows how real it is." I pointed to Dennis, sprawled across my bed. "He knows how grave this story is. It's sure getting too damn serious and scary for me."

"You know the whole story, don't you, Marti?" Paul asked.

I nodded an affirmative lie.

"Denny knows Wagner was with Natalie the entire time he said he was looking for her. There was no half hour that Wagner wasn't with her."

Again, I nodded, thinking, "Come on, Paul, tell me more."

But Paul said, "I ask him a lot of questions, but he only answers some of the time. Denny knows a lot that he'll take to his grave."

"Paul, let's camp out here tonight. I don't want to be alone, and we'll never wake up Denny. You take the other side of the bed, and I'll call for pillows and blankets to sleep on the floor."

"Do you think we would be safer back at the yacht?"

"No, there's a front desk close by, and I like knowing that."
I called room service, then told Paul, "I'll move the table in front
of the patio door. It doesn't sound like you had a car accident, Paul.
Have you had any trouble at the yacht?"

"No. Just a lamp that exploded one night."

"What?"

"It was so strange. A lamp in the main salon just burst
while we were watching TV. It was a lamp that came from
Splendour. Den and I just looked at each other with the same thought."

"Natalie?"

"Yep."

"Okay," I smiled, "this is too much like camp. Let's not
tell ghost stories on top of everything else, okay?" I laughed, trying
to lighten the mood.

There was a knock at the door. Paul and I jumped. It was
the extra linen. We turned in. I hardly slept, listening from the floor
for noises at the sliding glass doors. I was utterly relieved to see
the light of day. If I were overreacting, embellishing, and creating
drama, I checked my fear a hundred times over and still came up
scared. I reminded myself of an old friend, Phil Vaughn's, favorite
saying: *You never know nothin' for sure.*

Dennis called Tony Brenna to say he would finish the
interview after I left Los Angeles. Tony was upset, but Dennis
called the terms.

After Dennis, Paul, and I ate dinner, I packed my bags in
my room as we drank champagne, ordered snacks, played music,
and talked, laughed, and joked as though we were those carefree
teenagers back on the beach in Florida. Trying hard for relief, we
captured a few new moments, but our lives had surely changed.

Dennis and Paul rode with me to the airport with a
chauffeured driver. We did not say much during the ride. "Will you
finish the interview?" I asked Dennis.

"I think so. I'll be truthful and see what they do."

Feeling the champagne as I boarded the plane, I couldn't
wait to sleep. Oddly, the young woman seated next to me brought
up the subject of Hollywood mysteries, and I wanted to believe it
was coincidental but realized the strange trip would not end until
I was safely back home in New Jersey.

"Natalie Wood's death tops the list right now," she offered.
"The story circulating L.A. is that she left the boat, and when she
returned, she caught Robert Wagner in bed with Christopher
Walken. Then, mad as hell, she ran to leave, and fell into the water
and drowned."

Whether or not the woman worked for the *National Enquirer*, her slant seemed preposterous to me, and I never expected to hear the same rumor again, so I simply shrugged. I thought about Dennis's experience with Peter and Elizabeth, and how Elizabeth had gone the extra "smile" to get information. Then I slept all the way back to the East Coast.

A week later, our attorney said the *National Enquirer*'s contract appeared to be clean, but he still suggested we refrain. Dennis, whether on our attorney's advice, the threatening phone call, or pure change of venue, backed down from signing it. No article was published.

"I'm worried about those 'other things' George Kirvey said could happen if I go ahead with this, Marti," Dennis admitted weeks later.

Those other things worried me too.

Splendour
(From the authors' collection)

A view of *Splendour* taken from the dinghy approaching it. Where a person can be seen on the bridge in the photo is the location from which Dennis waited out RJ's and Natalie's final argument. RJ is at the swim step opening. (From the authors' collection)

Dennis is ready to mount the *Splendour* name to the stern of the Wagner's 60-ft. yacht. The sign was created from Natalie's design instructions. (From the authors' collection.)

Dennis and Natalie in *Splendour*'s wheelhouse. (From the authors' collection.)

Natalie Wood at the wheel of her *Splendour*.
(From the authors' collection)

Robert Wagner at his *Splendour* stateroom door. (From the authors' collection)

Natalie always teased RJ about fishing. He asked her to fish one day, and she caught her "prize fish" within minutes. This spot on the boat is the last location where Natalie was seen by Dennis, just minutes before she went missing. (From the authors' collection)

Robert Wagner with young daughters Natasha and Courtney on a Wagner family *Splendour* outing. (From the authors' collection)

Courtney Wagner is reluctant to swim in the ocean with her father. (From the authors' collection)

The Wagner family aboard *Valiant* with a family friend. The floating buoys attached to *Valiant* were used to keep the dinghy from banging against the mother boat, *Splendour*. (From the authors' collection)

Natalie with friends, actress Leigh Taylor-Young and husband Guy McElwaine, frequent guests aboard *Splendour*. Catalina Island is in the background. (From the authors' collection)

Robert Wagner and Natalie Wood onboard *Valiant* with friends, Guy McElwaine and wife Leigh Taylor-Young. (From the authors' collection)

Natalie enjoys her longtime friend Mart Crowley, scriptwriter and producer of *Hart to Hart*, aboard a festive *Splendour* outing. (From the authors' collection)

Sean Connery at *Splendour*'s wheel while RJ Wagner looks on. Sean liked the technical aspects of boating. (From the authors' collection)

Dr. Lyndon Taylor cruising around Two Harbors, Catalina Island. Lyn was moored near *Splendour* on his boat the *Catacean* the night of Wood's death. Lyn had earlier dined at Doug's Harbor Reef and noticed the trouble brewing at the Wagner party's table. (From the authors' collection)

The Sir Laurence Olivier outing. Olivier complimented Natalie's acting in *Cat on a Hot Tin Roof* this day. (From the authors' collection.)

Wagner and family friend makeup artist, Eddie Butterworth, aboard *Splendour*. Eddie made up Natalie for her final viewing and helped Dennis to retrieve *Splendour* from Catalina after Natalie's death. (From the authors' collection)

Robert Wagner and Dennis's brother, Paul Davern, after a day of fishing aboard *Splendour*. (From the authors' collection)

The walls in the Wagners' guesthouse were decorated with many Wagner/Wood accomplishments and photographs. (From the authors' collection)

In 1982, Dennis (right) poses with Detective Chuck Esser, his friend who believed the Wood case should be reopened. (From the authors' collection)

Natalie's sketch of daughter Courtney. (From the authors' collection)

Natalie's sketch of daughter Natasha.
(From the authors' collection)

Natalie's sketch of *Splendour*'s name design. (From the authors' collection)

Dennis Davern, Marti Rulli, and Paul Davern, taken on the first anniversary of Natalie's death when Dennis returned to his home-state New Jersey for a visit. (From the authors' collection)

Diagram of where boats were moored off Catalina Island on Nov. 28, 1981. (From the authors' collection)

Splendour's swim step that never collected algae and swim
step door, usually always left open.
(From the authors' collection)

Dennis Davern near his Captain's chair where he
would keep Natalie company in the wheelhouse.
(From the authors' collection)

Natalie Wood sitting in her perch on *Splendour*.
(From the authors' collection)

Chapter 22

Although Dennis had left the *National Enquirer* flat, his work at the studios came to a virtual halt. Our phone conversations subsided, and I tried to get back to a normal routine. I figured Dennis was reestablishing his marina career.

When I learned from a magazine article that Walken was married to Georgianne Thon, and had been since 1969, I called to ask if Dennis had known.

"No," he answered, surprised, "he struck me as a single guy."

"Well, he's not, Den," I said, "and I wonder what he told his wife."

That would be partially answered in *The Face* magazine in February 1985, which included an interview with Christopher Walken. According to the article, Walken remained reluctant to talk about the tragic weekend, especially after Lana Wood's book, which made claims about a possible Wood–Walken affair.

Walken states: "Everything that is known about what happened has been published. I don't know what happened." He continues, "Falling on your ass in the water.... I don't know. My silence about it has simply been the silence of ignorance."

Walken downplays the death's mystery factor by saying:

It doesn't sound kosher to me. You know, the curious thing about this is, certainly not to diminish it, I see things like that every day in the newspaper...every day. Somebody fell in their bathtub...somebody pulled out of a driveway...somebody ate a poisoned Mars bar. Who the hell knows? But these things happen constantly and I think when it happens to somebody famous it's a different story. We were all having a great weekend. We were at the end of a picture having finished our work and what were we going to do for the next two weeks? It was exactly three years ago today that we left. The weather wasn't very good. We went off for a nice weekend, having a very, very good time and I might add we were not the only people having a good time. It always sounds like we were all alone out on the high seas. We were actually fifty feet off the shore of Catalina in a harbor with many, many boats around us. The weather was shitty. Everybody was locked inside. There was a sort of cold drizzle. We were partying, there's no question about it, but very conservatively. Too much to drink. Who knows? In fact, I was asleep when it all happened. The fact is when somebody dies it's a very serious thing. No matter who dies, death gets your attention. You can pass out all you like. You can party. You can do all kinds of things...just don't die.

Walken's account made me think about Wagner's bottle smashing. "Do you want to fuck my wife? Is that what you want?"

In June 1985, Dennis called and said, "I have no studio work. P.V. and other extras are working every day because there is more than enough work to go around, but not for me. I guess R.J. got me the work in the first place just to keep me by his side. And now he doesn't want me anywhere near the studios even though *Hart to Hart* was canceled. But I'm back where I belong, on a boat."

"I guess Frank Westmore's happy now," I smirked.

Dennis told me, "Frank died just a few weeks ago. I didn't go to his funeral. I wanted to see his wife, a really nice woman, but I couldn't go."

"You would have seen R.J., no doubt."

"I never want to see him again."

"Is there any way to prove R.J. is behind your lack of work?" I asked.

"I doubt it. I'm just gonna lay low for a while."

But that would not happen.

A few weeks later came what I would dub the "Star Wars." A short article in the *Star* tabloid promoted Christopher Walken's new James Bond film, *A View to a Kill,* and the article sent Dennis into a frenzy and back on the phone to me. Walken's article described his film, then Walken stated that his cruise to Catalina Island, as the Wagners' guest the weekend Natalie died, had been a tragic end to a pleasant weekend.

"Why does he even mention the weekend Natalie died, Marti, to flat-out lie about it?" Dennis raged.

"Maybe because he's connected to that weekend, he felt he'd better mention it. This is a big movie, and he's not going to say it was the weekend from hell after he hadn't told the police the truth."

Dennis continued, "But why cover it with more lies? When I finally say something, it won't be lies. He should be truthful or say nothing at all."

"Geez, Den—like exactly what Mr. Sanford said to us?"

"To hell with them, Marti. They're not going to use Natalie's death to promote their latest projects. This time, I'll go through with the truth."

"Den, didn't we learn our lesson after the *Enquirer* episode?"

But there was nothing I could say to stop Dennis. He contacted the *Star*.

I refused to return to Los Angeles, so the *Star* flew Dennis to New Jersey. We met with *Star* reporter Brian Haugh and a *Star* technician at the Cherry Hill Hilton in my old hometown. We passed by the Country Squire, where big-name celebrities once lodged, but it was now surrounded by big-name hotels. The Latin Casino had been renamed and converted to a dance club. As a kid, I never saw a reporter come anywhere near the big stars who had once visited Cherry Hill. Now, reporters visited just to talk with someone who *knew* a big star.

Dennis offered his story without pause and finished with Wagner's bottle-smashing. Brian turned to me for answers I could not give. It was still enough.

With the final draft ready, Dennis and I drove to the *Star* home office in Tarrytown, New York, for Dennis to sign the contract and to shoot a television commercial for the story. Dennis was paid $26,000 upon publication. A good chunk of that would go toward taxes, and with some of his profit, Dennis paid some hefty phone bills—his and mine—that had accumulated. Money was not Dennis's motive for his story, and what he did profit would not last long, because Dennis now was scared enough to leave the country.

The *Star* paid me nothing. Although I understood Dennis's intentions, I worried that he might be viewed as capitalizing from Natalie's death. He had previously refused every reporter who had approached him, but Walken's press release had incited Dennis's cooperation with the *Star*. I believed Dennis acted out of pure emotion without considering the consequences. But Dennis wasn't selling lies. He was telling truth.

That his truth had been set in motion appeased me. A bonus for me was meeting George Carpozi, a *Star* senior editor. "George is a superb author who has written over fifty books, one a biography about Frank Sinatra," Brian Haugh told us. Carpozi took an immediate interest in Dennis's story and offered to help. He and I exchanged thoughts via telephone and mail over the next month, and I valued his purely professional input.

The first of Dennis's two-part article appeared in the July 23, 1985, *Star*. As usual, the paper hit the stands about a week before its actual issue date. The headlines took up the entire front page: *It was a night of drink, drugs & jealousy.... Natalie and*

*Walken sat together—R.J. got redder & redder and finally
exploded. He smashed a bottle of wine on the table....* "*What are
you trying to do, seduce my wife? Natalie Mystery Solved, Yacht
skipper breaks his silence...at last. World Exclusive.* The inside
article began by mentioning *Goodbye Natalie, Goodbye Splendour*,
associating me with Dennis, announcing a planned book.

Dennis waited in New Jersey for Wagner's reaction. We
never would have guessed that Wagner would respond with an
"answer article" in the *Star*!

"R.J. swore that he would never give a tabloid interview,"
Dennis told me. "Especially after Natalie died, R.J. avoided the
media. What scared him most was when Barbara Walters wanted
to interview him."

"Well, he sure sounds like a man with a lot to hide."

No doubt, Dennis's account would have carried more
weight if it had been published in a more credible magazine, but
the most far-fetched stories presented by tabloids often become
cover stories in more reputable publications. Our relationship with
the *Star* had been a professional one. There had been no push to
use inflammatory words. Brian Haugh and George Carpozi asked
the questions authorities should have asked long ago and
encouraged us to still present Dennis's truth in a more credible format.

Someone in Robert Wagner's circle—the studio we
presumed—or perhaps Wagner, himself—believed the *Star* article
credible enough to retaliate. R.J.'s answering article hit the stands
in the August 27, 1985, *Star*. Dennis and I sat at my dining room
table and read together.

Wagner's front-page coverage read: *Everybody thinks it
was one of those Hollywood love triangles. It was nothing like
that. It was a terrible, tragic accident I will have to live with it the
rest of my life.* In larger, reverse print, it read: *Robert Wagner: How
Natalie's Death Haunts Me...,* and in smaller, reverse print...*and
how his new show* Lime Street *is helping him recover.*

The *Lime Street* promotion said it all.

I said to Dennis, "R.J. has a new show, and a few weeks
before it airs, there's your world exclusive in the *Star*. Wagner uses
the same publication, just like you felt you had to answer Walken
in the same publication. R.J. never once responded to the media
or said a public word about Natalie's death until *you* talked. What's
that say, Den?"

"Damage control. But he can't control the truth. It's too big."

Reporter Fiona Manning wrote the article that primarily promoted *Lime Street*, R.J.'s first series since *Hart to Hart*'s cancellation. A promotional picture of Wagner with Maia Brewton and Samantha Smith, the two young girls who were to play the lead character's daughters in the series, accompanied the story.

Surprisingly, albeit unintentionally, Wagner corroborated Dennis's account. "I wasn't capable of identifying the body. Dennis did it," Wagner admits in his article. He also said he was "very uncomfortable with Walken being at Natalie's funeral." That statement warranted explanation, but there was none. If, indeed, it had been a pleasant weekend, why would Wagner feel uncomfortable in Walken's presence?

The article said that R.J. never set foot on *Splendour* again. "It was Davern who maintained it and skippered it after that fateful night," R.J. stated, and then warned again, now publicly, "But nobody will ever make a movie about her [Natalie] in my lifetime."

Of the past, R.J. says, "There is nothing to talk about. I know what happened and I keep saying it was an accident. Somebody is always going to blame me. Some of the versions of the stories I have heard have absolutely shocked me."

"So, Denny," I said, "R.J. doesn't deny one thing you said. He shades it by saying some versions shock him. Ironically, he says he knows what happened, so why doesn't he say what happened? Didn't he tell the police he *didn't* know?

"Marti," Dennis said, "he's not as smart as I thought."

After giving his story to the *Star*, R.J. went to Europe to film episodes of *Lime Street*, whose main character was a single father raising his two daughters, eerily close to Wagner's new real-life situation. Wagner claimed in several interviews that his grief had led him to the neutral grounds of Europe for work.

Dennis's *Star* article renewed media interest in the Natalie Wood story. Ellis Amburn, the editor who had worked with Lana Wood on her book, *Natalie: A Memoir by Her Sister* (1986), contacted me through the *Star*. Amburn's interest waned, however, after learning that I focused on Dennis's account; he did not comprehend the complicated message that needed to be told.

"You write about Dennis like he's a somebody," Amburn said. "He has to be a mouse in a corner for this story. Lana's her sister, Dennis was just an employee."

"Hold on, Mr. Amburn," I replied, "Dennis was an employee who at that time in Natalie's life was probably more familiar with her than any relative. He was there the night she died! He slept in her final bed with her!"

I read Lana Wood's book which was basically what she promoted it to be in her title: a memoir. In it, Lana owned up to a few thoughtless mistakes she had made throughout the years—the main mistake being that she and her ex-husband had sold photographs of R.J.'s and Natalie's second wedding ceremony to a magazine before the newly married couple had returned from their honeymoon.

Lana covered her acting career which began in 1956 when Lana played in *The Searchers* with Natalie. Natalie had been her mentor, and perhaps sometimes the object of jealousy, but rivalries and spats aside, they were sisters, and Lana surely sent the message through her book that she was bereft over losing Natalie.

Lana's celebrity later included numerous television series as cast characters and guest roles. From 1966 to 1967, she played Sandy Webber in the groundbreaking primetime soap opera *Peyton Place*. Familiar with the big screen, too, Lana is best known for her film role as Plenty O'Toole, a character many consider the most fascinating and gorgeous Bond Girl of them all.

Even if Amburn had recognized Dennis's importance in shedding light on the mystery of Natalie Wood's death, I doubt, after what transpired next, that Dennis would have cooperated in completing the manuscript.

Dennis flew back to California just days after Wagner's article finished our "Star Wars." He called a few days later and asked, "Marti, who is Samantha Smith?"

"She's the young girl who was starring in R.J.'s new show, *Lime Street*. She was killed in a plane crash last Sunday, along with her father, while they were on break. It's so sad. You heard, right?"

"Oh, I've heard, Marti," Dennis told me, with a strange quality to his voice. "What does she have to do with Russia?"

"A few years ago, she wrote a letter to the Soviet leader Yuri Andropov concerning world peace. Andropov invited her to Russia for a visit. It was big headlines all over the world. At just ten years old, she became a world peace ambassador of sorts. Her death is disturbing for reasons way beyond R.J.'s new show, but I'm sure he must be devastated. Why are you asking?"

"Some Mexican guy came up to me on the docks, anxious and looking over his shoulder. He asked, 'Do you know that little girl, Samantha Smith, who went to Russia?' I said I didn't—and I *really* couldn't connect her with anything. Then, he said, 'Well, she was just killed, and I'm here with a warning that you're *next* on the list.' I asked him what in the hell he was talking about, and he said, 'Just get as far away from here as you can if you know what's good for you.' What do you think of all this, Marti?"

I thought it peculiar that each time Dennis was involved with an interview, he met with some sort of threat, opposition, or warning, but I questioned this latest messenger. "Denny, maybe this guy knows who you are from being around the docks or even from the *Star* articles and got some morbid kick out of trying to scare you. What was your impression of him?"

"I thought he was a kook."

"Then he's probably just a kook. Forget it."

There was genuine fear in Dennis's voice. "I don't know, Marti. After the *Star* articles, the studio is probably mad at R.J., and R.J. no doubt is furious with me, then to have this weirdo telling me I'm next on the list, I'm really scared. My gut is telling me to get out of town, even if this is just a harmless, crazy guy."

You never know nothin' for sure, I thought.

Lime Street aired with a massive first-night draw because of the Samantha Smith tragedy, but it was pulled after a few episodes, never to return. Several publications, including *T.V. Guide*, mentioned how oddly the show had been yanked to oblivion.

And Dennis fled Los Angeles, never again to reside in the City of Angels.

He spent a few months overseas, in hiding, before I heard from him. "Marti, I can't go back to L.A.," he said. "I'm still scared. I have no regrets about talking, but I need time to really think things over. I feel worse about everything than I ever did. Can I come stay with you and George until I figure things out?"

George and I would never have denied Dennis a home— a refuge. Our home became his.

Chapter 23

Dennis worked odd jobs in painting and carpentry, sometimes with my husband, while living at our house. He longed for warm air, bodies of water, and boats. But he felt safer.

While Dennis had been traveling, before coming to live with us, I had immersed myself in my work and home and shelved our manuscript. I had made one important phone call, however, to Coroner Thomas T. Noguchi in Los Angeles, who had been extremely pleased to hear from me.

"Ms. Rulli," Noguchi said, "I'm so glad you called. I've tried to contact you since reading Mr. Davern's story in the *Star*. I need Mr. Davern's testimony to prove I was not lying about the fight that transpired the night Ms. Wood died. I lost my job soon after she died because I'd told the truth about that night. I did my job to the best of my abilities. Mr. Davern's story confirms that I was telling the truth. And I'd like to reevaluate. Can you convince him to testify for me? I'm filing suit to get my job back, or for retribution. And I can change my theory on Natalie."

"I wish we could help you, but I can't get in touch with Dennis," I explained. "Dr. Noguchi, I've read your book and your account of what happened to Natalie, and I question the changes in your theory."

"Ms. Rulli, I had to base my findings on the evidence presented to me. Mr. Davern now owns up to a fight, and it changes everything. I did my best, based upon evidence. This is new evidence!"

"Perhaps you should have stuck to your original findings."

"My original findings got me fired, Ms. Rulli."

"Why did you retract your original belief that Natalie may have been unconscious before she hit the water? And who was your source about the fight?"

"Natalie could have been unconscious, but that changed with new evidence. As for the fight, I believed it. I was forced to deny the fight, pressured and threatened with the loss of my job, which I lost anyway. Frank Sinatra wrote a letter blasting my findings in the Wood investigation. I am powerless without evidence. Are you certain you can't persuade Mr. Davern to help me, Ms. Rulli?"

"Not just yet, Dr. Noguchi. Again, I'm sorry."

How skewed a picture is that—Thomas Noguchi asking *me* for help? When I told Dennis about my conversation with Noguchi, he did agree to help, and I called Noguchi many times but never received a return call.

Privately, I kept reading articles and excerpts of interest about Natalie's death. Two from Wagner and Walken stunned me. In an article in *People* magazine, "From Any Distance, AT CLOSE RANGE, Star Christopher Walken Comes Off as Edgy, Electric and Elusive," Andrea Chambers wrote:

When a topic rankles, he stonewalls. Tops on that list is the matter of Natalie Wood, his co-star in the 1983 film Brainstorm. *Walken was on board the yacht with Natalie and her husband, Robert Wagner, the night she drowned. "I don't know what happened," snaps Walken. "She slipped and fell in the water. I was in bed then. It was a terrible thing. Look," he continues, his eyes icy, "we're in a conversation I won't have. It's a —ing bore."*

Countering Dennis's recent *Star* article, Robert Wagner's account, used in Diana Maychick's *Heart to Heart* with Robert Wagner (St. Martin's Press, 1986), was a bit more specific.

According to Wagner:

We reached the boat in a happy frame of mind after spending a few hours at the restaurant eating and drinking. During dinner, I got into a political debate with Walken and we continued it aboard the yacht. There was no fight, no anger. Just a lot of words thrown around like you hear in most political discussions such as "you don't know what you are talking about!" Natalie sat there not saying much of anything and looking bored. She left us after about a half hour, and we sat there talking for almost another hour. Then I went to kiss her good night, and found her missing.

It was only after I was told that she was dressed in a sleeping gown, heavy socks, and a parka that it dawned on me what had really occurred. Natalie obviously had trouble sleeping with that dinghy slamming up against the boat. It happened many, many times before, and I had always gone out and pulled the ropes tighter to keep the dinghy flush against the yacht. She probably skidded on one of the steps after untying the ropes. The steps are slick as ice because of the algae and seaweed that's always clinging to them. After slipping on the steps, she hit her head against the boat.... I only hope she was unconscious when she hit the water.

* * *

Natalie had not been "bored" the night of November 28, 1981, after returning from the restaurant. She had lit her beeswax candles and started chatting with Walken. No one talked politics. Wagner, in a rage, smashed a wine bottle. Natalie looked *mortified*.

Although Dennis and I did not discuss Natalie's death much while he lived in my home, I asked him about Wagner's theory. Dennis explained why the dinghy does not slam against the boat. "First of all, the dinghy would only swish against the boat, never bang," he said. Long before the tragic weekend, Dennis had purchased dinghy "fenders" to prevent the problem. They were attached to adjustable lines that could be dropped over the side as a cushion between the dinghy and the yacht. The fenders, which Dennis described as looking like large sausages, were used only when it was windy or when the seas were rough. There had been no need to use them the night of November 29, 1981, as the wind was low and the sea was not rough; *Valiant* was not banging against the yacht. There existed no algae or seaweed on *Splendour's* swim step.

It took a good three months for Dennis to feel normal again. In April 1986, my first grandchild, Jessica West, was born. I was a young grandmother at 34, but the joy could not have occurred at a better time. I had been immersed in the mystery of a tragic death, and this new beautiful baby focused our attention on life and hope. Her birth seemed a turning point for Dennis as well. He seemed to realize, finally, that life must be lived in forward motion. Dennis started seeing friends and socializing. He met Rita—a girl he dated for a few months—and it seemed that the Dennis Davern we had all once known was back. Dennis's high school friend Arnie Felderman, with his wife Carol, and Paul Davern, visited every weekend. Friends brought normalcy back to Dennis's life. Socializing relieved the stress. I had hosted huge Halloween parties for years. This year, 1986, Dennis, dressed as a pirate, attended my party with Rita. It felt good to see him cheerful, upbeat, and healing.

After a year as our house guest, Dennis missed the sea. It was time to move on. His drinking was under control, he had gained weight, worked, and saved, and he seemed less burdened. He packed up his few belongings and drove his newly purchased used car to Fort Lauderdale, Florida, where the events of the past fifteen years had begun for him aboard *Dizzy Izzy* in 1972.

It had been one hell of a fifteen years, including a fascinating sea adventure, interesting new friendships, a job and close relationship with two of the most famous people in Hollywood, a tragedy felt around the globe, a short-lived acting career, a media frenzy—extraordinary experiences that would always be a part of him. I wished Dennis every best thing for his next fifteen years and beyond.

As we hugged goodbye, my tears flowed. I was glad Dennis was moving on, but it seemed to be the end of our "something big."

I tried to get back to life, but my marriage started to fall apart. Some family members and friends blamed my obsession with the Natalie Wood project, and some guessed that becoming a grandmother had spun me into an early midlife crisis. I felt as if I needed to escape all of my confusion. There was never more than friendship between Dennis and me but some asked why I devotedly put myself at Dennis's beck and call. That was easy to answer: a legend named Natalie Wood and her tragic, mysterious death bound Dennis and me even closer than the connection we had made the first time we met.

Chapter 24

I had little contact with Dennis throughout 1987. I began seeing someone I worked with, Robert Mooney, and the relationship became serious. Dennis backed off as I focused on other areas of my life, and he had his new start in Florida to focus on.

Dennis called my new residence on February 4, 1988, and told me, "I've been talking to Steve Dunleavy from Maury Povich's *A Current Affair*. He hunted me down and wants to interview us about the book."

I did not disguise my cynicism. "Denny, this is getting ridiculous. The unfinished book?" I answered. "The one I don't know the ending to?"

"Marti, I'm sorry about your divorce, but we have to get moving. An entire year has passed."

And so had my blatant sarcasm, right over his head. But that was Dennis, so I smiled.

"Denny, it's going to start looking like you're making a living doing these interviews."

"There's absolutely no payment. People are forgetting, and I still want the truth in a book, but we need to keep Natalie's memory alive."

"Denny, let me confess something," I said. "Last October, I drove to New York to talk to a producer from *A Current Affair* who had contacted me after the *Star* article. Over lunch, he told me that Lana Wood had dined at the same restaurant with him just weeks before. She agreed to do their show, but then backed down because she feared retaliation from R.J. The producer ordered plenty of wine for our table, and his heavy questioning increased with each sip I took. I didn't like his tactics. Let's stay away from this, okay?"

"I'm really comfortable with Steve, and now that I'm out of California, I'm not afraid of R.J."

"I'll resume working on the book, and maybe later we can do an interview."

"Marti, please, fly down tomorrow. They'll take care of everything."

Why I allowed Dennis to again persuade me into participation, I could not answer, other than that I still sought the truth myself.

There was a seven-hour flight delay out of Philadelphia, so I did not arrive at Fort Lauderdale Airport until five in the morning, February 6, 1988. A frustrated and tired Steve Dunleavy, holding a sign with my name on it, stood alone in the empty airport corridor.

On the drive to the hotel, Steve's trick questions started. "So, Marti, luv," he asked, his thick Australian accent and expression full of concern, "I'm shocked to learn from Dennis that he actually slept with Natalie the night before she died."

"Yes, Steve," I said, anticipating where he was going with the statement. "He only slept with her, though."

"He told me he had sex with her," Steve said.

"Well, he never told me that, and I've never known him to lie."

"You can tell me all about it, luv. I already know he had sex with her."

He escorted me to my hotel room door and gave it one last try. "Luv, why not tell me about Dennis and Natalie having sex?"

"Steve, I need sleep. We'll talk later."

Dennis called me by ten o'clock the next morning. My first question escaped my mouth before he finished his greeting.

"Denny, did you tell Steve you had sex with Natalie?"

"No way. Why?"

I explained and Dennis laughed. He found Steve amusing.

"Denny, I'm worried about this interview."

"He's okay, Marti. He'll be fair with us. You'll see."

We met with Steve and his technical crew around noon. The cameraman first took some footage of Dennis walking the docks. Then we gathered in the film crew's hotel room. Steve first interviewed me. I was extremely nervous at first, then relaxed and covered important points—none of which would air.

Dennis was calm and articulate and told everything he knew up to R.J.'s smashing of the wine bottle. Steve accepted that as the extent of the story and did not pursue how Natalie got into the water.

Steve went harder after Dennis's night with Natalie in a motel room. Slowly, Steve asked, "You...spent the night with...Natalie...in the same room?" Dunleavy's face filled with concern. "I have to ask this question because of certain mysteries surrounding that weekend. What is a captain doing in a motel room with Natalie Wood?"

It was a good question.

Dennis explained that trouble had been brewing, and when Natalie wanted to leave the boat, he escorted her as a bodyguard.

Dunleavy says, "You had plenty to drink. She had plenty to drink. I have to ask the question: Did you have an affair with her?"

"No."

"Did you stay in the same bed?"

"Yes."

"This is pretty hard for me to work out," says Dunleavy. "You do have to concede that it does to the outside world look a little bizarre."

Dennis conceded, talked about respect and caring for Natalie, but did not change his story. Perhaps Steve had hoped Dennis, like a nervous witness on the stand, would have finally broken down. But Dennis was not lying. It would have been so easy for him to say he did have sex with Natalie. Sex with Natalie would have enhanced any story he had created, but Dennis was not being creative. Dennis was being truthful.

Steve Dunleavy and his technical crew treated us to dinner after taping. Steve still was not satisfied. "Now that the interview is over," he leaned over and whispered to me, "you can tell me. Did Dennis have sex with Natalie?"

By this time, even I found Steve amusing. I smiled and said, "Steve, I promise, if I find out that Dennis and Natalie did it, you'll be the first person I call."

Steve then whispered, "Have you and Dennis ever had sex?" Although I thought it an extremely personal question, I realized that many people might think I would lie for Dennis if we were romantically involved, so I answered, "Dennis and I are longtime friends," I said. "We're like family."

Despite Steve Dunleavy's bloodhound reputation, it was a respectable reputation. I like Steve. He believed us. Most reporters did.

I was not disappointed with the *Current Affair* episode that aired in late February 1988. My few moments of air time showed my nervousness and offered nothing pertinent, but Dennis covered important information.

Duane Rasure, the lead detective of the Natalie Wood case, had been separately interviewed for the show and was featured right after Dennis talked about the wine bottle smashing. Steve Dunleavy's voiceover during Rasure's spot went, "Rasure swallowed the first story he was told"—concerning the shattered glass from the broken wine bottle. Rasure then admits, "There was some broken glass around. This happens on a boat...rough seas. No furniture was moved around. It didn't look like a fight or anything."

Yet when Dennis had retrieved *Splendour* with Frank Westmore, Eddie Butterworth, and Tommy Thompson, each one had witnessed blatant signs of a disturbance in the master stateroom. And, if Rasure had checked, he would have learned that the furniture could not "move around" as most of the furniture on *Splendour* was *built-in* furniture.

The show closed with Dunleavy asking Dennis, "How will you remember Natalie?"

Dennis's expression went somewhere far away. Perhaps he was thinking about Natalie in her perch as she stitched her pillows, or giggling over breakfast, and he answered with a slight stutter and pure recall: "A b-beautiful woman," he breathed out.

Perhaps it was the time to begin picking Dennis's brain again, but I chose to let it go. I was too drained to chase after what Dennis had buried in the deepest core of his being. Only time would bring those details to the surface. There would be no contact between us for a long time.

In mid-1988, Bob Mooney and I moved into a new home in Columbus, New Jersey, near our jobs. It wasn't always smooth sailing with my teenage kids but we all adjusted, and life went on.

Still, in the back of my mind, Natalie was always there, haunting me. When I saw the gigantic headline *Natalie Wood Was Murdered* spread across the cover of the *Globe* tabloid in October 1989, I called not Dennis but investigator Milo Speriglio, the source behind the headline. Natalie Wood's sister, Lana Wood, had hired Speriglio, director of the Nick Harris Detective Agency in Los Angeles. I thought it sad that Lana had to resort to a private investigator because the public servants had failed to investigate the tragedy thoroughly.

In the article, Speriglio asked the tough questions: Why wouldn't Wagner allow Dennis to search for Natalie? Why did Wagner, instead of worrying about his missing wife, drink with Dennis until her body was found? What happened during the mysterious 30 minutes Wagner went below deck? Why did no one try to rescue Natalie as she screamed for help?

The article said Coroner Noguchi lost his job because of his outspoken doubts about the case. Speriglio is quoted in the article: "If the sheriff's department doesn't reopen the case, it will be a mockery of justice. There was no accident that night. Natalie Wood was murdered."

Then, I read the next line with disappointment: a claim that the tragic weekend had been jam-packed with kinky and bizarre sex. When I had Speriglio on the phone, I asked where he had obtained his information.

"I've been investigating Natalie Wood's death for seven years," Speriglio told me in his gravelly voice. "I've talked to witnesses on the island who saw R.J. and Natalie arguing over lunches and dinners that weekend. I've spoken to the authorities and the coroner."

"And what information led you to believe that Natalie was murdered?" I asked.

"I was misquoted on that," Speriglio told me. "I've settled with the *Globe*, out of court, for their misquoting me. I believe her death was an accidental homicide. They twisted the words of my conclusion."

Accidental homicide. What an oxymoron for Natalie's legacy.

"Did they misquote you concerning your statement of kinky and bizarre sex?" I asked.

"No," Speriglio went on slowly. "I spoke to a blonde who claims to have received that information from Davern one night in the Polo Lounge. She was investigating Natalie's death undercover at the time. She said she had sex with Dennis and that he told her Natalie had caught R.J. and Christopher Walken in bed that weekend, and that's what made her leave the yacht in a rage."

That rumor again! *Elizabeth*.

"I know who you spoke with, Milo. She tricked Dennis, and he *didn't* give her *any* information. Too bad it didn't occur to you that perhaps the blonde was lying because that scenario never happened!"

"Marti, let me explain," Speriglio continued. "I've investigated Natalie's death minus eyewitnesses. My conclusions are based on secondhand information. You have the key in Davern to unlock the mystery. I've always wanted to talk to him. I encourage you to pursue any information he gives you. It's a Hollywood mystery that I would like to see cleared up. If I can be of any help, please don't hesitate to call. I wish you all the luck in the world with your endeavors."

I gave Speriglio my number, then chatted with him about his work. He seemed proud of the high-profile cases he had worked in Hollywood. He had written books on Marilyn Monroe's death, and he had worked a case involving George Reeves, who played Superman on television. The 1959 death of Reeves, whose gunshot wound to the head in his upstairs bedroom was ruled suicide, still bothered the detective because the drunken partiers downstairs delayed in calling for help after hearing the gun go off. Reeves's houseguests said they saw him lying naked on the bed, dead, and they panicked.

Speriglio explained that most suicidal people still have enough humility to remain fully clothed when they end their lives. "Natalie wearing her nightgown, minus underwear, suggests to me it wasn't suicide," he said.

Speriglio obviously was trained to see extraordinary clues. He understood the intrinsic value of Dennis's knowledge, but Elizabeth had apparently convinced him of an untruth.

If Dennis had seen the *Globe* article, he did not call. My interest in the Natalie Wood story had been rekindled. I wondered how Dennis was doing and missed him, but I avoided calling him. Months passed with no word from him, even at Thanksgiving, a time we always tried to spend together.

Robert Wagner hosted a *Saturday Night Live* broadcast in early December, and I watched with mounting frustration. His hosting of the comedy show somehow seemed the epitome of arrogance to me.

Chapter 25

On an October morning in 1990, as I arrived at work, there was a personal ad from the local newspaper's classified section taped to my phone. A coworker had seen it and passed it on. It read: "Marti Rulli or Dennis Davern, please contact Brian Haugh at the *Star*."

The ad, ironically, had been placed in one of the daily newspapers owned by the corporation for which I worked. I assumed Brian was interested in another article, but I did not call. I felt obliged, and happily relieved, however, to pass on the message to Dennis. I dialed his Florida number.

"Denny, hi. It's me, Marti."

"Marti? Marti who? I don't remember a Marti. Do I know you?"

We laughed.

I told him about Brian's ad.

"What do you think he wants?" Dennis asked.

"A story, no doubt," I said. "The ninth anniversary of Natalie's death is coming up; what else would he want?"

"Well, what's the sense in doing a story? There's no book now. Why haven't you called me, Marti?"

"Lots of changes, but everything's fine. Bob and I live in Columbus now. And, I'm sorry about your dad's passing. I heard after the funeral."

"He was such a help to us, Marti."

"I still follow things closely and look for anything published about Natalie, like that private detective's murder headline—I hope you saw it." I explained about Milo Speriglio.

"I'll be in Jersey for Thanksgiving. Maybe we can pick up where we left off. I miss you."

"Same here, Den. Are you going to call Brian?"

"I'll see what he wants."

Two days later, Dennis called me. "Brian wants another story—says he wants to do something on Natalie every Thanksgiving so that people remember."

The article appeared in a November edition of the *Star*. It focused on the aftermath of Natalie's death and how, nine years later, Dennis was still haunted by that night. And, indeed, he was. Brian's interview awakened Dennis's desire to tell his secrets—his beast inside. Natalie suddenly loomed as large as ever, and Dennis started calling constantly.

"Marti, I thought I was doing all right, but it's still so hard," Dennis said. "I love my job. I'm skippering a beautiful yacht for a great couple, and they pay well. I have good friends, but not a day goes by that I don't think of her."

"I guess you're just going to have to live with that, Denny," I told him, "because it won't go away by itself, ever—you're still avoiding the whole truth."

"I've never lied to you, Marti—not once! Everything I told you is true."

"I didn't say you lied. You never revealed the *whole* truth. Natalie didn't untie the dinghy. How do you know that? There was foul play involved. What do you mean by that? All the reports are bullshit. Then what's not bullshit? Nothing you've told me answers the question: Why is Natalie Wood dead?"

"All right, let's talk about this when I come up, okay?"

Dennis came and went. The entire truth went with him—again. Our telephone calls continued, but so did Dennis's reticence, and he told me something that angered me.

"Marti, I talked to the *Globe* a couple of times. I don't want Natalie to be forgotten. The *Globe* wants to talk to you too."

The *Globe* reporter called me—about 50 times—but I stood firm, and Dennis agreed to not tell anything more to reporters.

Dennis's new boss, Mark Forstein, found out about Dennis's former job as *Splendour* captain through a previous *Globe* article, and Dennis told Mark about our manuscript. Mark was so intrigued that he offered to invest his own money to get the compelling story to the public. Although appreciative, I said that so much more needed to be explored.

By March 1991, I was thoroughly frustrated. This time, however, I could not avoid the manuscript. Dennis had not told me enough, but he had said way too much. For the first time, I felt my obligation extended beyond him. A dead woman cried out in my mind for justice, and her story needed an ending.

I contacted a local writing teacher and freelance editor, Carol Lallier, whom a colleague highly recommended, to help me edit the manuscript. One night at her kitchen table, I blurted out everything Dennis had told me, whether he had intended it for publication or not.

"So you see, Carol, it's a moral issue to me now. I know there's more; but I'm as lost as Denny was the first night he called me to ask for help."

Carol's ability to listen to details and absorb and remember information amazed me. She said little as she listened to me night after night, then would astound me with insights she processed from my input.

She called one afternoon, so excited she could barely form words: "Marti, ducks float! Ducks float!"

My mind drew a blank.

"Ducks float. They *float!*" she repeated, as if no other words were possible or necessary.

Then I got it. "I'll be right there," is all I said.

I rushed to her house, and despite the seriousness of the project we were working on, Carol and I stood in her living room and laughed ourselves silly over how that conversation would have sounded to anyone listening in. We had gone beyond a working relationship, for only true friends could have had—and understood—such an absurd telephone conversation.

Ducks float. The realization had hit Carol as she tried to stuff a down comforter into her washing machine and couldn't get it saturated. Then she dragged it out of the washer and into the bathtub, where she rolled up her pant legs and stomped it like grapes, but still couldn't keep the comforter underwater. Wouldn't it be just as hard to sink a down jacket? she thought.

Natalie's red down jacket did not pull her down and sap her strength, as Noguchi had claimed. It kept her afloat—and it could have saved her life if anyone had tried to help her!

Carol's insight magnified Noguchi's neglect, but refuting Noguchi's theory only clarified what had not happened. Carol and I sharpened up my manuscript, but we hit the same brick walls.

Dennis's original intention was to clear up the mystery surrounding Natalie's death, but as the tenth anniversary approached, it seemed that Natalie's death now rested on my shoulders. I felt I had enough information to cast stronger doubt on the official version of what really happened, and I would have traded all thoughts of publishing a book if I had believed for a second that the authorities might take my information seriously. But my word, legally, was only hearsay.

I called Dennis to convince him to take back his courage— to contact the authorities and tell them the entire truth. Dennis, afraid of repercussions, refused. He still wanted truth exposed, believing it would both unburden and protect him. He asked me to find credible publicity for the tenth anniversary of Natalie's death and to accept no monetary payment. He wanted to tell it all this time.

Although the nation harbored mixed emotions for Geraldo Rivera because of the antics of his daytime talk show, Rivera had started a new news magazine program called *Now It Can Be Told*. I remembered and admired Geraldo from his early 1970s television start with *Good Night America* and then *Good Morning America*, and I appreciated his work on ABC's *20/20*.

I met with one of the show's producers, Alexander Johnson, at the Café Society restaurant in New York City. He convinced me that he would treat the mystery and lack of professional investigation with sensitivity.

I arranged for Dennis to meet with Alexander, who traveled to Florida for the interview. Alexander waited with a camera crew for four hours at a Miami hotel. Dennis pulled a no-show. I was embarrassed for having wasted their time and money, but I blamed myself. Dennis had pleaded with me to attend the interview, and I had refused, hoping Dennis could take charge.

Unable to reach Dennis at home after numerous calls, I phoned the yacht he captained. "Denny, we have to talk—seriously," I said when he answered.

"Marti, I understand if you're mad, but I couldn't go through with it."

"I understand, Denny, and that's why I'm calling. I shouldn't be pushing you into anything. Your silence says it all, and I haven't paid attention to that."

"Did you see R.J.'s 'I still grieve for Natalie' piece in the *Star* this week?"

"No. For someone who hates tabloids, he's there enough," I said.

"He repeated that crap about his taking his personal speedboat out to search for Natalie. Goddammit, he wouldn't even let me turn on the searchlight to look for her. He didn't try to find her in a nonexistent boat! In the middle of that night, an island worker cruised out to *Splendour* to help. He cruised R.J. to shore and back in about fifteen minutes. R.J. now twists that into looking for Natalie? R.J. had already said to me, 'She's gone, she's gone,' and he meant *dead*.

"Soon after R.J. got back to the yacht, Doug Oudin, the harbormaster, cruised out to *Splendour* and told us to call the Coast Guard. R.J. said he didn't want to. I stood there dumbfounded. Why wouldn't you want to call the Coast Guard to find your missing wife in the ocean? *Why*?"

"Damn it, Denny, you should have never covered for this man. I didn't know any of this. Can't we call the authorities?"

"If they wanted the truth, Marti, they would have discovered it years ago. They could pursue *me*. Reporters find me any time they want."

Dennis was right. Authorities didn't seem interested even after all of the published information including Dennis's revelations, Wagner's quotes, and Walken's confusing information.

"If the authorities don't act, it's their continued neglect," I said. "I don't know how seriously to take this, but Milo Speriglio called me a few days ago to see how we're progressing. He said he recently heard more threats against your life. This is ten years later, Den! I think he might have heard about *Now It Can Be Told*. Milo said to tell you to be careful."

"Is he still working this case for Lana?"

"He reached a dead end, but told me Lana wants to talk to you and gave me her number. I called her. Her Hollywood career ended with Natalie's death. She can't get acting jobs, or anything in the industry. She said R.J. was so furious about her book that he won't let her see Courtney and Natasha. She's been taking care of her mother. She says R.J. 'put the word out on her,' which is what you believed when your acting jobs stopped. Now Lana works in telephone sales. She talked about us possibly collaborating with her on Natalie's life story. She has the beginning, she said, and we have the ending. She said it doesn't matter what stories are told—that nothing will bring her sister back. I told her Natalie had tried to call her that Saturday morning, hoping she might find comfort in knowing Natalie reached out to her when experiencing an emotional crisis."

"Marti, I hardly even know Lana, so I can't collaborate with her," Dennis said, "but I will call her. I owe her that."

"In the meantime, Den, think about everything. I'll call you soon."

"I knew it would come to this, Marti. Do me a favor? Call the attorney and find out where I legally stand with *all* of the truth. Don't kid yourself. You know what I mean. Then ask him how I would go about acquiring citizenship in another country."

Citizenship in another country?

What on earth had happened that night?

Chapter 26

Ten more days would mark a decade since Natalie Wood's death. For eight years, I had sympathized with, listened to, lectured, and pleaded with Dennis to tell what happened on November 29, 1981. I had fought beside him against his personal demons, leading the charge when he lacked the strength, retreating when he lacked the courage. I was battle weary. As I dialed our attorney, whom we had not spoken with in years, I hung up before connecting, realizing my conviction that the truth must be told grew weak in the shadow of my concern for Dennis, so I dialed Dennis instead.

When he answered, I said, "I lost sight of your fear, and I sure as hell don't want you leaving the country. Most importantly, I don't want to put you in any kind of danger. And, in all honesty, I don't think the authorities will do anything for you. You would probably end up in more trouble than Wagner ever would. You're the common participant, not worth believing, and probably not even worth silencing, if that sad comment makes you feel any better. So let's give it up, okay, Den?"

Dennis exhaled a long, quick breath. "Marti, I always wanted to believe that Natalie was unconscious when she drowned because I couldn't bear thinking about her being alive and aware of her worst fear. She wouldn't have gone near the water on her own, so that leaves me with only one conclusion."

I sensed that Dennis was not going to censor himself for this conversation. I quickly said, "You're about to tell me something I won't be able to keep to myself, Den."

"The half hour I told you about—when R.J. was in the stateroom with Natalie—they had a terrible fight, *after* R.J. smashed the wine bottle. Natalie was never alone. R.J. was involved with what happened to her.

"It all happened fast. I stayed in the main salon, and they were in their stateroom a few steps down. I heard them screaming at each other so loudly that I couldn't even make out the words. I heard things being thrown around, hitting the walls, and it sounded like they were going at each other. So I ran up to the bridge. I heard things hitting their ceiling, right under my feet where I stood, and it really got out of hand. I kept thinking, no, he won't hit her."

"You think he did?"

"When I saw her body the next day, that's what it looked like to me. And that's sure what it sounded like as I listened to them fight. Water doesn't cause bruises like that. I heard a physical fight when they argued, but I didn't see it. But when we cleaned that stateroom and Natalie's pieces-of-eight earring was in the corner of the bedroom, I was so pissed off the cops hadn't scrutinized that room. Natalie was always careful with her jewelry—that earring was thrown there, or pulled out of her ear right there, somehow."

"Well, Den, sometimes you don't have to see something to know what it is. My blind friend taught me that long ago."

Den continued, "Well, I didn't need to see what I heard to know what was happening. I had everything figured out that night, but as time went on and I put other pieces of it together, I felt even worse. I questioned myself to make sure I didn't miss a single detail until I couldn't think about it anymore. I fooled myself into believing R.J.'s actions were forgivable."

"And now you're telling me you think her bruises came from things flying around, or from R.J.—how could you have held back something this big?"

"I was scared to death, Marti, that's how. I didn't know what to do. And the truth was so much worse than what we all told the police. I thought I'd go to jail, even though I just followed the attorneys' advice. The R.J. who fought with Natalie was not the R.J. I knew. Smashing that wine bottle was crazy, but just a start. He was *so* drunk."

"Den, sorry, but it's too weird that he wanted to go to the Isthmus the night before, where it's quiet. It almost looks like planning. Right after Natalie died, a *Hart to Hart* show aired about a murder victim who, of all things, drowned. When had he worked on that episode? That always bothered me too. I can't get past how desperate he was to go to Isthmus Friday night."

"Marti, he wanted the quiet of Isthmus so no one would see his wife flirting with her costar at lunch in Avalon the next day. That whole scene embarrassed R.J. That's why, on Saturday night, he wanted to get the hell out of the restaurant. He thought Natalie was making a spectacle of their marriage. He covered her with his coat when we left the restaurant, to protect her, then he turned into a madman back on the boat. I don't think anything was premeditated. It all just happened."

Dennis's defense for R.J. gave me a view of how confused Dennis must have been throughout the years. "I understand," I said, half believing it.

He hesitated, then said, "If only Natalie would have forgiven him, it wouldn't have happened. But I don't blame her. Natalie had no clue, no warning, that R.J. was about to go ballistic."

I had always dreaded Dennis's answers that suggested more, yet served as stop signs in the middle of details. But his voice this time was different, charged with apprehension. His breath came like that of a diver preparing for his first leap off a cliff. After several long seconds, he gathered his nerve and made the leap, and suddenly there was no stopping or slowing the torrent of words that poured from him.

"After R.J. smashed the bottle, he was suddenly scared. When it came down to it, Natalie really hadn't acted much different than if Mart Crowley had been sitting there with her on the sofa, but Walken was a threat to R.J.

"In the middle of all the broken glass and embarrassment, Chris—and I respect Chris for this—didn't say a word. He was shaking, though, real hard. He walked outside for a few seconds, then right back in, went to his room, and stayed there the rest of the night.

"After Natalie stormed off, and I made her tea, R.J. said he was embarrassed. He looked as shocked at himself as the rest of us were. I really felt sorry for him as he sat there feeling like a fool."

"What time did all of this happen, Den?"

"We got back from Doug's before ten-thirty. The bottle smashing happened right after that, maybe about ten forty. R.J. waited about ten minutes to follow Natalie to their stateroom. Then, everything happened real fast. When R.J. and I were in the main salon, and he was fidgeting, I could tell he wanted to go to Natalie to assess the damage. He told me to wait there because he didn't really expect her to accept his apology. She'd probably throw him out of the stateroom."

"So, he was in their stateroom by ten fifty?"

"Yes, no later than that, and as soon as he got there, the yelling started. I couldn't hear clear sentences, though, but all the curse words seemed magnified. Natalie screamed. I remember thinking their marriage might not survive that fight. It was like that doomed feeling you get out at sea watching a storm in the distance. You hope it won't come your way, but the winds shift and you catch the smell of ozone, then the black clouds are bearing down on you. That's what it felt like. There was hatred coming from that stateroom. They humiliated each other. They had never crossed that line before, at least not in front of me."

"Then what happened, Den?" The blank half hour he was now confronting was the missing link that could help solve the mystery. I sat on the edge of my chair, anxious for what Dennis would tell.

"The fighting got louder, and then I heard R.J. yell, 'Get off my fucking boat,' or 'You can fucking leave the boat,' or something like that. Natalie screamed out again, so I headed down to check things out. That was around eleven. I knocked on their stateroom door. It took about thirty seconds for R.J. to open it. He looked horrible, just horrible, like he'd been in a fight. He wedged himself in the door and told me to go wait for him. He said he would be up in a bit. I didn't hear Natalie, I didn't see Natalie. Everything was quiet then, and that bothered me. R.J. closed the door. I stood there for a few seconds but heard nothing. I went up to the bridge and turned on a light.

"Then, I heard their voices again, and their stateroom door to the back deck opened and shut. I ran to the window to see if I could get a look at why they were outside. I wanted to do something, but R.J. had just told me to leave the situation alone. At that point, I felt like an intruding employee. Here are these big-time celebrities, out there on the deck going at it, and I felt helpless to intrude. I peeked out and R.J. looked up, so I ducked back real fast. They started yelling again, so I put on loud music so they wouldn't think I was trying to listen to them. I thought the music would help cover their voices so nearby boaters wouldn't hear, either. Big mistake.

"They were under the ledge—the bridge extends out over the deck, so I couldn't really see them, and the isinglass—plastic window—reflected the light inside the bridge, but I saw shadows and could see that Natalie was in her nightgown. These quick moments always confused me. But I know what I saw, and I didn't think anyone was going anywhere, just that the fight was outside now. It was loud again. Natalie was screaming—or yelling, then I heard *nothing*.

"R.J. would call me to take Natalie ashore, if that's what she wanted, but there was nowhere on the island to go, so I just waited it out. I waited a few minutes, then looked out again, and I saw them together. This was a quick look, but I thought—and I don't know why—that he had gone to get her coat to keep her warm. I thought they might be making up. I didn't hear screaming anymore, but I kept the music on just in case. About ten to fifteen minutes passed.

"I turned off the music and heard what I can only consider boat sounds, the kind you get used to and don't really think about. But everything seemed weird. I think this is when the dinghy was being released.

Something was wrong. I headed back down. I didn't go through their stateroom, though, like I usually would to get to the back deck. I went through the salon to the side door. I walked out onto the deck and came up behind R.J. and there was no Natalie. R.J. turned around and looked at me like he saw a ghost. He was panting and sweating, and disheveled—he had just been in a wicked fight, and there was no denying it from his appearance. He rushed me off the deck, back through his stateroom, which was a *total* disaster. 'Natalie's missing,' he said quickly. 'I've been looking all over for her, and she's not here. Help me find her, Dennis. You go forward and check the rooms.'"

"God, Den, what did you say to him?"

"What could I say? I was dumbfounded. I couldn't figure out what in the hell he was talking about. Natalie wouldn't have left in her nightgown. I had just heard them fighting and saw them on the deck. I felt a tremendous panic, and I asked, 'What do you mean, she's missing?' He cut me off and said, 'She's missing, Dennis,' and he looked straight into my eyes. He froze my insides with that look."

"Did he say the dinghy was gone?"

"No. He told me to search forward while he checked the back again, so I didn't even check for the dinghy. Those first few minutes were crucial to save her. And insane. It was unthinkable that she was in the water, and R.J. was so convincing that I ran off to search the boat like he asked. I ran to my quarters, where I really expected to see her. She could have gone through the salon below me when I was on the bridge to get to my room up front. I thought I would see her sitting there waiting for me in my cabin. She wasn't there.

"Then I checked the empty cabin. I hoped it was all a crazy mistake. I checked every head. I even checked Chris's room. He was sound asleep. I thought of waking him up to help, but with what went down already, I was afraid it would be worse if Chris got involved.

"I ran out to the bow, and I looked in the water. It was dark, and I couldn't see very far. I needed the searchlight. I heard nothing coming from the water. I ran down the side decks, checking the water. And I went back out to the deck and saw the dinghy was gone. Now, I'm *scared*.

"This all took less than ten minutes. I went back up to the wheelhouse where R.J. was, and he told me the dinghy was gone, and that Natalie must have gone to the island. I said we should put on the searchlight, but he said, 'No!' I told him to get on the radio for help. I reached for the searchlight anyway. He grabbed my hand and said 'No' again. Then, believe it or not, he opened a bottle of scotch.

"That's when I got pissed. I *knew* Natalie didn't take the dinghy. She never did, and she wouldn't know how to start it. Maybe *one* time, in broad daylight with someone next to her, Natalie steered the dinghy. No way was she cruising in the dark, in the rain, using a flashlight for a headlight. *No way*. She didn't untie that dinghy, and Chris was sleeping. Who does that leave?"

"R.J." I remained silent for a minute. We both absorbed that revelation, me for the first time, Dennis for who knows how many times?

"What happened next?" I asked.

"R.J. poured me a drink! I drank some of it, but knew I needed to stay alert. At that point, even though all the signs were there, I still wondered. My mind couldn't fathom much. Natalie was either in the dinghy or in the water, and one was as illogical as the other. So I *had* to believe she was in the dinghy. I didn't want R.J. to think I suspected him, so I drank to keep his trust. Doesn't that sound sick? I kept jumping up saying, 'Let's call a search,' but R.J. kept refusing, saying that he couldn't afford the bad publicity.

"I almost believed him, but I was scared out of my mind. I was in a state of shock. Nothing made sense. R.J.'s behavior was bizarre. But, I had to go along with what he said. At one point, I asked if we could gun the engines so we could go look for her, but he wouldn't let me. He said we couldn't panic and cause a scene. In the meantime, he kept telling me to drink up, and I felt like he wanted me drunk on my ass. His image meant more than his wife's safety. I even thought about using that sonar we installed years ago. It could've helped by showing if anything was beneath the yacht or along side of it."

It chilled me, imagining the sonar capturing an image of Natalie floating beneath the yacht and projecting it to the wheelhouse video screen. "Denny, this is much worse than I expected," I broke in. "You've been carrying this around with you and blaming yourself? Please, listen to me. You did what anyone would have done. You didn't interfere because you thought it would make them defensive and prolong the fight. You interfered when you thought it was necessary, and R.J. told you lies. Maybe you drank too much, but you were a victim too. He was using you. Do you hear what I'm saying?"

"I hear you," he said flatly.

"Tell me what happened next."

"I just sat there, almost believing him, but I just couldn't. I tried to sort things out as a separate voice in my head kept repeating, 'He's lying. He was fighting with her, not looking for her.' Somehow, inside, I knew the truth, but I couldn't face it. My mind refused to put it all together, to face that she might be dead, and that R.J. refused to do anything about it. I remember thinking that R.J. had every reason to *not* want to find her. He knew how pissed Natalie was. She was talking to me the night before about seeing a lawyer.

"You don't treat Natalie Wood the way R.J. treated her that weekend—embarrassing her, smashing a wine bottle in her face—and get away with it. R.J. *knew* that. I was the closest thing to a witness as you can get, and I was *petrified*. This man wanted me obliterated with booze. Why? So I wouldn't remember anything? Or *worse*? I mean, that's how I was thinking, and I was afraid if I didn't go along with the program, that my life was in danger. I slept in the same bed with Natalie the night before. Easy enough to prove, right? It wouldn't have meant anything more than another Hollywood scandal if I had shown up dead in the water the next morning too. That's how I was thinking. I didn't know what to do, Marti." Then Dennis asked me, "What would you have done?"

"I don't have a clue. What in the hell is the right thing in a situation like that? To safeguard your own life? To try to save Natalie, who was probably already beyond saving?"

I *didn't* have a clue. I was in awe, listening to his details, unable to fathom how frightening it must have been on that boat with Wagner. I encouraged Dennis to continue.

"I stopped drinking and tried to sort things out. But nothing made sense. I just kept my eyes peeled and my ears open, hoping he would call a search. After more than an hour, R.J. regained some sense and realized the horror of what was happening. He suddenly started crying—really crying and saying 'Dennis, I know it. *She's gone, she's gone, she's gone.*' Before that, he didn't once say the normal kind of things you'd expect, like 'I wonder where she went,' or 'She should be back by now. I'm worried.'

"I held him while he cried. It was weird: I wanted to comfort him, yet I was repulsed. I thought about everything that happened over the weekend and how R.J. believed Natalie made a fool of him, how he had tried to control himself. And I thought about Natasha and Courtney, and I knew I had to keep my mouth shut and let R.J. handle it his way. Those girls were going to be devastated, and they would need their father more than ever. I even wondered if Natasha would be taken away and have to go live with her real dad. How could I add to their pain by telling what I knew, when what I knew would make R.J. look guilty as all hell?

"I told R.J. he'd better notify the Coast Guard. He still waited, though. He finally made a call around one-thirty, and Paul Miller, who was moored next to us on his boat, *Easy Rider*, and Don Whiting, the restaurant manager, picked up on the call. R.J. slurred that 'someone was missing'—he didn't even use Natalie's name! Then, Whiting talked to him, and R.J. asked Whiting to help but insisted that Whiting keep it 'low-key.'

"So Don Whiting said he would get the restaurant cook, Bill Coleman, and they would go looking for her. About half an hour later, some island worker brought a small patrol boat to *Splendour* and took R.J. ashore. They were gone for only about fifteen minutes.

"The harbormaster, Doug Oudin, cruised out and came back after three in the morning, *insisting* R.J. call the Coast Guard. R.J. *still* didn't want to go that route, but he finally gave in and Doug called. Then R.J. made a phone call, and he was crying. Probably to his lawyer. Doug Bombard, the restaurant owner, took a boat out to look for her, too, near daybreak.

"Next I was identifying her. When I saw her bruises, I realized it was a convenient escape for R.J. to not have to react to her bruises in front of the authorities. When I saw how bad she looked, all I could think about were those thumps and screams I heard from their stateroom the night before. The rest is history."

"History that needs correcting, Den. Natalie deserves that much."

"I agree." In his voice he held the acceptance and relief of a man finally facing truth.

It all made such sad sense.

I had expected a feeling of triumph to accompany my learning, at long last, the mysterious details surrounding Natalie Wood's death. Instead, I found myself grappling with the questions Dennis had struggled with for a decade. I had held onto my unwavering conviction that the truth must prevail. Now I asked myself, why? I tried to distinguish between the triumphs of finishing a book I had started long ago and the life-altering impact the horrible truth would have. What would be the triumph? That Robert Wagner would publicly be suspected? No more would come of it than that. Dennis confessed a lot of incriminating details but nothing that R.J.'s lawyers wouldn't be able to diminish.

According to Dennis's observations, Wagner was a kind and loving father. His actions that fateful Thanksgiving weekend were of a man who, under extreme stress and what he perceived as provocation, had behaved out of character, but that conduct did not change his basic disposition. Wagner had not suddenly been transformed into a malicious monster who presented a danger to others. He was still the man whom Dennis, in the six years before the tragic cruise, had grown to respect. That is part of why Dennis had stood by him. The truth would certainly cause pain for Robert Wagner. He had buried his wife but probably had not buried whatever guilt or remorse he may have felt. He had sidestepped all legal consequences, squelching official suspicion and overcoming public skepticism to continue with his life and career. He still worked. He had married again to actress Jill St. John.

No one can know what secret demons have tormented Wagner. Perhaps he had paid his price not through the law but through the grief of his daughters who experienced life's ultimate loss at such tender ages. Was their pain his punishment? Or was it one more grave injustice for which he escaped accountability? Their pain would have been intensified had their father been implicated in the death of their mother. Wagner was, no doubt, their principal source of comfort and strength in coping with the tragedy. To have compounded their distress by incriminating their father was unthinkable to Dennis. Dennis cared about Natalie's girls, and of the entire, unbearable tragedy, their grief was the hardest part for Dennis to deal with. Would it be fair to Natalie's daughters to now cast doubt in their minds? Could it benefit them in any way to learn what their "Uncle Dennis" had seen and heard in their mother's last moments? Dennis had never been allowed to see them after being released from under R.J.'s wing. Lana Wood had also been barred from the Wagner home—the two people who most reminded Wagner of his guilt. Through the years, Dennis has regretted his silence as much as he has regretted releasing a portion of the truth. There were only two choices now. Finish with the complete truth or forever hold his silence.

Wagner's celebrity factored highly. Would John Q. Public have been as fortunate to escape legal questioning and accusations? That injustice bothered me tremendously.

There was Natalie's family to consider. Surely they wondered about the contradictions and inconsistencies in the statements made about Natalie's death. Did they not deserve to know the entire truth as Dennis had experienced it?

Truth holds a healing power. That is why, after more than a decade, Dennis's need to tell the truth was still so powerful. For years, Dennis felt he had betrayed Natalie, not just by allowing lies and rumors to spread uncontested but by hiding behind those lies and by releasing only parts of the truth. When Natalie's mother blamed Dennis for the death of her daughter, it had pierced him to the core because, in his heart, he believed she was right. As the skipper of *Splendour*, her passengers were his responsibility. Dennis had failed his passenger, his beautiful friend Natalie. That is the sad truth he lived with.

Questions, so many of them, spun through my head. I had to accept, however, that some of my questions could never be answered; they would only damage me, as they had Dennis. I realized that only one answer mattered. Sometimes things really are black or white, good or evil, right or wrong. Despite my tendency to look for shades of gray, it came down to this: Natalie Wood's death was *wrong*.

A woman ended up dead, and the three men who had been on board *Splendour* had described a pleasant weekend—three men who played ignorant when asked, "What happened?" The banging-dinghy theory was certainly unfounded after what Dennis had just confessed to me. Natalie Wood died after a terrible fight, and her husband had been by her side the entire time.

And *everyone* should have been told.

Chapter 27

Certainly, Dennis could not be holding back more. But I had an aching suspicion.

For backup, I asked Dennis to tell Carol Lallier all he had told me. I wanted more than my ears to absorb this horrible truth. Dennis and Carol met when he had spent Thanksgiving weekend with me on the tenth anniversary of Natalie Wood's death, and he trusted my trust in her.

The new details Dennis had revealed cast a pall over this holiday season every bit as saddening as Natalie's death a decade earlier had. On Christmas morning, I thought about Natasha and Courtney, now young women. I had attended my mother's viewing on my twelfth birthday, about the same age Natasha was when she lost Natalie. I wondered if Natasha and Courtney had accepted the "accident" theory. I thought of my own children: In the same situation Natalie had experienced, would I want them to know— and would they want to know—what really happened to me? *Yes*.

I was in a spell I could not shake, but the media was about to shake it for me. In January 1992, Susan Levit, a producer from Geraldo's *Now It Can Be Told*, called Dennis, still wanting an interview. I talked with Susan, and our conversations left me drained. I could not manage for Susan the trust I had acquired for Alexander Johnson, but Johnson was on other projects.

I did not like Susan, but she pulled the ace from her sleeve, as all devious players eventually do. She said that Geraldo Rivera could help publish our manuscript, claiming our high-profile story could, as she put it, "draw millions." The possibility of publishing drew me in. Dennis's account was lost to the public without a book, so despite my misgivings about Susan herself, I listened.

I asked for a news format to present the story for her show. Susan promised we could have that. Susan asked what our big revelation might be. I told her that Natalie Wood was not in the habit of taking the dinghy out alone. That fact, according to Susan, was a tremendous revelation. The potential for "making millions" became the prominent bait behind her every plea. It was not money we wanted—it was exposure. Ten years had passed, and perhaps *Now It Can Be Told* would draw attention to the shabby investigation into Natalie's death—and they promised they would, with a panel of attorneys. We had never had that kind of opportunity.

Arrangements were made, and *Now It Can Be Told* financed Dennis's flight from Florida to New York for January 26, 1992. Since I lived just an hour south of the city, I drove myself to the hotel where the show booked our rooms. It was late on Super Bowl Sunday, around eleven o'clock, when I arrived. Carol Lallier planned to meet up with us the next morning.

After checking in, I went to the hotel lobby to wait for Dennis, who arrived around eleven-thirty, looking weary. We sat in the lobby with coffee, not wanting to talk in either of our rooms. We were not prepared: the interview had been arranged too quickly, and my apprehension resurfaced. Susan would not budge on giving us more time. The media train that had always chased us down the track was about to run us over. We had heard the warning signals, yet we stayed on the track.

Our sincerest motivations were about to be compromised—without our permission. Had I only known that because of Susan's cunning, deceitful practices, I was about to fall into our biggest media blunder, just by mocking her reference to "making millions"—and being secretly taped while doing it—I would have run as fast as I could back home.

Each media publication or production had a preconceived notion of what they wanted Dennis to say—what would generate them the most profit. Dennis and I had been through it too many times, and we were wearing thin.

Dennis and I walked a few blocks to the St. Moritz Hotel at Central Park. The place was virtually empty, but we took a booth far from the bar after ordering wine.

"Okay, let's decide now, Den. Should we cancel this interview?"

Dennis shrugged his shoulders, and I shrugged mine. Suddenly, we laughed. Pure, nervous laughter.

"Marti, we've been through a lot," Dennis noted.

"And I just don't feel right about this one, Den. I don't like Susan, but I hope she'll be fair."

The bartender was closing up, so we left and hailed a cab. We went to Callahans on the East Side, only because we saw their advertisement. The bar was packed with a partying crowd, not yet winding down from Super Bowl excitement. The noise provided a buffer, and Dennis and I were able to talk without fear of our voices carrying. We had a death to discuss. Again.

We sat at the bar with wine and tried to go over details, which seemed a chore, oddly more for me than for Dennis.

"You know what, Marti?" Dennis said. "Let's just have some fun tonight—they don't want us until ten. Let's stay a little longer."

I agreed, and we sat at the bar and talked about whose support we appreciated over the years, because we shared an ominous feeling that our "something big" may never manifest. We talked about my relationship with Bob, into its fifth year. Dennis and Bob got along great. We were pleased that Dennis's mother had finally come around to at least understand Dennis's burden. There was Dennis's brother, Paul, who had recently undergone cancer surgery, and we hoped he would stay well. I bragged about my new grandson, Josh Singleton, who was in Bob's and my care. We lingered over old times and fun memories, and when I brought up our ancient "jail time," we laughed.

My friends Frank and Mary Greco had listened to me every weekend for over a year, and they had warned me not to take this particular trip to New York, as they worried about repercussions of premature publicity. When I had said to Mary that it was long overdue to expose a ten-year-old lie in a book, she played the devil's advocate and said, "Do you really think people will just believe what you and Den have to say?"

Her comment was insightful because that was exactly what I had thought: that because *I* believed Dennis, *everyone* would believe him. Despite my faith in Dennis, I needed to explore his details. Nothing made sense about Natalie's death, except for Dennis's story. But Mary helped me to realize that if I couldn't substantiate Dennis's claims, I would look like his parrot.

Dennis and I talked with the twenty-two-year-old bartender who had overheard us mention the name Natalie Wood and said, "The name sounds familiar, but I can't place it." The bartender instantly recognized the names Marilyn Monroe, Elizabeth Taylor, Bette Davis, and Judy Garland when we "tested" him. Within that genre, he should have known the name Natalie Wood. I suggested some of Natalie's classic movies for him. We were ready to leave when the bartender gave us a refill of wine, on the house.

Suddenly, I was startled by tears in Dennis's eyes.

"What's wrong, Den?" I asked.

"He's an evil man, Marti," he whispered.

"Wagner?"

"Yeah, Wagner. He's an evil, *evil* man."

Within seconds, Dennis's mood had switched from relaxed and animated to burdened and depressed. Obviously, his comment had sprung from talking about Natalie.

"Well, let's not say that tomorrow," I said.

Dennis looked straight into my eyes, his solemn eyes piercing. What he said next caused me to lose my balance, and I almost fell off my barstool.

"He put her coat on her."

He did? I grabbed my wine and drank it straight down, unable to respond to such information. My suspicions were confirmed. There *is* more.

"My God, Denny, this thing doesn't end, does it? You know we can't do this interview tomorrow. Is that why you told me this now?"

"I don't know, Marti."

He put her coat on her. He put her coat on her. He put her coat on her. The words spun my brain, screaming at me. What could I ask about it? What could I say? Those words pretty much said it all.

And changed everything.

Chapter 28

Carol Lallier's loud knocks at my hotel room door woke me. I let her in, then rushed to shower, still dizzy from wine and Dennis's words. I needed to talk to Dennis. I said nothing to Carol about the night before.

Running late, Carol and I met Dennis in the lobby, caught a cab, ran two blocks, and had no time to talk things over. I had not wanted to disappoint the show once more, so I remained quiet until we were seated in front of a large camera that rested on a tripod, and that's when it hit me for certain that it was imperative to *not* tell Dennis's story here. But the interview had started.

Susan Levit had planned, without informing us, to let Dennis run with the story—to just tell it rather than to have a question–answer session, as promised. Dennis mentioned Natalie's flirting, which led to Wagner smashing the wine bottle. Then he stopped. I kept my eyes on the floor. Everything seemed wrong. Then Dennis and I exchanged knowing glances. We wanted off.

Carol, still under the impression that Dennis was prepared to finally reveal important details, looked as confused as the entire crew did. Susan encouraged us on by asking, "How did Natalie get into the water?"

Dennis finally said, "I don't know if I can say that—"

Then Carol, from where she stood in the background, said, "Den, you can tell them how she got into the water. It's okay to mention the fight.... Go ahead and tell them. You can tell them that Wagner told her to 'get off his f-ing boat.'"

Carol believed she was helping a reluctant Dennis to release his truth, and I needed to update her, so I asked for private time, thinking Carol would stay, but she walked away with the producer and crew, probably in an attempt to smooth things over. We watched the cameraman unplug the camera from the wall outlet before they left the room. The camera was right there, unplugged, but had a battery-backup system. Susan blatantly lied to us, assuring us we would not be filmed when we were left alone.

I said things to Dennis, worried thoughts that came rushing out—things that should haunt me—such as, "Den, we have to eventually say how she got in the water, but not *here*, not *now*. Don't tell *them*...tell *me*. We have to tell it, but tell it *right*...we're not prepared."

I now wanted to talk with an attorney before revealing sensitive details. Why tell the sensitive components of Natalie Wood's death to a producer who might exploit the information, one who tried to manipulate us with intimations of money and exposure for our book?

At that moment, Dennis reached in his pocket and pulled out a mini bottle of vodka he had taken from the hotel room mini bar.

"Calm down, Mart. Here, have this," he said jokingly to lighten my distress.

I needed a joke. I smiled and patted Dennis's shoulder, then looked at the camera and remarked that I hoped it wasn't secretly on. Dennis and I had behaved in the studio room as the friends that we are—the same kind of friends who had sat on barstools the night before in the same mood—and we looked like friends—friends who found Susan Levit to be our biggest mistake, and we nervously laughed at our mistake because it wasn't yet worth our energy to find her repulsive. We had enough repulsive things to deal with.

When Carol returned to talk with us, she stood in front of the camera, facing Dennis and me. She said, "They're through," and I said, "Good, why should we give away the book here? How can we say things without incriminating ourselves?"

We needed to be *understood*. A five-minute explanation on a television show couldn't begin to encompass the complexity of a decade-long mystery, and as I sat in front of that huge, unplugged camera, it was my moment of truth. As much as I had always wanted Dennis to tell *all,* another part of me was always proud of him for his ability to keep such a deep, dark secret—even from me. It was a protective instinct.

Dennis was an innocent bystander who had initially called me because he trusted me. I had never taken one opportunist cent in return for information about Natalie's death, but I would never compromise my right to a manuscript no matter how many unethical reporters would try to portray my intentions to the contrary. Susan's little production was for money and for herself, not for Natalie.

No one would ever be able to capture the raw honesty, emotion, and desperation that had poured out with that August 17, 1983, phone call Dennis had placed in the middle of the night to a "nobody" who had no ulterior motive for listening to his story, no interest in scooping other media sources or sensationalizing a tragedy. That call had come to a friend who would offer loyalty and emotional support to help an exploited, frightened young man to take back his life. That call had come to *me*.

And now this nobody knew that Natalie Wood had not gone out on deck to quiet a banging dinghy, that Robert Wagner had been fighting with her the entire time he claimed she had gone to bed, that Robert Wagner was a liar. And this nobody would do everything in her power to bring this injustice to light.

Chapter 29

I called Susan Levit a few days later. She was smug when I explained the timing was not right.

"Oh, we're still airing a story," she cattily warned.

"Well, what will you use? We canceled the interview. We walked out."

"I gotta go. Watch the show and see," she smirked.

The show begins with Geraldo Rivera introducing the abrupt, tragic, and mysterious end to Natalie Wood's life, then looks into "a glamorous life cut short" by showing some footage of Natalie's roles, then builds upon three theories—the first from Duane Rasure, the lead detective in the Natalie Wood case; the second from private investigator Milo Speriglio; and the last from an "eye witness to the circumstances leading to Natalie Wood's death."

Duane Rasure explains away the broken glass in the main salon by citing "rough seas." He claims he had interviewed Wagner, Walken, and Davern several times each, could detect no signs of foul play, and so concluded that although a brief argument might have taken place, Natalie's death was an accidental drowning that occurred as she had tried to quiet a dinghy and fell.

Warren G. Harris, author of *R.J. and Natalie* (1988), a bland biography focusing on the duo's Hollywood histories, then insists that Natalie's death was an accident—the popular dinghy theory. Harris adds that Natalie, as tiny as she was, had sunk quickly in the ocean because her jacket, when saturated with water, became a heavy thirty to forty pounds and weighed her down.

A dramatization shows Natalie walking a swim step near a dinghy, which is tied with a loose, swooping rope to the back of a yacht.

Then Milo Speriglio's theory is introduced, obviously offered through pure speculation and "Elizabeth." When I had spoken with Milo, I had clearly let him know that Elizabeth's account had nothing to do with truth. I now realized that Milo had probably been Geraldo's source for the Marilyn Monroe segment that had *20/20* executives balking when Geraldo left that show. Milo's books on Marilyn suggested that John F. Kennedy and his father hired mafia hit men to kill her. Milo, smart as he seemed, reminded me of someone who played private eye to the hilt. I wished I had talked with him more because he was a fascinating hybrid of the real deal and a Sam Spade. But, with his record of solving over 30,000 private cases to date, I was sure counting on Milo to save this show—unfortunately, he failed miserably.

Milo's scenario involved Wagner and Walken fighting, then chasing Natalie who, in her anger, ran from the two actors, fell overboard, and was not rescued. Milo said the two actors were "out of their minds," thus would not call for help right away. Then, the dinghy rope had been cut—shown in dramatization with a knife's blade slicing through a single rope. Milo's reputation far surpassed him for this show. He clearly stated that no crime had been committed, a statement in contrast with the dramatization of cutting the dinghy rope.

The show then returns to focus on the secret camera on Dennis and me. Carol's voiceover is heard, encouraging Dennis to talk, then a quick show of Carol walking away with the crew, to her returning and talking with us. The segment ends with me saying, "How can we say anything without incriminating ourselves?"

It was at the television airing that we learned how we were duped. Yet Geraldo Rivera, good investigative reporter he still could be, makes it clear with his facial expressions and words that Dennis was a voice to eventually be heard.

For the close of the show, a panel of three respected attorneys, Barry Slotnick, Ralph Felder, and Gus Newman, individually and collectively agreed and strongly recommended that the case be reopened. Slotnik said that the public had always "bought accident" but that the "snippet of tape" including Dennis and me took it away from accident. Felder, a matrimonial lawyer, said that the combination of drinking, jealousy, and anger could very well indicate that Natalie Wood was killed and that the answer seems to "rest with the skipper." Gus Newman, a criminal attorney, said that the official version simply does not seem accurate.

I appreciated Geraldo's choice to include the attorneys in the show, which I thought had been the original intention—to have Dennis and me answer to them. I hoped the authorities might take the attorneys' advice to reopen the case.

In closing, Geraldo speculates that Dennis's big revelation might have been that Natalie never took the dinghy out alone: I expected Geraldo to have been more perceptive. It would have made more sense to pursue how the dinghy had been released, but Geraldo had shown Milo's unlikely scenario for that.

Geraldo offered an audience participation vote, the results to be aired on his next show. People could vote for "official version" or "nonaccidental death." When the votes were tallied, it came in at 9 to 1 in favor of *nonaccidental* death.

Geraldo, by allowing the unfair portrayal of Dennis and me, had only postponed a chance for justice, as the show simultaneously hurt the case while pushing for it to be reopened. Many of our comments were not aired—comments that would have shown the seriousness of our dilemma—but Susan Levit seemed out for revenge because we did not work with someone of her ilk.

After the show aired, friends, family, and acquaintances called, their concerns similar: "Are you embarrassed? Are you mad?"

"No," I answered to each. "We didn't do anything wrong. *They* did. Hopefully, that panel of attorneys will help to bring attention to this mystery."

Of all the incoming calls, it was my no-nonsense sister-in-law, Shirley Carter, who made the most sense: "Marti, get your head screwed on right concerning this show. Go see Glenn Cochran, an attorney I highly recommend. They unjustly portrayed you, and people can vouch for that. Dave [my brother] is really upset over this."

Excellent advice. It was not long after the show that other kinds of calls started coming in, and we heard from Wagner's attorneys. The letter claimed that Frank Salerno, the supervising detective on Wood's case, had said the case "speaks for itself" and that Davern was sensationalizing, possibly for money.

We had been interviewed for no payment. Wouldn't Salerno want to know the details behind the *Now It Can Be Told* show?

We signed with a reputable literary agent. In July 1992, Dennis and I visited publishing houses with our agent's New York partner. We felt privileged to meet with several publishing house executives. Thousands of talented writers struggle and produce wonderful work yet never come close to the advantage that now stared us in the face. I did not kid myself: it was the mystery of Natalie Wood—not two nobodies from New Jersey—who attracted the interest of these publishers.

Our agent's partner had warned us we might encounter an "attack-the-messenger" attitude, but Dennis and I were relieved that it seemed not to even occur to the publishers and editors we met with to question our motives—or more plainly, to accuse us of capitalizing on a tragedy. Nor did these professionals question our purpose—to reveal a hidden truth. The only people who condemned us were those who might benefit by casting doubt on Dennis's and my credibility.

While Dennis and I hit the New York City pavement with our agent, we learned in one publisher's office that "word was out"—that our mission was common knowledge throughout the industry and that it might leak to Wagner.

As we waited to meet our final publisher of the day, the only one we hadn't visited at the publisher's actual location but instead at the Gramercy Hotel, Dennis and I sat at the bar, and Dennis told me he had met a girl he was seriously considering marrying. Before he could say more, the representatives from the publishing house walked in. For this meeting, I did most of the talking and explained honestly that I still had avenues to explore with the manuscript.

An uneasy feeling crept up on me that if a publishing offer developed now, Dennis would still withhold his deepest, darkest secrets. He had received enough threats to make it an understandable choice. I wanted him to tell me everything he knew—and that was the point: if we went forward with a book now, Dennis might come to regret omissions made solely out of fear. Here, on the brink of finding some sort of justice for Natalie Wood—and of holding Wagner accountable for his part in Natalie's death—I wished the opportunity for publication were a little further down the road.

The meeting at the Gramercy Hotel was positive, and we all clinked glasses to our project. I was filled with mixed emotions.

Dennis and I went home and waited. Months passed. I was distracted by a job change and a move to a small town in New Jersey where Bob Mooney and I took over a turnkey printing business attached to the front of a four-bedroom home. There was family to attend to and hard work in keeping a business going. Normalcy returned to my life, and I was better for it.

Publishers were afraid of Dennis's truth. It was an obvious time to prioritize. And Dennis and I would do just that.

A few months later, in March 1993, Dennis called to announce he had married Ellen, a woman ten years his junior but, according to Dennis, *a perfect match, a perfect catch*. Ellen hailed from England. She and Dennis had met during her travels to the United States. She could not have entered Dennis's life at a more perfect time.

"We're so in love, Marti, that we don't even know what's going on in the world right now," Dennis boasted.

Dennis had come close to marrying before but waited for the right time and person. Natalie Wood had tried to warn Dennis about certain relationships, and Dennis usually recognized relationship flaws, which is why so few lasted.

That summer, over the Fourth of July holiday, Dennis visited my home with Ellen and his brother Paul. Carol Lallier and our friend John Levandowski were visiting, and we all sat around our kitchen table talking.

Ellen, a blonde-haired, brown-eyed beauty, outdoorsy with the perfect touch of class and elegance, radiated charm with her fascinating stories. Where else might I meet someone who had literally taken a slow boat to China? What I had thought was an ancient practice-turned-metaphor was actually a way to travel on a low budget. Ellen's fare had taken her from Hong Kong to Shanghai on a freighter with only a few cabins available for passenger travel. She had also experienced the Siberian Express on a seven-day trip from Beijing to Russia. Ellen had sung, too, during her travels, with a popular, inspirational singing group called Breathe.

Dennis and Ellen started a family right away. Their first daughter was born just eleven months after their marriage ceremony. They named her Natasha.

The family moved from Ft. Lauderdale to St. Augustine, Florida, where Dennis resumed his marina business. Dennis became a true family man and a good businessman, and he cherished every second of it.

I saw Robert Wagner on the *Phil Donahue Show* during one of his rare public appearances. With Stefanie Powers by his side, they promoted the play "Love Letters" that had them traveling to cities around the world for special performances. An audience member asked Wagner who he considered his most influential Hollywood figure throughout his life. Everyone obviously expected to hear the name Natalie Wood, because when Wagner answered, "Spencer Tracy," a collective gasp sounded from the audience.

Paul Davern saw "Love Letters" in Philadelphia and gathered the nerve to ask to visit Wagner backstage after the performance. To Paul's great surprise, Wagner met with him, embraced him, and seemed genuinely happy to see him. Wagner did not ask about Dennis.

Paul called me to tell me about it and said he had a secret to reveal about the visit but that it would have to wait. In February 1994, however, I received a shocking call from my sister, Mary Haines, who told me she had read Paul Davern's obituary.

Dennis called. "Ellen and I are leaving tomorrow for Jersey," he told me. "I'm my mother's only son now, Marti."

The viewing was difficult, but with his life force gone, Paul looked like a stranger. When I looked for Dennis, he was nowhere to be found. I asked his sister Rita if she minded my stopping by her house, where Dennis was staying.

Chuck Esser, Bob, and I left the viewing to go be with Dennis. He greeted us at the door and explained that his one-year-old Natasha had developed an earache during the flight, so he stayed with Ellen to help with Natasha, who was irritable from pain. We talked late into the night. Dennis had now lost another brother, but no death ate away at him more than Natalie's.

Chapter 30

In June 1994, I watched the infamous white Bronco ride and waited anxiously for the O.J. Simpson trial of the century. The media met their heyday. I learned a lot about criminal trial procedure but concluded that justice is selective. I did note that O.J. Simpson was handcuffed on the morning of his wife's death—quite a contrast to R.J. being hurried away in a helicopter after his wife's bruised, dead body was discovered.

I did not talk much with Dennis about the Simpson trial except to tell him about the young woman who had seen Simpson's white Bronco near Nicole Brown-Simpson's condo at the established time of the murders. The woman was scratched from the prosecution's witness list, however, for telling her story to a tabloid reporter.

Writer Dominick Dunne followed the Simpson trial and reported his courtroom accounts to *Vanity Fair* magazine. That was the venue to go with, I told Dennis. I wanted to contact Dunne but was aware that his daughter, promising actress Dominique Dunne, had been strangled to death by her boyfriend just one year after Natalie Wood died. She was only 22 years old. Dennis knew that Robert Wagner had provided Dunne with home bodyguards at the time of Dominique's funeral so that Dunne would not experience the reporter frenzy that had occurred at the Wagner home after Natalie died. Dominique was buried near Natalie.

Dominick Dunne, one of the most outspoken critics of the Simpson trial and an advocate for the Goldman family, could be of no help to me. Dunne became one of my favorite writers, and my profound regard for his perspectives and insights prevented me from imposing upon him with questions and information about his friend, Robert Wagner.

My new burning desire to bring Natalie Wood justice had all but fizzled.

In November 1994, I learned about the remake of *Miracle on 34th Street*, Natalie's first classic film. I agreed with many critics that there was no need to remake this classic. Macy's, in a public statement, concluded that the "original version—like our store in Herald Square—is a one-of-a-kind classic that just gets better with age."

I tried again to contact Coroner Noguchi in 1995, to no avail. Carol Lallier took her teenage daughter, Melanie, for a vacation in Los Angeles. Carol tried to make headway with Noguchi in person, but was unable to arrange an interview.

Carol visited Natalie's grave and took pictures of the marker, a flat stone:

NATALIE WOOD WAGNER
BELOVED DAUGHTER, SISTER, WIFE, MOTHER & FRIEND
1938 – 1981
"MORE THAN LOVE"

It struck me that on her gravestone, by failing to add the simple word "Actress"—for her fans—Wagner failed to acknowledge Natalie's brilliant career.

Dennis and I stayed busy with work and family, which left little time for the manuscript, now moved to a back burner, but not put off, just simmering. Natalie's death still ate away at me, but only in nibbles, so I was able to deal with not dealing with it. The next three years would be mystery free.

In July 1997, Bob Mooney's mother, Josephine "Mama Moon," passed away from cancer. Nearing her time, she said to me, "I'm thinking about Natalie, and what you told me, and her fans deserve to know what happened to her. I hope you can give her justice one day." Then she added, with a smile, "I think about you dancing on that desk, playing *Gypsy*."

Mama Moon was an extraordinary woman with a keen sense of justice. She was the first to make me pause and actually sympathize with Natalie's fans.

* * *

Robert Wagner's career moved steadily along. He was creeping back into various television shows, even had a part in the classic yada-yada-yada episode of *Seinfeld* with his wife, Jill St. John. There were many fans and colleagues who still offered him devotion and never questioned his part in Natalie's death.

When I saw Wagner in rare television interviews, the shows appeared to follow pre-established guidelines: Don't bring up Natalie Wood. Otherwise, what interviewer would avoid asking about his late wife? Yet, Wagner usually appeared on edge, in anticipation of a possible surprise "Natalie question."

While many fans were happy to see Wagner back in action, in movies and on television, I was more interested in testing the durability of Natalie's socks and coat. In September 1997, while planning a weekend beach getaway, I packed a pair of wool socks and an old down jacket. Bob and I stayed at a Surf City beach house with our friend John Levandowski. While Bob and John watched football, I slipped away in the late afternoon with my coat and socks. Being the fall season, the temperature was no more than 65 degrees, and no one was in sight.

I chickened out with the coat. What if Noguchi was right, and the coat sapped my strength when it became saturated? I passed the cold breakers with my socks on, and then I treaded water strongly. Within a minute, one sock came off. I relaxed my body and floated. The other sock remained on my foot. If Natalie had kicked and struggled much, or had tried to climb into a dinghy, I was now certain her socks could never have remained on her feet.

Next, I returned to the beach and pulled out the September 1997 issue of *Playboy* to read Christopher Walken's interview, in which he told a more detailed account of the night Natalie Wood died.

When asked about the strict silence he has maintained, Walken opens up for this *Playboy* exposé, claiming he has not spoken about the tragedy previously out of respect for the Wagner family.

But, in fact, Walken had previously spoken about it and had said he was sleeping. This new version, however, seemed a confused mix of both Friday and Saturday nights, a loss of memory, and new information too confusing to decipher. Walken says Natalie went to bed before the other three on board, that he was in the main salon with Wagner and Davern. He says the dinghy was banging, and only Natalie knows what happened because she was alone. He recalled slipping on the "ski ramp" himself, and surmised that's what happened to Natalie. He confirms Natalie's fear of water by telling that a scene involving water was cut from *Brainstorm* due to Natalie's apprehension.

Walken, who for fifteen years claimed to have been sleeping when all of this happened, says in the *Playboy* interview, "I remember distinctly that about forty-five minutes after she had gone to bed, R.J. went down to her room, came back and said, 'Natalie's not there.' And then the Coast Guard was called."

Walken says he feels "funny" talking about that night in detail. He states that Natalie had gone ashore in the dinghy the night before to call her kids because the phone on the boat wasn't working properly, so he surmised that was where she might have gone on Saturday night, the night she died. According to Walken, they were not on "high seas" but just fifty feet from the shore, near a hotel and a restaurant, so to go call her kids was not so "far-fetched." The first reaction was that "everything was okay, but then, time passed."

When asked by the *Playboy* interviewer about Noguchi's release of an argument between Wagner and Walken, Walken replies: "Wasn't that guy, Noguchi, kicked out as chief medical examiner for being an asshole?"

When pursued, Walken defends himself by rambling on about Noguchi's credibility and calls him a "bad man," asking "how in the hell would Noguchi know what went on?" He says that if a "policeman" said there was an argument, it would "be different" because the police investigated thoroughly, and if there had been anything wrong, the police would have pursued it. Walken tries to end the topic by, ironically, using Noguchi's official account. "The story I just told is the absolute truth. Nobody can know, but I believe she went to move that dinghy, slipped, fell, hit her head, and died. Not a good way to go."

Playboy persists, asking Walken's reaction to that fateful night. "Oh, man, forget it," he says, "My reaction was for R.J. To receive that kind of news...."

Walken gets hold of himself to further explain that the Wagner family was nice to him, having invited him to their home and on their yacht for a cruise. He says they had a lot of fun, and for something like the tragedy to happen to someone who really was loved and legendary is "just too hard to talk about."

Walken's *Playboy* statements are nonsensical—had he been sleeping or not? He didn't know? The truth is, Walken was *not* present when Natalie "went missing," so perhaps Walken was reciting previously written accounts instead of what actually happened. There never existed a moment when Wagner left the main salon to "go discover Natalie missing." That part of this tragic tale was nothing but a lie—as was the banging dinghy theory—a lie that stuck so well, now Walken used it.

As for Natalie leaving in the dinghy Friday night to "call her kids," perhaps that is what Natalie told Walken in an effort to smooth over the embarrassment of having to leave the yacht Friday night because the Wagner/Wood marital argument had escalated. Walken was already in bed Friday night when the arguing got out of control. After returning to the yacht Saturday morning, with R.J. apologizing and wanting to continue the cruise to Two Harbors, Natalie may have taken advantage of the opportunity to salvage the outing. The last thing Natalie would have wanted was for Christopher Walken, her guest, her new friend and co-star, to be uncomfortable.

In the whole picture, it was difficult to understand why Walken would not have asked to end the unpleasant cruise on Saturday if he had known that Natalie had left the yacht on Friday night because of tension with her husband. It is possible that Walken truly had not recognized the volatile situation until the wine bottle was smashed and he was accused of wanting to have sex with Natalie. After Walken learned that Natalie's body was found in the ocean, he no doubt realized the horrific consequences. Perhaps he felt guilty that he had not remained awake to help smooth things over either night. His *Playboy* interview appeared to be blatant lies, even in comparison to what was thus far publicly known.

Walken's disdain for Noguchi is stunning. Too call Noguchi "an asshole," as Walken had, was downright arrogant and rude. Noguchi's career as a conscientious, *chief* medical examiner spoke for itself. He was condemned for his every attempt to seek truth in the Wood case. As for Walken saying, "If a policeman asked...," in fact, policemen *had* asked. Walken, Wagner, and Davern, hadn't been forthcoming.

Everything got scrambled about in this case, and the confusion prevented people from working together. Wagner and Davern immediately secured attorneys. Noguchi changed his initial report, and according to new media information, had indeed intended to conduct a further psychological report, which may have revealed a more comprehensive account of Natalie's death. Such a report, however, would depend heavily on the cooperation of the entire Wagner family, especially R.J. That would never happen. Noguchi was fired, and Wagner was never investigated beyond two short interviews with Detective Rasure. Celebrity weighed heavily on anyone suggesting there might be something amiss.

Would honesty have ended Walken's career? Would his scruples have been interpreted as traitorous by the Hollywood powers that be? Why does Walken, decades later, still play dumb? Was his career simply too important to risk for justice? If I had been in his place, I would have realized that even if I shouted the truth from the Hollywood Hills, the odds of a celebrity such as Robert Wagner being prosecuted were mighty slim—as would be my career choices after opening my mouth.

It's what constitutes an actor: self preservation.

Chapter 31

Life moved forward. Dennis added to his family: a son, Travis. Natalie's mystery became a subconscious thought for me when I took on a full-time job with a national trade magazine for which Carol Lallier was editor in chief, and still worked hard at my own advertising business. Dennis and I saw each other only for Thanksgiving reunions.

At my friend Mary Greco's daughter's wedding in early 2000, I saw Mary's sister-in-law, Colleen Sumption, Chuck Esser's daughter—Dennis's godchild. "Marti, are you upset with Uncle Denny for giving his story to *Vanity Fair*?" she asked me.

Colleen recognized from my expression that I knew nothing about the article. It was Dennis's prerogative to tell his story as he chose, but I was upset at being blindsided. I explained that I had not seriously touched my manuscript in years, so, "No, I'm not upset," I told Colleen. But I was upset.

I stopped at a convenience store on the way home, and there was one last copy of *Vanity Fair* (March 2000) available. I bought it and did not sleep until I finished the article titled, "Natalie Wood's Final, Fatal Hours," by Sam Kashner. Not only did I feel betrayed by Dennis, but also I realized that, right or wrong, I felt possessive of what seemed at the moment to be Natalie's story, not Dennis's.

I called Dennis the next morning. He explained that he had allowed Kashner to read parts of my unfinished manuscript. Dennis had volunteered his information and was not paid for his interview. Kashner had insisted that it would lend credibility to Dennis that way. "I did this for us, Marti," Dennis told me.

Instead of questioning Dennis, I admitted that his decision to talk with a respected publication such as *Vanity Fair* was a good one. But I could not help wondering why on earth, considering my years of close involvement with Dennis's efforts to tell his story, he or Kashner had not contacted me.

In Kashner's article, he mentions Dennis's former tabloid journey, implying its intent was "for profit." Yes, I did want to write a book that would sell worldwide—and that was okay, because foremost, I wanted truth and justice for Natalie Wood, and Dennis had never compromised his motives for money. Most of his interviews *were* given for free. Dennis spoke with a heavy heart when he spoke of Natalie. He wanted her mystery death cleared up. Dennis was a man of principle, a naïve and impulsive one at times, but it ripped me apart knowing that only a few right words, or information, could explain his straightforwardness. Kashner did see this in Dennis, and I considered Kashner a credible and excellent, persuasive writer who obviously cared.

Because of Robert Wagner's wrath, writers' motives regarding Natalie would always be questioned and condemned if connected to Dennis. Sam, no doubt, had worked hard, but he presented nothing in his article that was news to me—and a lot of what I did know was missing—things that could have substantiated Dennis's claims.

With the *Vanity Fair* interview, Dennis had offered his most detailed account of the circumstances leading to Natalie Wood's death—beyond the wine bottle smashing. Natalie Wood magazine segments were scheduled by television networks, and Kashner appeared on *Good Morning America* after his article was published. He remained steadfast in his belief that there was a lot more to Natalie's death than had ever been told.

I called *Vanity Fair* and left a message for Kashner. A week later, he called. He complimented what he had read of my material and told me he truly believed in Dennis's story.

"Marti, it is never too late for truth," Sam said. He encouraged me and smoothed away any concern I had building about getting all of the truth conveyed.

Sam and I talked about Duane Rasure. Neither of us could understand Rasure's continued defense of his investigation. Kashner had interviewed Rasure at his Arizona ranch, and told me he thought it odd that a retired detective could afford such a beautiful ranch with top-bred, Arabian horses to complement the spread. "R.J. was raising Arabians after Natalie died," Sam reminded me.

It didn't bother me to hear this pseudo-accusation from Kashner because I understood fully why sensible people would question Rasure's choice to keep looking the other way. I had also heard the same speculation before in odd postcards I had received from a private investigator in England, Peter Rydyn. Rydyn seemed obsessed with promoting an allegation that Wagner and Walken had murdered Natalie and that Rasure had accepted a payoff from Wagner. I would be surprised if Wagner ever took Rydyn seriously enough to have his attorneys put Rydyn on notice, so the way was clear for Rydyn to promote himself as the "international retributor." He hosted a Web site filled with bizarre conjecture about the deaths of various celebrities. For instance, he accused Stefanie Powers of killing William Holden. I never became involved with Rydyn's outrageous theories, and I never told Dennis about Rydyn, either.

I thought it too farfetched that Rasure compromised his investigation for horses. It seemed more logical that Rasure believed Wagner had nothing to do with Natalie's death because he misinterpreted Wagner's hangover, delirium, and remorse and believed the lies he was told.

"Rumors and innuendos," I told Kashner. Sam and I agreed, however, that many questions lingered of the hurried Wood death investigation.

Kashner mentioned, too, that a California KNBC producer had called *Vanity Fair* and wanted to get in touch with Dennis. I asked about other feedback and learned about Dr. Lyndon Taylor, who had contacted the magazine immediately after Kashner's article was published.

"Taylor was on the island that night," Kashner informed me, "and has always had an unsettled feeling about what really went down. He ate dinner at Doug's and saw the *Splendour* gang in there. He taught at USC, and his graduating dissertation was on nonverbal communication. We checked him out, and he's for real. He's an interesting fellow—so much so that I plan to meet him when I get out to California soon. He was moored near *Splendour* that night, and I gave him Dennis's number. Let Dennis know."

Kashner's agent told me the story was the most difficult he ever worked and that he wouldn't touch the Wood story again with a ten-foot pole. "Sam's article had to be rewritten four times because of legal problems," he complained. "You will have to wait for Wagner to die. Truth isn't easy to tell."

Because Rasure had been misled by an actor's tears in 1981?

I phoned the Catalina Island witness and recognized immediately that I had met a complete gentleman in Dr. Lyndon Taylor. Dr. Taylor had contacted Dennis before I had had a chance to alert Dennis to the pending call, and Dennis had been a bit rude to him. After all, Dennis didn't know him, and Dr. Taylor had come on strong, immediately asking questions about *Splendour's* layout.

Dr. Taylor had been moored on his boat, the *Catacean*, near *Splendour*—not even a football field away—and had seen the Wagner party dining at Doug's just hours before Natalie's death. His restaurant seat gave him a perfect view of the troublesome

Wagner table. He passed Wagner in the men's room and did not like what he saw in Wagner's eyes that night. A doctor of nonverbal communication, he immediately recognized the bitter anger emitting from R.J.'s glazed-over eyes. After reading Kashner's article, Dr. Taylor's perceptions had been confirmed, and he was more anxious than ever to talk with Dennis.

Dennis called to tell me about Dr. Taylor's contact, and I took his number to call and apologize for Dennis's abruptness. Dr. Taylor explained that he had waited over twenty years for the opportunity to learn more about Wood's death, so he apologized for his exuberance in finally being able to connect with Dennis.

Dr. Taylor had boated for over fifty years. He had owned and operated numerous boats, both sail and power, had constructed a sailboat, and now spent his free time aboard his forty-three-foot, high-speed power boat.

Dr. Taylor resided with his wife in Yorba Linda, California. His first trip to Catalina Island was at a mere three months old with his father. He spent a good portion of his life enjoying Catalina's beaches, and the events that took place there were important to him—*personal.*

His education included a B.A. in biological science from Whittier College in California; an M.S. from Simmons College in Boston, Massachusetts; and a Ph.D. from Claremont Graduate School in California. What inspired his dissertation on nonverbal communication was his association and work with a brilliant anthropologist interested in linguistics and paralinguistics. Taylor became fascinated with the topic. His dissertation was well received and has since been the stimulus for further studies in the area.

Dr. Taylor taught biology at high schools and community colleges and once served as vice president of Cypress College in Southern California. Currently, he was a successful businessman.

If all of that wasn't enough to learn about Dr. Taylor, I chuckled when he told me he never drinks coffee. He prefers hot chocolate. He asked me to call him Lyn.

Lyn always believed that Natalie Wood's death was anything but accidental. Because he was one of the few people who last saw Natalie alive and was within hearing distance of where her death occurred, and being an inquisitive, educated doctor and teacher, it was difficult for him to quell his curiosity.

He told me, "I have thought about her death every time I've gone to Catalina since that weekend. I knew from the start that the story released in the papers was a lie. It was too easy to see through, and I could never understand why an investigation didn't ensue. I knew that the conclusions reached by the coroner were incomplete." Here, Lyn's emotions intensified. "It was hogwash, what they expected people to believe. Total bullshit. I was there, and there's no way someone falls off a boat like *Splendour* without a huge splash. I would've heard a splash. She had to have gone into the water from the swim step, but I doubted it was while securing a dinghy. It was a quiet night. No wind. A drizzle. I didn't see *any* of those reported parties right on the beach, and I was closer to the beach than *Splendour* was."

It's bullshit, Marti, total bullshit, I recalled Dennis telling me in 1983. Two people, close to the scene, voiced the same reaction to the official report.

My friendship with Lyn grew over the next few months. In between, the KNBC reporter Sam Kashner had told me about called Dennis and Lyn Taylor. When talking with Dennis, the reporter mentioned something confusing about a movie deal. Dennis talked with him briefly before asking him to call me. *Vanity Fair* had also connected the reporter with Dr. Taylor, and Lyn told me he had talked with the reporter, too, but Lyn disliked him. There was a message on my answering machine when I arrived home from work one evening:

Hey, uh, this is a message for Marti. This is Tom Snyder at NBC. I got some news I think you're gonna be very interested in. I talked to some of the people who are involved in producing the NBC movie of the week and, uh, I told them about this, and, uh, you know what? I think they may be interested in this. I think this may be it. I talked to Dennis last night about interviewing Saturday. I want to set up a conference call, but we're gonna have to move on this. It's gonna work out real good; won't take very long...checking with you. I think it'll be a great thing for you. Okay, bye.

He left his number. I did not return his call. Another message was left the next day:

I found out some interesting information as far as what other people are gonna do with this story in the future. You're gonna wanna know this.

The media started chasing Dennis again. No matter who stirred up the Natalie mystery, no matter their status—established author, journalist, producer—it was still Dennis who drew the most interest.

I dreaded another media barrage. Reporter Tom Snyder was not the respected, famous Tom Snyder from the *Tomorrow Show* and *Late Late Show*, who had been with NBC forever. Although this Tom Snyder did not differentiate his identity as he should have—or mention the "K" before the "NBC"—I was well seasoned by now on the tricks of the media trade. I returned the lesser-known Snyder's call, and he dismissed Dr. Taylor by calling him "a kook." I already knew that Lyn Taylor was anything but a kook, so I immediately disliked Snyder. Snyder proceeded to expand on his "great news" about a "movie offer" in the works—just as Susan from *Now It Can Be Told* had had a publishing opportunity involving potential millions.

Dennis and I declined to participate, but Tom came on strong, calling daily. I was plain sick of it all. When he finally stopped calling, I left a message for Snyder, telling him I hoped he understood our reluctance, and that I wished him the best for his project. I received a return call from Snyder: a stern message in which he made it clear that if I ever called him again, he would report me for harassment and that any further contact should go through his New York attorney.

Because Snyder's segment aired in Los Angeles, I did not see it, but Lyn Taylor sent me a video tape with a written message that the show was a whitewash. Lyn wrote that Rasure defended Wagner, that they even had the location of Wagner's table at Doug's Harbor Reef wrong, and that Lana Wood waned by saying there was no mystery and that Natalie's death was an accident.

The show talked about Dennis doing a tell-all book and concluded with: "We contacted Dennis Davern for an interview, but he declined unless we could arrange an interview with producers for a possible movie."

It was a disturbing thought that many news reports are contrived by the tactics of reporters and producers the likes of Tom Snyder and Susan Levit. How relieved I was that we hadn't been taken by this latest, lying snake.

Lyn and I continued discussing Natalie Wood's final night by phone, fax, and e-mail because Lyn believed that Kashner's *Vanity Fair* article was by far the only published information about Natalie's death that made sense. Lyn asked various long-term boaters about procedure when someone is overboard or missing from a boat. Not one of their answers matched Wagner's procedure for Natalie. Lyn disagreed with the coroner's theory that neither Natalie nor the dinghy could have ended up where they were found unless Natalie had propelled the dinghy. Lyn was hell bent on proving that theory wrong. He created a diagram of the known facts involved in Natalie's case showing the suspicious information available that led to "accidental death."

I still followed news about Wagner. I read that he was suing Aaron Spelling Productions for $20 million, claiming he was cheated out of profits on the extremely successful television hit *Beverly Hills 90210*. Wagner believed he was entitled to profits from *90210* based on a ten-year-old settlement between Spelling and Fox Television under which Spelling obtained the right to produce the show in exchange for *Angels 88*—the never-produced series in which Wagner was involved.

Rumors abounded of Wagner's dislike for Lana Wood, particularly after she published her memoir of Natalie. Lana's book was extremely unbiased in recounting her sister's death, but it seemed to give Wagner an excuse to cut her out of his family's life. His family, however, included two of Lana's nieces, and Wagner refused to let her visit Natalie's daughters. Their Aunt Lana could have told Natasha and Courtney interesting anecdotes from Natalie's childhood that they would learn from no one else. Natalie's daughters may never know if they might have loved their Aunt Lana despite their father's dislike for her. They were not allowed to choose. Natalie had wanted freedom of choice for her daughters. Robert Wagner, who was fully aware of the way Natalie had been influenced in childhood, now, in essence, was guilty of the same type of control Mud, Natalie's mother, had exerted over Natalie.

In spring 2000, a *Vanity Fair* cover shoot featuring all past actresses playing Bond girls in every Bond film was broken up after an encounter between Lana Wood and Wagner's present-day wife, Jill St. John, resulted in a major argument on the set. Jill had been a Bond Girl too. Jill reportedly refused to participate if Lana Wood was involved in the *Vanity Fair* piece, and it was Jill, reportedly, who caused the problem at the shoot.

It was probably a small percentage of the public that followed this type of information, but behind the scenes, a private, and sometimes public, Wagner–Wood family feud continued to affect lives.

On July 4, 2000, my friend Mary Greco called and invited Bob and me to a barbecue at her friends Nita and Alex Clark's house in Pennsylvania. While there, conversation drifted to Kashner's recent *Vanity Fair* article. I mentioned my previous ocean "sock test." Nita, whom I barely knew, was intrigued and encouraged a sock test right then and there. So we performed a more detailed and documented test in Nita's in-ground swimming pool, in calm water. Nita happened to be a "sock person" and brought every variety of sock available to the poolside. I swam while wearing polyester, wool, cotton, and every style of sock available, from ankle to knee-highs. Every sock came off my feet within thirty seconds to two minutes of regular, easy swimming.

This test reinforced my conclusion that Natalie could not have "kicked her way [anywhere] in the ocean, or tried to mount a dinghy," as Noguchi claimed. Had Natalie clung to the dinghy and tried repeatedly to mount it, she would have been found sockless. She was not trying to mount a dinghy, which also negates Noguchi's explanation for her bruising. Natalie did not have to move her body much to stay afloat, because of the buoyancy of her down jacket—which I planned to prove next.

Chapter 32

Suzanne Finstad, an attorney, had written several books, including the bestsellers *Sleeping with the Devil* (1991) and *Child Bride: The Untold Story of Priscilla Beaulieu Presley* (1997). When she happened to see Natalie Wood's daughters on television, Suzanne was touched by them and wanted to explore Natalie's life and death.

When Suzanne called me in 1999, she wanted an accurate closing for her account of Natalie's death. She wanted to interview Dennis. We sympathized with Suzanne's frustration but offered her little information. I had worked diligently to present Dennis's story and still had confidence in my ability to do so.

Suzanne called me again on March 28, 2001. Her manuscript was completed, ready for the most accurate ending she could get. She and Lana Wood had first called Dennis, who refused to discuss details about the weekend Natalie died. Suzanne suggested that because I had gone on record with Dennis, my version of that tragic weekend would suffice for her book. Lana was on the extension, pleading with me to tell all. I considered the repercussions of telling what I knew. Disloyalty to Dennis aside, I would be revealing something that I had wanted to tell for eighteen years—but for someone else to use as a partial part of her work. I wanted the story presented a certain way—no one ever offered in their telling a hint of sympathy for Dennis's experience. Now, here was Suzanne, not long after Sam Kashner, suggesting that I would never be able to tell it.

Suzanne and Lana told me that Sam Kashner had "tricked them." Lana claimed Kashner had approached her for an article about a Bond Girl story. Lana thought Kashner's interview was for that purpose, but Sam had used her instead for his Natalie investigative piece. Suzanne said that Kashner had resorted to the same tactic with Duane Rasure, the lead detective in the Natalie case. Kashner supposedly had told Rasure he was working on a "hero detective" type story. I do not know why Suzanne and Lana thought this information mattered to me. Sam Kashner had been completely ethical with Dennis. His confidence in me gave me the courage to present what I knew on my own terms. I appreciated that Suzanne valued my input, but it was time to work alone.

I wanted to be in Kashner's and Finstad's good graces, but it seemed overly ironic that tabloids, magazines, television shows,

producers, journalists, and authors could tell about and profit from
Natalie's mysterious death, but the two people who knew the truth
and wanted to present it in depth were prevented from doing so
and were ridiculed for their efforts. Did none of them see the
double standard in their approaches to us: *Okay, Marti and
Dennis, tell us the truth, and we'll make sure you're responsible
for what you tell us, and we'll make sure it gets to the public, and
we'll make sure you get nothing for it so that you can look credible.
Hand over your years of work, now that I'm on the phone.*

Suzanne did not want all of her hard work spoiled by the
wrong conclusion. She was on an extremely tight schedule, as her
publisher was giving her only a few extra days to convince either
Dennis or me to cooperate. It was the most difficult refusal I ever
gave, but I did offer verification of a few extraneous details as our
conversation continued. I sensed Suzanne's frustration, but I could
not trust another's few paragraphs to ever offer an accurate
enough "ending."

Suzanne told me she had interviewed people at Doug's
Harbor Reef, but not Lyn Taylor. She had heard of him through
Kashner.

Lana's pleading got to me—she was at a breaking point.
Suzanne then informed me that Dennis, years ago, had
corroborated to Lana part of the Marilyn Wayne and John Payne
account—that in fact Natalie was in the water crying for help as
R.J. argued with her. She said Dennis had told Lana that R.J.
"might have" pushed Natalie into the water and that R.J. decided
to teach Natalie a lesson by not helping—taunting her when she
was in the water.

I told Suzanne and Lana that I would not, because I *could
not*, confirm that account, and I pleaded with Suzanne not to place
Dennis in that scenario if she truly wanted an accurate ending.

After our conversation, I e-mailed Lana, telling her I
sympathized and that I also hoped for closure. She replied,

Marti...

*I must tell you that I am even more puzzled, frustrated
and upset, as I am sure you know how very much I love my
sister....*
*I thought I knew what happened, and oddly enough it
gave me a modicum of closure all these years. Now I feel as though
another entirely different scenario has risen to the surface, and I
can no longer believe in anything.*

My head is spinning.... I am confused and upset (not at you or Dennis, but with life!)

At this point, I am not sure what to believe from Dennis, I am just being really honest with you. I feel like I cannot trust what he says, and I suppose this is what happened to other people speaking with him. I wish things were different, I wish my sister was still here. I dream about her, and the dreams aren't good; they are usually showing her unhappy.

Let me know if I can help you deliver the truth someday. This is the only way I will ever have any peace in my life....

If it helps at all, the public is on your side, as they don't trust R.J. and want the truth too.

This entire thing is driving me crazy.... I will try and not think about it today!

Much love to you, Lana

I replied, letting Lana know that I truly sympathized with her twenty years of frustration. I mentioned our troubles with attorneys and our fears about moving forward. I made it clear that Dennis did not recall telling her anything about knowing Natalie was in the water needing to be saved. I wondered why Lana had recently told the KNBC reporter that her sister's death was an accident yet now claimed to know differently from Dennis's phone call years ago.

I wanted to believe her statement that the public was on our side, and I appreciated Lana's encouragement.

I awaited Suzanne Finstad's book, relieved that Robert Wagner was under her scrutiny. My mission was rekindled.

Chapter 33

On May 12, 2001, Dr. Lyn Taylor went to sleep thinking about his pending "drift test," that would be conducted midweek, when fewer boats are moored at Two Harbors, to best simulate the weekend of November 29, 1981.

He would conduct more drift tests later in the year, in case currents varied from spring to autumn. He watched the weather forecast to determine when the seas and weather conditions would be similar to those of November 28, 1981.

Regarding the theory that the wind carried the dinghy and Natalie out to sea, Lyn told me the conditions for that to have happened occur only in the afternoons. Generally, in the early morning, the wind blows toward shore from the mainland to the island. In the afternoon, it shifts and blows from the island to the mainland, and by ten o'clock until about midnight, the wind dies altogether, and the prime force is the ocean current, which would have carried Natalie exactly to where she and the dinghy were found.

By midweek, the weather cooperated, and Lyn Taylor cruised to Catalina Island to begin his first drift test, which was designed to determine the likely direction of drift for a simulated body (plastic bags filled with life jackets and weights equivalent to approximately 120 lbs.) to see exactly where the "body" would end up.

He released his makeshift body from mooring can "Oscar One" at Two Harbors at Catalina Island, where *Splendour* had been moored in November 1981, at approximately the same time (just after eleven o'clock at night) as Natalie's body was believed to have entered the water. The design of this test was to track the floating object to establish the likely drift of an object that was not self-powered. By seven forty-five the next morning, Lyn's simulated body wound up exactly where Natalie's body was discovered the morning of November 29, 1981.

Lyn next would attempt a dinghy test to prove Natalie and the dinghy could have separately floated to their destinations. This test would suggest that Natalie had not "stayed with the dinghy for a good amount of time," if at all. That Natalie still was wearing socks when found already supported this idea. That the dinghy had not been found with Natalie indicated one of several possibilities. It could have been released after Natalie was in the water. Because its weight and proportions were different from a human body, it would have drifted with a heavier current.

The dinghy, *Valiant*, found hours before Natalie's body was discovered, had been used in the search. How many times the dinghy's rubber sides were "touched" by people that morning is impossible to determine, which completely eliminates the evidentiary value of the dinghy except for the state in which it was discovered—key in ignition, oars in place, engine in neutral. Scratches that were said to be visible on *Valiant's* rubber sides could easily have been incurred with normal use.

Lyn was not surprised that his test showed nothing different from what actually happened the night Natalie died.

When I asked him if Natalie would have been able to fight the current to make it to the beach—had she been clinging to the dinghy—Lyn insisted that it would not only have been easier, because of the vast difference in distance, but that the current could have helped Natalie to go in the direction of the close-by beach, or to nearby boats if she propelled herself. It would have been the logical thing to do. Lyn doubted she was ever with the dinghy. "She probably was terrified, and panicked, and drowned quickly, or the jacket's buoyancy made it difficult for her to fight drifting out to sea."

* * *

While driving to work the day after Memorial Day, and thinking about Lyn's recent drift test results and subsequent questions, a revelation hit me, a burst of complete clarity, the kind that explodes in your brain causing extraordinary despair, elation, or relief. I felt all three.

Finally, an *answer*. I had never felt more secure and in tune with my convictions. I called Dennis and Lyn Taylor the minute I arrived at my office. Dennis was unavailable, but Dr. Taylor answered my call and commended my revelation. He said, "Get hold of Dennis as soon as you can. If you're right, it blows their irresponsible official theory out the window once and for all!"

Lyn Taylor's urgency reminded me that here I was, in the middle of a marketing/advertising workday, feeling like a detective trying to solve a case. That's how Natalie's story always made me feel—as if my every action in relation to it was smothered in urgency. It would be years before I could release my findings, but still I worked on her mystery, in one capacity or another, with a sense of urgency I lived with daily. Lyn, apparently, felt the same way.

All the years I had poured over Dennis's words until I could recite them verbatim, all the restless nights I lay pondering those words scrambling around in the back of my mind trying to make sense of a senseless death, all came down to an eight-word sentence that could completely obliterate the final, standard, accepted explanation to Natalie's death. Dennis called me back within minutes and confirmed my answer. How could I have missed it all those years? How could anyone, especially detectives, have missed something so trivial yet so significant?

I tied the lines tight that night, Marti.

Just one word in that sentence could expose the preposterous explanation to the mystery of November 29, 1981: *lines*.

Dennis had said those words to me throughout the years, as far back as 1983. Now, he told me again that he had tied the dinghy lines tight. *Two of them*, at opposite sides of *Splendour's* stern, as was always the routine for securing the dinghy, when in for the night.

In television dramatizations involving the dinghy—showing the dinghy being cut loose or set free or showing Natalie retying it—a single rope attached to the dinghy is shown. When nonboaters think about Natalie securing the dinghy, they probably visualize a rope—one rope. Yet in all the discussions of and writings about this theory, the plural *lines* or *ropes* is used in reference to the dinghy being attached to the yacht.

If Natalie's purpose for being on deck near the water had anything to do with retying a noisy, disturbing dinghy, and she fell into the water while doing so, there is no way the dinghy could have floated away with her! No one securing or tightening a dinghy would—or could—untie both lines at once unless they had a natural arm span of twelve feet! To untie both lines before retying one would require extra trips across the swim step, which made absolutely no sense. Dennis now told me that the cleats the ropes are fastened to are located at the *top* of the transom (the rear wall of the stern), about twelve feet apart, and that the dinghy can be and usually is re-tied *from the deck*! Dennis, from the safety of *Splendour's* deck, had tied *two* lines after returning from Doug's Harbor Reef that night.

This was new and startling information! Wagner knows that no one has to leave the boat and step out to the swim step to secure the dinghy, but he never once mentioned that fact in all of his "ponderings" and suggested theories. Wagner seems to have purposely led everyone to believe that the dinghy had to be adjusted from the outside of the boat. It is an outrageous lie that only a few people—primarily boaters—might ever detect. But I doubted that the majority of boaters of the world spent their time trying to solve the mystery of Natalie Wood's death. Dennis had always suggested to me that R.J. had released the dinghy. I now, without a doubt, believe that he did.

Piece by piece, the official theory was falling apart. A detective with nautical experience or knowledge should have been brought in to study the circumstances surrounding Wood's death. How could authorities have not questioned the steps involved in tying/untying the dinghy, whether they were pursuing the possibility that Natalie had gotten in the dinghy to leave or that she had tried to secure it? How could they not have poured over these essential details in the wake of such a famous woman's death?

Add to this the fact that Natalie was never known to operate the dinghy alone due to a fear of water. Certainly she was capable of operating it, but Natalie was not nautically inclined. She enjoyed her yacht for socializing but had no interest in performing her skipper's tasks. When planning a dinghy ride, it is not as simple as preparing for a car ride. You do not hop in, turn the key, and cruise away. Dennis explained the process:

1.   Purge
2.   Choke
3.   Rev
4.   Untie

First, you need to prime the fuel by squeezing a rubber purge that brings gas into the fuel lines. After turning the key to start the engine, you usually have to "choke it" because there can be engine hesitation if the gas has not been primed properly, or the engine may stall if too much gas is pumped. You push a button, which is simple enough, to choke the engine, but at the same time, at just the right moment, your experience tells you when to rev up the engine, then to idle it, to get the engine running properly. Then you untie the lines securing the dinghy to the mother boat.

Furthermore, rubber boats simply don't "slam." They are somewhat like large balloons, although made of heavier rubber. The "slamming theory" makes no sense, particularly since the sea was rather calm that night with slight wind—another fact the authorities could have checked into. They might have learned about the dinghy fenders and the *two* lines.

Chapter 34

A few weeks before Suzanne Finstad's biography on Natalie Wood was to hit the book stores, I read an excerpt from *Natasha* in *People* magazine (June 11, 2001). The excerpt involved circumstances surrounding Natalie Wood's death.

I was livid. And I flipped out on Lana Wood.

I was so furious that the scenario Suzanne and Lana had discussed with me was published—the scenario that included Dennis having seen Natalie in the water while R.J. argued with her. I knew, that had Dennis been aware of Natalie's grave position, he would definitely have attempted to rescue her. Dennis had been drinking, but always insisted that he would have jumped into the ocean to try to save Natalie without hesitation, acting purely on instinct, but he hadn't known Natalie's exact whereabouts that night.

Although Dennis thought taking the dinghy was totally out of character for Natalie, he also knew that nothing had been in character that night for R.J. or Natalie, so he could only hope she was safe in the dinghy and would return soon, as Wagner suggested. Dennis suspected Wagner was lying, but he had not seen Natalie in the water, nor had he heard her.

I figured that Dennis had told Lana he knew R.J. had argued with Natalie while she begged to be saved from the ocean, because that's the only possible conclusion, but having seen or heard that scenario surely is different from suspecting it. Dennis was not an accomplice to Natalie's death. I had been the one who encouraged Dennis to phone Lana years ago. Dennis now reiterated that he had confessed to her that Natalie and R.J. had argued, but he had offered no details.

Lana told me about Cheryl Quarmyne, a receptionist where she had worked who had taken one of Dennis's calls in 1991. While waiting for Lana to get to the phone, Dennis supposedly told Quarmyne the same scenario—that he saw Natalie in the water.

It amazed me that because Dennis had once been a torn man over the death of his dear friend, and had drunk to cover the pain, he would be forever maligned as "the drunk." His heavy drinking had lasted only a few years after Natalie's death. By 1986, when Dennis had been my houseguest, his drinking was under control.

I shot off an impulsive e-mail to Lana and tore into her. I felt that because I had not cooperated with Suzanne and Lana, the published account was some sort of payback. Near tears, I wrote, "How dare this story be told? It's a blatant lie!"

Lana seemed so adamant that Dennis, in fact, had confessed the published scenario to her—and to three others—that I never felt more confused, but the Cheryl Quarmyne "back-up" would never feel right to me. I realized that Quarmyne—or someone similar—was legally "necessary" in order for Finstad to have published such incriminating information, and perhaps Dennis had chatted with Quarmyne while waiting for Lana to get to the phone. Lana's words sent my antenna into a whirlwind.

Telling the truth about Natalie's death was not about stealing thunder or scooping a story or about who could present the truth first. It was about a mother of two young girls who lay in a grave because of irresponsible drinking and fighting that led to a tragic, shocking death, and it was about an injustice that occurred because authorities failed to look closely at the circumstances of that death and failed to *interrogate* the husband of the dead, bruised-up wife. Dennis was captain, but he had a boss, and Dennis obeyed his boss. Dennis's full story may never get told unless it is twice removed, and that is why I wanted to cooperate with Suzanne, but no matter how Lana or Suzanne defended it, if Dennis had known Natalie was in the water while R.J. argued with her, that scenario, if true, made Dennis an accomplice.

And then I realized I was acting like an angry, spoiled, pompous insider and taking it out on the sister of the terribly missed woman who actually lay in a grave. No matter what Lana believed, no matter what she had heard or had not heard, and no matter what she tells or does not tell, what right did I have to argue with her about anything she might feel or believe about the three men, in her eyes, who had *let her sister die*?

I felt ashamed. Dennis had called me so many times, drunk and in agony. He very likely could have done the same with Lana and out of pure guilt had confessed more to Natalie's sister than he had released to me. I had always suspected Dennis held back. I just did not want it to be true that Dennis would not have tried to save Natalie had he known she was in grave danger. Perhaps Dennis had said something that Lana misunderstood, perhaps she had misunderstood nothing. Finstad's chapter, based on Lana's information, certainly seemed a likely scenario.

I wrote Lana a long and heartfelt apology, and it still did not feel like enough, but no matter how many words poured out of me, nothing would ever erase the guilt I felt for having chastised her for wanting nothing more than closure on her sister's death. Lana accepted my apology, and we became closer.

Then, I directed my anger more appropriately, just as Lana had suggested, but it was not toward Suzanne Finstad who had done a superb investigation into Natalie's death—but toward Robert Wagner.

I continued to learn more about Lana and Natalie through correspondence with Lana. She told me she had recently been given a long-lost autobiography that Natalie had begun writing in 1966. Natalie apparently stated—in her own handwriting—that she was such a product of make-believe she felt that she had to perpetuate the image even if it made her unhappy. She claimed that she was not completely happy in her first marriage to R.J. and that she left him then over an incident "so shattering, it destroyed the relationship."

I was sure this incident referenced the coming revelation in Suzanne's book that the Wagners' first marriage ended in divorce because Natalie had discovered R.J. in a compromising position with another man. If that were true, Natalie was quite a woman to let all the rumors and media stampede go wild at that time and to shoulder the blame that her attraction to Warren Beatty was the reason for the troubled marriage.

When I asked Lana about the New York *Current Affair* producer who had mentioned her fear of R.J. to me, Lana explained, "I can't help but fear R.J. because I now know for sure that he has prevented me from working in the only industry I love. I was told by a very important agent at ICM that I had been blackballed. And R.J. has cut me off from all the friends I thought were mine too," she revealed. "You know what else is really sad? People I work with, who are in their thirties and twenties, don't even know who Natalie is! It hurts me enormously. I just discovered, too, that for the past who knows how many years, R.J. has been telling Natasha to 'stay away from your crazy aunt!' What would be the purpose of telling a child something like that? He continues to hurt people who do not serve his purpose! I am aghast!"

"Could R.J.'s contempt be related to money?" I asked.

Lana insisted it could not be because she had never asked R.J. for money. He seemingly saw Lana the way he chose to see her because he preferred not having to deal with her unwillingness to settle for the vague explanation offered for her sister's death, and although Lana never pushed for information, R.J. feared she one day would.

Lana told me that R.J. kept telling her, in the days before Natalie was buried, that Natalie's death was an accident. R.J. pleaded with Lana to believe him. After she did believe him, he eliminated her from his life and excluded her from her nieces' lives. R.J. seemed to disregard or misinterpret Lana's true sadness over losing the one person she had loved and admired most for all of her life. Natalie had treated Lana to occasional shopping outings or lunches, but Natalie was not overly generous with Lana, either. They were sisters who had fun being together. R.J. saw Lana as a taker, but Natalie saw Lana as one of few people on earth she could truly trust, and Natalie understood how she, too, had been at fault for enabling her entire family. After having the kind of security Natalie provided to her birth family, it is quite devastating to lose it, even though Lana had never intended to "live off" her famous sister. If certain advantages in the show business industry could derive from Natalie and R.J., Lana did not mind the favor, but Lana had never been financially supported in adulthood by Natalie. Natalie and R.J. had never been Lana's keepers.

Lana struggles financially. She preferred to work in an industry she was certain Wagner now helped to ban her from. George Kirvey had told Dennis he would be banned from that same industry if he did not do as Wagner wished. Could Wagner truly wield such influence?

Lana told me, "I don't know if anyone will ever know exactly how I feel, but my entire life has been agony. My entire life's savings was eaten away taking care of my mom for the five years she had Alzheimer's, as I couldn't work for taking care of her. It has only been a couple of years since she passed away, and once again, the small amount of money I had saved went to my daughter's doctor bills for her cancer treatments...the stuff insurance wouldn't cover. We live from paycheck to paycheck. I work at Barney's Outlet selling clothing! I have hope for the future, but I feel as though my life has been destroyed, and I just want a quiet corner. Natalie won't rest, and I will be in a constant state of turmoil until she can."

Lana agreed that Natalie could have been aware of her actions that fateful weekend, and how R.J. might respond to them. Although Dennis said Natalie had flirted with Walken, he also clarified it with statements suggesting that Natalie was a gracious hostess to *all* guests who came aboard *Splendour*.

Lana remembered Thanksgiving night, 1981, all too well. "I remember the entire holiday as strange," she claims, "and

Natalie was forcing merriment. R.J. was rather sullen, and the kids, well, specifically Natasha, was literally begging Natalie not to go away on *Splendour* the next day. But Natalie was unmoved and determined that Natasha go to her friends and Nat was to go on the boat. I remember pouring and very insistent rain. It was a real stinker. It was not a pleasant Thanksgiving, and just for the record, Natalie did not ask our mother to go on the boat. My mom would tell this to people later, but it was a fabrication on her part. Probably some unconscious wish."

Lana, I highly suspected, had a lot of her sister in her too. She is a survivor. She was approaching her breaking point and told me, "R.J.'s just afraid of me, as he knows someday he will have to answer to me for what happened. I wish I had my sister back."

Chapter 35

Suzanne Finstad's book, *Natasha*, was published in June 2001 and brought out the media again. This time, *Inside Edition* was interested in doing an interview with Dennis and me because the show had located *Splendour* with its new owner in Hawaii. *Inside Edition* producer, Josh Paris, informed me that the Sea Scouts had sold *Splendour* to a nice family in California who named her the *Graceful Lady* in honor of Natalie. When the family sold *Splendour* to its current owner in Hawaii, she was renamed *Splendour*, again in honor of Natalie. Dennis was glad to learn she had "sold with dignity" and was finally able to say his goodbye to *Splendour* with pride that her overall décor and layout had never been changed.

Josh Paris was extremely helpful to me and offered contact information for Marilyn Wayne. He told me he had gone to Rasure's ranch and interviewed him. He liked Rasure and believed Rasure truly felt bad about Natalie's death. He said Rasure's wife was one of Natalie's biggest fans. He confessed that Rasure showed him a picture of Natalie's body. I asked why, and he surmised that Rasure felt a need to show graphic evidence of how horrible a death it had been and to show that if he had had something to go on, he never would have let the case go.

Dennis and I decided not to interview with *Inside Edition*, but Josh gave me Rasure's number; however, I was too timid to call. I did, however, contact Marilyn Wayne, even though authorities had always dismissed her claims, and Josh Paris had told me she might be reluctant to talk.

Apprehensively, on July 29, 2001, I dialed Marilyn's number. After a touch of awkwardness while explaining my identity and mission, I was surprised to hear Marilyn say that just a few nights before, she had been thinking about the Natalie Wood story and decided that she *needs* to continue talking about it. She was willing to cooperate with me fully. "Apparently," she said, "Finstad's book didn't help the case, and this case needs to be reopened."

Marilyn explained that Finstad's interview with her had been her only opportunity to offer her complete account. "The day Finstad's book was available in bookstores, I went to a private party that night," she said, "and when someone walked in with a copy of *Natasha*, a bunch of us ran to the bedroom, opened to the end of the book, and looked for information about the night

Natalie died. It's what people want and deserve to know." Then, without prompting, she determinedly offered, "I believe Wagner knows what happened to her, but I still keep an open mind about Dennis. Please get this story out there!"

"Dennis witnessed what led up to her death," I told her, "but he didn't see Natalie in the water, as Suzanne reports."

"Well, I've changed my mind about keeping quiet because I'm *also* one of the witnesses. I have no doubt that it was Natalie I heard crying for help, but authorities could care less. How can they just not care?" she asked, her voice wavering, and I pictured her eyes swelling with frustrating tears.

This was only two minutes into our conversation. Although I could not answer Marilyn's question, I poured much of my same frustration into the receiver. Then I listened to Marilyn's account.

She and her fiancé, businessman John Payne, were sleeping in their stateroom aboard John's forty-two-foot sailboat, the *Capricorn*, which was equipped with a silent generator. John always slept with an open window in his cabin, and this night, despite the rain, was no exception. A distant voice, crying for help, awakened him. John sat up to listen intently. "Help me, someone please help me," he heard again. He awakened Marilyn and asked her to listen. Alarmed, Marilyn called out to her young son, Anthony, who also heard the cries. He wore a digital watch, and Marilyn asked him for the time. It was just minutes after eleven o'clock.

The cries for help continued. John went to the control panel and switched on their beam light. Marilyn went on deck to look toward the sound, but it was dark and damp, and she could not see anything. Marilyn had a bead on the plaintive cry for help, though, and thought if she swam just about forty feet, she might be able to help. Marilyn, an avid and strong swimmer, told John she wanted to jump into the water and swim toward the cries, but John convinced her it could be too dangerous. "You have Anthony to think of. Whoever's out there could pull you under too." He persuaded her to stay on board. They called the harbor patrol but no one answered. They called the sheriff's office in Avalon, twelve miles away, and the person who answered told them a helicopter would be sent. They heard loud music, too, so they thought there was a party on a nearby boat.

Then they heard a man's voice, slurred, and in an aggravated tone, say something to the effect of "Oh, hold on, we're coming to get you." Marilyn was not sure of the exact words used, but there was no mistaking that it was a man's voice, and he sounded miserable.

But the woman's cries continued: "Someone please help me, I'm drowning, please help me." The voice did not seem to be moving further away. It was clear and concise.

For fifteen minutes, John and Marilyn felt helpless as they waited for a helicopter that never arrived. Their dinghy had already been deflated for the night and would take more than a half hour to prepare, so they were at a loss to help. After a fifteen to twenty minute wait, the cries for help ended. A few minutes later, the music ended too. There was utter silence—a haunting kind of silence. Terribly disturbed, John and Marilyn could only hope that the pleas had stopped because of a rescue. They went back to their stateroom for a terribly restless sleep.

Marilyn was up by five the next morning and went right out to the deck, afraid of what she might see in the water. To her relief, only the ocean flowed between the *Capricorn* and the boat moored closest to it—*Splendour*. She jotted down *Splendour*'s name, as that was the exact area from which the cries had originated. *Splendour* was moored about seventy to eighty feet away, starboard, facing in the same direction as the *Capricorn*, toward the island, no more than a five-minute swim to the shoreline. Marilyn calculated that the cries came from no more than ten to thirty feet from *Splendour*. Whoever had cried for help did so from between the two boats.

About a half hour later, Marilyn noticed a police boat near *Splendour*. At this time, the harbormaster's employee—a teenage boy—arrived at the *Capricorn* to collect the mooring fee. The police boat lingered at *Splendour*, so Marilyn asked the young rent collector, "What's going on over on that boat?" He answered, "Maybe you should mind your own business!"

"Keep it low key" obviously had generated its way through the island. Had the rent collector answered that Natalie Wood was missing, Marilyn probably would have been able to immediately offer solid information to the authorities.

When John and Marilyn arrived back at Newport Beach a couple of hours later and learned that Natalie Wood's body had been found, they felt sickened by the news and had no doubt that it had been Natalie crying for help.

Marilyn had always wanted to believe that Natalie's death was an accident, and she always felt sorry for Wagner. But then things started to change. The police never interviewed her or John, although they claimed to have done so. Marilyn never reported anything to the authorities. She talked at work about the experience, and someone from the *L.A. Times* called to interview her. She became more known when she placed a call to Noguchi after he published his official theory. She simply wanted to correct him on his "timeline," which she knew was off. Noguchi talked with her and would later revolve his "clinging to the dinghy" theory around both Marilyn Wayne's account and Wagner's December statement about the "banging dinghy." Authorities were fully aware of Marilyn Wayne's account, yet they ignored her. When investigating a death—especially under the bizarre circumstances surrounding Wood's death—should not the authorities have jumped at the opportunity to talk with anyone who might shed light on the case?

But there was no "case."

Detective Rasure was reported to have said that Marilyn Wayne was just someone who wanted her name in the papers—to be connected to a celebrity's legend. Marilyn, like Dennis, had been bombarded with requests for interviews, but she never talked to anyone again until Suzanne Finstad contacted her while researching information for her book, *Natasha*.

Marilyn Wayne was a commodities/stock broker in November 1981, and she worked in the same firm as Red Reeder, who was Robert Wagner's broker at the time. She saw Red Reeder on an almost daily basis. They had "client boxes'" at work that were designed for clients to drop off their messages through a slot in the front. The boxes were opened in the back, labeled by broker name on each end. Three days after Natalie died, Marilyn found a scribbled message on a torn piece of paper in her box that read, "If you value your life, keep quiet about what you know." She immediately knew it was related to Natalie Wood's death because that's all anyone had been talking about. She suddenly became pretty vocal about letting everyone know she believed Natalie's death to be accidental.

Marilyn Wayne was afraid.

When threats continued, she contacted her attorney to let him know about it and went so far as to make provisions in the event something might happen to her. John Payne did not experience any of that same kind of trouble, but John was a highly respected businessman, far wealthier than Robert Wagner. No one would bother John because of his status. Marilyn suspected she was targeted because she was the more vulnerable of the two.

Then, a few weeks after Natalie died, Marilyn and John had dinner at a Beverly Hills restaurant, and in walked Robert Wagner with his mother. Oddly, the maitre d' asked Marilyn and John if they were uncomfortable and wanted to move to another table. They declined, saying they were fine. Wagner looked over and saw them. They wondered if they should approach Wagner to offer condolences but decided that might be an intrusion. They thought Wagner would have wanted to approach *them* to ask, "What happened that night? What do you know?" They believed at that time that Wagner was totally innocent. They knew Wagner in passing, from around the docks and clubs. They were stunned that Wagner said nothing to them—not then, not ever. That was when their own suspicions about Wagner started. They asked themselves: Why wouldn't a loving husband want to ask a question of the people who possibly last heard his wife's voice? Why wouldn't he have wanted to thank them for their concern? Something was far too odd for Marilyn's better senses.

"It wasn't until Sam Kashner's article," Marilyn said, "that John Payne was brought into it. After reading Suzanne's book, I've called Wagner a liar and a son of a bitch, and I don't believe anything he says."

Marilyn said she thinks the biggest disgrace is the way the authorities handled the case, and she wouldn't doubt there was a far deeper cover-up than with Detective Rasure. She also said that she would fear for her life if she were in my shoes, knowing what I know.

"I have no agenda, Marti, and you can use anything I've just told you," she said. "Call me anytime with questions, and I am also willing to take a lie detector test to help substantiate anything I've said. I have no doubt I would pass it." Then, she added, "There's no way Wagner would ever agree to a polygraph. But, if I take one and Dennis takes one—well, that would show who's willing to back up their claims. If Wagner wanted the world to know he'd done nothing wrong, he should try to prove it too. He doesn't need to ask questions because he already knows what happened!"

I called Marilyn again on August 15, 2001, to reconfirm it was only one man's voice she had heard answering the cries for help. She confirmed it was one voice, a miserable one, saying, "Hold on, we're coming to get you." She said the word "we're" may have thrown her off and contributed to her assumption that it might have been a party. She said she always wondered how

Natalie's socks had remained on her feet, and she explained that the buoyancy of the West and East coast water is different. The salt in the Pacific offers more buoyancy, which requires less movement when treading or floating water.

I mentioned Rasure's question in *The Final Day* documentary about why Marilyn and John had not used their dinghy to help. "We had deflated it before going to bed," she explained. "We were planning an early departure the next morning, so we packed up everything before going to bed. There was no time to use it."

Marilyn no longer connected those cries for help she had heard the night of November 28, 1981, with an anonymous person. I asked, "After learning that Natalie had drowned, did you mentally compare the sound of the woman's voice to the sound of Natalie's voice?"

"Yes. I heard *Natalie's* voice that night crying for help. I'm *sure* of it."

"And Rasure wasn't interested in this information?"

"I never heard from Rasure or any investigator, and I called several times to officially report my account. We started hearing the cries at exactly 11:05. Rasure closed this case way too fast. Something was very wrong about this case from day one, and I won't keep quiet about that any longer."

Then I asked Marilyn to tell me a little more about herself. She impressed me as a vibrant, conscientious person, and I was curious about her. She told me she was an avid swimmer and truly regretted not diving into the water that night. She used to be an actress and had met Natalie when she was eighteen. Nick Adams, Sal Mineo, and Elvis were once her friends.

"But that was a short period in my life," she claimed. "I became interested in business and have had a successful career. John Payne and I never married, but we're friends to this day. He would vouch for me on everything I've told you."

After talking with Marilyn, I realized how much the conversations reminded me of talking with Dennis. The conviction in her voice left no doubt in my mind that I had talked to another witness to the death of Natalie—an honest one who had also received threats because of her connection with the death.

Her timeframe matched every single piece of Dennis's account. It was just after ten-thirty when Wagner had smashed the wine bottle. Natalie had gone to her room. Wagner shortly followed. The arguing started immediately; they moved out to the deck by eleven o'clock and then Dennis put on the music—right about the time John and Marilyn heard music and confused the music with a possible party nearby—also the exact time Dennis would not have heard cries for help because he was near the music and fifteen feet above the water.

Marilyn claimed those cries lasted for fifteen to twenty minutes.

Chapter 36

I ordered Natalie's autopsy report and acquired the police report. The Anatomical Summary on the first page of the autopsy read:

1. Drowning.
2. Superficial skin bruises on the extremities and abrasions
*   on the left side of the face.*

I was shocked to see the many bruises on her legs and arms, as indicated on the autopsy's body diagrams. The second page of the report summarized the external and internal examination of the body, revealing the body as a "well-developed and well-nourished Caucasian female appearing to be about the stated age of 43 years old, weighing approximately 120 pounds, and measuring approximately 64 inches in height, showing a moderate generalized rigor mortis. The hair is brown and long. The eyes are brown. The nostrils and mouth show white froth."

The report records Natalie's old surgical scar on the lower midline of the abdominal wall and her well-known wrist deformity, but it records that "the right forearm shows a diffuse recent bruise over the lateral aspect measuring approximately 4 inches × 1 inch area above the wrist." The report mentions a fresh bruise near her deformed wrist: "a slight superficial fresh bruise is noted in this area measuring approximately ½ inch in diameter." The report states: "There are numerous small superficial skin bruises over the right and left lower legs measuring approximately ½ inch to 1 inch in diameter. They appear to be relatively fresh. The left knee area shows a recent bruise measuring approximately 2 inches in diameter. The right ankle area shows a recent bruise measuring approximately 2 inches in diameter. There are superficial bruises on the posterior aspect of the lower legs. They are small, superficial and measuring approximately ½ inch to 2 inches in diameter. There is no particular pattern." No contusion or hemorrhage was noted internally. No fractures were noted.

Natalie's body had far too many bruises and scratches in too many places—the autopsy diagrams showed more than twenty-five bruises on the fronts and backs of her arms and legs—to be explained by a fall off of a boat into *water*.

The body showed only mild arteriosclerosis (hardening of the arteries). The respiratory system showed the larynx, trachea, and bronchi were filled "with a large amount of white froth. The lungs are voluminous and heavy. The surface of the lungs are smooth with a few petechial hemorrhages. The sections of the lungs show abundant amount of watery fluid with froth."

The liver was noted as about normal in size, noted as grossly normal, with no cirrhosis or "fatty change." The spleen, stomach, adrenal glands, thyroid, and kidneys showed nothing abnormal.

Natalie Wood was a healthy woman. Only the bruises weren't normal.

The autopsy report noted Natalie's clothing:

The body was clad with a wet flannel type gown and wool socks. No underwear was on the body. One (1) red down jacket is accompanied with the body but it was not on the body. The examination of the clothing revealed no tear or blood. They are all wet.

Nail scrapings and nail clippings were not collected. "Sexual Assault Evidence Collection" was completed.

The report noted under "Historical sections":

Representative sections are taken for the hold jar and sections from the bruised area of the extremities are taken for the microscopic examination.

The report was signed by Joseph H. Choi, M.D., Deputy Medical Examiner; Thomas T. Noguchi, M.D., Chief Medical Examiner-Coroner; and Ronald N. Kornblum, M.D., Deputy Medical Examiner. It was dated December 4, 1981.

A report by investigator Pamela Eaker, dated November 29, 1981, was written at the scene where the body was brought ashore.

Eaker's report states that Wagner called for help immediately. How this kind of information can become documented, be treated as irrefutable, and go uncorrected is astounding. Wagner waited two hours to call for local help, then another two hours to call for official help. Yet Eaker's report reads as if every private searcher and official team were in on the search all together at the same time, from the moment Wagner noticed Natalie missing.

Numerous bruises were noted in Eaker's report, and if Eaker had observed similar bruising on a child, she would have been legally bound to report suspected abuse. Yet Robert Wagner and Christopher Walken were offered the private, official helicopter to leave the island. No one had a clue how Natalie's bruises could have occurred, yet every effort was made to look for the least culpable way she could have received them.

Deputy R. W. Kroll of the Avalon Sheriff's Department visited *Splendour* after an official report of Natalie's disappearance was announced. Kroll wrote in his report on Sunday, November 29, at 6:30 a.m.: "I observed pieces of a broken wine bottle laying on the deck carpeting of the main salon. I also observed partially eaten food, empty wine bottles, and clothing scattered about the cabin." (The mentioned cabin in Kroll's report refers to R.J.'s and Natalie's stateroom.)

As for what Wagner, Walken, and Davern officially told Rasure, there was a vague timeframe available from their statements, and Rasure, as his reports indicated, asked nothing that could pinpoint the time Natalie went missing. Wagner had told Rasure that Natalie went to bed and disappeared not long afterwards. Walken admitted a "beef" with Wagner, said he went on deck for a few minutes, talked to Wagner, then not much later heard the captain say the dinghy was missing. Davern told Rasure in his first interview that Natalie had gone to bed and shortly afterwards he noticed the dinghy gone. Sheriff's reports also included a "phone-call" witness to trouble. A fellow Doug's restaurant customer, Warren Archer, who spoke with and exchanged bottles of champagne with the Wagner's party at Doug's, had called the *Splendour* from his boat, *Vantage*, to invite the Wagners for a nightcap shortly after eleven o'clock. Archer told investigators that while Robert Wagner refused his invitation, Archer heard background noise that led him to believe R.J. and Natalie "were arguing or fighting."

I asked Dennis about Archer. Dennis does not remember the call and said it would have come through the boat's radio. I told Dennis that Archer's account confirms Dennis's account of an argument, but Dennis said he doesn't know how Archer could have talked with Wagner while Wagner was arguing with Natalie. Wagner would have needed to take such a call in the wheelhouse.

Walken's statement appears that he was aware of Natalie's disappearance before he had gone to sleep, although Davern was not aware of Walken's presence from the time of the bottle smashing through the morning discovery. With all of the confusing information available, along with Archer's suggestion of a marital dispute, you would think Rasure would have pushed for more specific timing and details. You would think—but he didn't. He was satisfied. Thousands of Wood fans were not. Marilyn Wayne and dozens of other participants were dazed by the official close of the case.

Dr. Lyn Taylor was a longtime friend of harbormaster Doug Oudin, and offered to interview Doug for me. I did not have the advantage of giving up my home and work responsibilities to conduct an onsite investigation into Wood's death. With Davern as my source, I never saw the need. I believed Dennis, but believing and proving are two different things. I was grateful for outside help.

Oudin recalled Natalie's bruises—everyone who saw the bruises recalls how numerous they were. Doug Oudin had seen how drunk Wagner was, so why hadn't Rasure recognized Wagner's inebriation?

With a little Internet research, I learned about characteristic domestic violence injuries. Quite common are "bilateral injuries"—injuries involving both sides of the body, usually the arms and legs—which is exactly where most of Natalie's bruises were located. As reported in Natalie's autopsy, there was no particular pattern to her bruises. There is usually no particular pattern to a husband and wife going at each other, either. If Natalie had managed to get one of her legs up far enough to straddle the dinghy rail (the only part of the dinghy that could cause bruises), and the wet jacket's weight, out of water, did pull her back down, we would expect to see significant elongated bruising on the inside of the straddling leg, caused by her leg hitting the rail and sliding back off. If she attempted to hoist her upper body first into the dinghy, the bruises on the fronts of her legs, which are primarily from the kneecap down, could only have occurred as her torso slid safely into the dinghy, dragging her shins across the dinghy rail. That would not explain the bruising on the backs of her legs—but at least she would be alive to tell us how they got there. There is no way the bruises on Natalie's legs could have come from "trying to mount the dinghy" without her having landed safely inside it. Even if she had hit her legs on *Splendour*'s swim step, there would not have been the many small "circular" bruises, as shown on the autopsy sketches—and the bruises would have been either on the fronts or on the backs of her legs, not on both.

The bruises had Lyn Taylor thinking hard. The four-inch bruise on Natalie's left wrist was particularly consistent with striking someone or being held tightly by the wrist. Lots of people, including Rasure, claim that a person gets bruised up while boating, but Natalie had far too many bruises in far too many areas of her body to be explained by recreational boating. Of the twenty-five bruises sketched on the autopsy diagram, twenty-two of them were labeled "fresh" or "recent." Dr. Taylor was particularly interested in the small circular bruises: he noticed a pattern in them that looked as if someone had grabbed or held onto Natalie's legs. The autopsy also noted "sharp scratches" at Natalie's ankles. Lyn thought about fingernails, a watch, or a ring that could cause scratching. He could think of nothing else. *Splendour*'s smooth surfaces would not have caused sharp scratches.

The facial abrasions, which ran vertically on Natalie's left cheek and on her left forehead between her eyebrow and hair line, also caught Lyn's attention. He told me a story that could perhaps explain the abrasions, which could only have resulted from some surface scraping in an upward or downward motion against her face. Nothing in the water could have abraded Natalie's face in such a way, nor did Noguchi's suggestion that she tried to climb into the dinghy explain it. Lyn said that when he prepared to wash the deck and hull of his boat, he inadvertently kicked over the bucket of soapy water and slipped on this slick mixture and fell to the deck. Landing on one knee, he immediately felt pain and saw that he had skinned his knee on the "nonskid" that coated the deck. Nonskid is a mixture of paint and coarsely ground walnut shells or sand that creates a texture similar to coarse sandpaper to prevent boaters from slipping on a wet deck. As the paint wears, the nonskid becomes less effective, and the deck becomes smoother. This means that the painting process with the sand or walnut shell additive must be repeated to renew the surface. On newer fiberglass boats, this rough surface is molded into the fiberglass itself.

I asked Dennis when nonskid was last applied to the back deck of *Splendour*: he had applied it just weeks before the Thanksgiving outing.

In Lyn's mind, he envisioned a reluctant Natalie, kicking and screaming—or a semiconscious Natalie being pulled along the back deck by the ankles. Dennis had heard screaming while R.J. and Natalie fought on the deck.

Lyn was now convinced that had they checked Natalie's abrasion for particles, they would have discovered traces of nonskid even though she had been in the ocean for up to seven hours. But it was way too late for tests like that.

Lyn could only speculate, but his speculation made more sense than the speculative answers that had come from authorities. His conclusions were so enlightening that it prompted two more "evidence tests," as he called them.

He attempted to mount a dinghy similar to the Zodiac dinghy the Wagner's had owned. It was difficult for Lyn to hoist his legs to the top of the dinghy, and when he did, it still did not cause any bruising, as his legs could not even get into the position Natalie's legs would had to have been in given the pattern of her bruising. The dinghies are made of inflatable rubber, with few hard surfaces that can cause bruises. After ten attempts, Lyn finally hoisted himself into a position that could cause leg bruising, but it was also a position that left it impossible to not end up in the dinghy!

His next test required help. Lyn drew marks on the legs of a model following the sketches included in Natalie's autopsy. When placing his hands over the marked "bruises," his fingertips aligned with the bruises as indicated on Natalie's autopsy report. Other bruises, according to Dr. Taylor, appeared to come from a physical altercation such as a fighting couple may have, hitting back and forth at one another.

Lyn asked me if I knew whether Wagner had been checked for bruises. I was sure that Dennis had not been checked and was virtually sure Wagner had not been either. Checking for bruises on Wagner, Walken, and Davern should have been the authorities' number one priority. Instead, they summoned a helicopter to take Wagner and Walken from the disturbing scene.

Chapter 37

I purchased a down jacket and a flannel nightgown.

I had planned to attempt the down jacket test in the Delaware River, where I had once almost drowned, but became too frightened of dangerous currents, and I was deathly afraid to test the ocean, even though I would have been attached to a safety rope with an experienced boater, Bob Hall, to assist me. I decided on a swimming pool, where I could tiptoe to safety if necessary.

On September 27, 2001, a cool Northeast night, equivalent to the temperature near Catalina Island the night of Natalie's death, with water temperature a bit less than 60 degrees, I was ready to see if I would float while wearing a down jacket. First, over a three-hour period, I drank six glasses of wine.

I donned my down jacket with sleeves (irrelevant, I know, but the jacket happened to be red). I jumped into the water, and the jacket immediately kept me at the surface. For over half an hour, I tried everything in my power, even dunking my head to try to swim underwater. Eleven-year-old Erik Holtz joined me in the pool as his parents, Rita Vermeer and John Tonnessen, videotaped the test. Erik created waves and whirlpools. Still, my head stayed completely above water.

To duplicate Natalie Wood's entire outfit the night she died, I also wore a flannel nightgown and socks for this experiment. The socks remained on my feet while I floated, and the buoyancy of the jacket held my upper body in such a position that my legs were drawn up almost in a sitting position. Kicking my legs in this position was difficult and ineffective; it was less difficult, although not easy, to propel myself with my arms.

After exiting the swimming pool, I took off the jacket and weighed it: it weighed just about fifteen pounds! In the water, the jacket served as a flotation device, and I had no problem pulling myself out of the pool while wearing the jacket (I did not use the ladder). Its saturated weight did not affect my movement until I was completely out of the water and standing, and then its weight was only mildly burdensome.

To test the effects of hypothermia, still wet and cold, I put the wet down jacket on and jumped back into the pool. Although I felt drunk from the wine, the cold water sobered me somewhat. I intended to stay in the water for another half hour to test how my motor reactions could withstand the environment.

Within twenty minutes, my sight became foggy and objects appeared distorted. I lost the desire to talk. Forty-five minutes into the test, trees, fences, people, and the nearby house seemed surrounded by a hazy glow. I reached what is known as tunnel vision. I could barely see the shape of the house that was about eighty feet away, and the people standing on the pool deck appeared as stick shadows with a glow surrounding them.

This is hypothermia. Your internal temperature decreases, and without treatment, this drop in core body temperature leads to stupor, collapse, and death. Feeling numb, I was helped out of the pool. I felt ill for over twenty-four hours after this test.

As reported, wine may have distorted Natalie's obvious choices, yet it is more likely that Natalie kept the jacket on because she recognized it was her life preserver. However, Natalie was prone to the strong ocean currents that could have pulled her out to sea further, just as Lyn Taylor's drift tests proved. Her alcohol level (reported to have been approximately 0.14) was not high enough to have rendered her insensible. Fear and hypothermia probably overcame Natalie.

It was because of Natalie's down jacket that her body had been discovered so quickly after a full search was called. It kept her afloat even after she died. Had she not been wearing the jacket, she may have sunk and not been found for days, weeks, or ever: the cove is known to be shark infested.

My test proves that there was an immediate window of time to search for and possibly find Natalie Wood alive. The down jacket would have also insulated her, trapping heat and prolonging the effects of hypothermia. Yet it took over four hours to *convince* Robert Wagner to call in the Coast Guard. Seven other men, including Dennis Davern, knew that Natalie was missing, yet none of them had the courage to override Wagner's order to "keep it low key." Even the harbormaster deferred to Wagner.

I learned that saltwater drowning is known to be painful. According to my research, saltwater drowning takes five to thirty minutes, while freshwater drowning takes five to twenty minutes. The difference is because a body does not respond the same to every liquid that fills the lungs.

In freshwater, the water filling a person's lungs can enter the bloodstream quickly, causing blood cells to swell and burst. Also, the fluid filling the person's lungs prevents the body from taking in enough air, which leads to cardiac arrest (when the heart stops because it lacks enough oxygen). The only good thing to say about drowning in freshwater is that the drowned person is more than likely unconscious by the time the heart stops.

In saltwater, drowning is a different story. The lungs fill with saltwater, which draws blood out of the bloodstream and into the lungs. This liquid buildup in the air sacs stops oxygen from reaching the blood and causes death. In other words, in saltwater, you basically drown in your own fluids, and it is usually more painful. It is not just lack of oxygen that causes drowning. Saltwater has higher concentrations of dissolved substances than blood and body tissues, so it is unlikely to enter the circulation. This means water is more likely to move from the capillaries of the lungs into the air spaces containing the saltwater (due to what is called osmosis), and the drowning victim feels this happening.

In one respect, however, saltwater drowning is less painful because seas and oceans tend to be cooler than freshwater, so victims are more likely to develop hypothermia, which causes drowsiness and confusion, thus less awareness of the watery end awaiting them.

If water enters the airways of a conscious victim, the victim will try to cough up the water or swallow it, thus inhaling more water involuntarily. Upon water entering the airways, both conscious and unconscious victims experience laryngospasm; that is, the larynx or the vocal cords in the throat constrict and seal the air tube. This prevents water from entering the lungs. Because of this laryngospasm, water enters the stomach in the initial phase of drowning, and very little water enters the lungs. In most victims, the laryngospasm relaxes some time after unconsciousness and water can enter the lungs, causing a wet drowning. However, about 10 to 15 percent of victims maintain this seal until cardiac arrest; this is called dry drowning, because no water enters the lungs.

In forensic pathology, water in the lungs indicates that the victim was still alive at the point of submersion; the absence of water in the lungs may indicate either a dry drowning or a death before submersion.

Natalie had water in her lungs.

A continued lack of oxygen in the brain, hypoxia, will quickly render a victim unconscious. An unconscious victim rescued with an airway still sealed from laryngospasm stands a good chance of a full recovery.

Cardiac arrest used to be considered the point of death, but at this point, there is still a chance of recovery. The brain will die after approximately six minutes without oxygen, but special conditions (such as cold-water drowning) may prolong this time. After death, rigor mortis sets in and remains for about two days, depending on many factors, including water temperature.

At the active part of drowning, victims will stop calling for help simply because they lack the air to do so. When Natalie stopped calling for help, either she was actively drowning or was being carried by a current to a point where her cries for help were no longer heard. Since it is necessary to breathe to yell, human physiology will not allow the body to waste any air when it is starving for it.

Natalie was not actively drowning when Marilyn Wayne heard her calls.

There can be splashing involved during drowning, but because Natalie was wearing her buoyant jacket, she probably did not drown underwater—hers was most likely a surface drowning. Astonishingly, this was not recognized or announced by anyone on the medical examiner's staff because they assumed her jacket weighed her down.

Factors used in determining the length of time a body has been submerged include maceration of the skin, cooling of the body, rigor mortis, livor mortis, water temperature, clothing, and decomposition.

The cooling rate in drowning victims depends upon water temperature and movement. Rapid cooling retards development of postmortem changes. A naked body submerged in cold water can cool twice as fast as a body on land. Waters with heavy current accelerate cooling. Thus, submersion in cold water will retard the rate of rigor mortis. The body usually floats face down, buttocks up, and extremities dangling in a downward fashion—just as Natalie was found. Due to absorption of water into the skin, the color ranges from blue-red to pink.

Natalie was discovered before decomposition began, but when a submerged body has been brought ashore, decomposition will proceed at an accelerated rate. Even after just a few hours, the appearance of the body may be completely changed. The body should be examined as soon as possible after the body is brought ashore.

A froth cone is produced when mucous, air, and water mix during respirations. Therefore, if a froth cone is present in the victim's airway, this indicates consciousness at the time of submersion. A froth cone may be present about the nose and/or mouth of the drowning victim, as was the case with Natalie.

As for drowning while under the influence of alcohol, intoxication causes vasodilation of skin and causes a rise in the skin temperature. A strong reaction occurs when the person enters the cold water. The person undergoes very rapid skin cooling, which may cause him or her to inhale water or suffer sudden cardiovascular collapse.

Because of the condition of Natalie's lungs, indicating she had by legal definition drowned, and because the coroner decided the drowning must have been "accidental," the cause of her entry into the water was neglected. There was no way to know it her death was accidental, and in view of all her bruises, "undetermined" was the only logical choice.

But we had a chief coroner being chased by celebrity.

Chapter 38

It was time to contact the investigating detective on the Natalie Wood case, Duane Rasure. I dialed his number expecting an answering machine and/or uncooperativeness. I received neither. Rasure offered all the time I needed. "I'm retired," he said.

"I hope happily," I answered.

He was. I asked him to tell me about himself and the case.

Detective Rasure does not have a Texan drawl, but he does own and alternate two Texan hats: a straw cowboy hat and a black cowboy hat. On his ranch, he usually wears the straw hat. He also wears a belt with an engraved number 187 on the buckle—the California penal code for murder. Detective Rasure despises murderers.

Catalina played a big part in Duane Rasure's life since childhood. He used to dive for coins when the steamships pulled in, and his many other happy memories of the beautiful island *were* tainted by having been called in to handle the Wood death case there.

He keeps in touch with his retired friends from the department. He had worked as a homicide detective for the Los Angeles County Sheriff's Department and had solved many crucial crimes. His jurisdiction included Catalina Island. His longtime partner had just been promoted when Duane was called to investigate the Wood drowning. Roy Hamilton went with him, but according to Rasure, 90 percent of the workload was left on him. He had "little help or cooperation."

Pam Eaker had been first on the scene and had talked to Wagner, Walken, and Dennis, and via her report and information that had been gathered by first responders, Rasure learned that a helicopter pilot first spotted Natalie, that Davern had spent Friday night with Natalie in Avalon, and that Wagner and Walken were already on their way to the mainland by helicopter. Rasure rushed to the mainland heliport drop to catch Walken and Wagner. He was waiting for them as the exited the helicopter, and he led them into the captain's office there.

"Wagner was really hurting. I had heard that Natalie had fallen overboard and drowned, so I had no reason to suspect anything else. When Wagner got off the helicopter, I was about fifty feet away, and I could see that he could barely pull himself upright to walk. He was shook up, *really* in bad shape. He got a cup of coffee, and I asked only a few questions, thinking I could get back to him. He wanted to get home, and I wanted to get to the island. It just worked out that way. He said she was gone, he didn't know how. He cried. I did what any decent person would do."

"Mr. Rasure," I said, and he interrupted to suggest I call him Duane, as I was mispronouncing his last name anyhow. "Duane, you might think I'm your biggest opposition, but I'm not. Some people claim you were on the take and received Arabian horses plus cash to close the case quickly. I don't think that. I know you were a good detective, and I know you were stifled. From what I've learned, including from one of the principles involved, you've had every reason to stand by your initial call."

Rasure remained silent.

"Wagner, Walken, and Davern all lied to your face. When you last interviewed Dennis, his attorney saw you approaching his office, and he ridiculed you, as if you were the enemy. He deliberately made you wait in his office. Then, you had trouble getting through to Wagner for your second interview with him because Wagner *didn't* want to talk with you. Wagner told Davern, right before you were scheduled to meet Wagner at his house, that he hoped 'fucking Rasure doesn't start playing detective.' You were the plague from the start for Davern and Wagner. I don't know how Walken reacted to you, but he lied to you too."

"Walken called me a couple of weeks after the case closed to thank me for not treating him like a suspect," Rasure said.

"Well, I'm sure his gratitude was mixed with relief—he held back information that may have made you look closer into this case. As for Dennis, he knows he made a big mistake, which scared him then and *still* scares him. You know he lied. I wish that had been more of a clue to you, but I understand that Wagner and Walken seemed credible to you because of their status. But they're actors and better than Dennis at lying. I can't blame you for the way you feel about Dennis, but he is a victim of this case too. The thing is, Dennis admits his mistake—at least, he's trying to!—and he is willing to take a lie detector test to prove the truth about the Natalie Wood case."

"I don't put much stock in lie detector tests," Rasure told me.

"Okay, I appreciate that, but many professionals do. And Dennis's willingness to take a polygraph should give him some credibility. There was another witness, though, who is also willing to take a polygraph: Marilyn Wayne. I know you discount her testimony, but I believe her. You would, too, if you spoke with her. She had no reason to lie. Ask Wagner or Walken if *they* would be tested, and I think you already know the answer."

"I have it in one of my reports that I did contact Marilyn Wayne on December third. First she said she 'may have heard...' so I thought her later claims were exaggerations."

"Well, she doesn't recall ever speaking with you, and she was scared, and she did lay low because she didn't want to bring John Payne into it, but now she's not holding back. I truly believe she heard Natalie, but I understand how this is just another part of the case that got scrambled. Sam Kashner didn't talk much with her, but Suzanne Finstad did."

"Sam Kashner just wanted a sensationalized story," Duane insisted.

"What he learned from Dennis is not a lie, Duane." I went on to explain the most important of my findings and Lyn Taylor's drift tests. Duane respectfully listened. When I started telling him about Noguchi's oversight with the socks and the jacket, Duane told me something that almost floored me.

"Noguchi is a liar too!" he said. "There were no scratches on the dinghy—none—nada. The coroner made it up to fit his report. Pure lie!"

"Did you see the dinghy?"

"Yes, and there were no scratches!"

"Duane, didn't this tell you something?"

"Yes, but I didn't know at that time he was going to use a lie in his report. That came way down the road, after the case was closed. It wasn't enough to reopen the case."

"Maybe he lied about the algae on the swim step, too, because Den says it didn't exist. But why didn't you mention this on the shows you've been interviewed on? I've been on a couple of those shows with you. I would have liked to have learned that."

"Those shows—the reporters—they keep coming at me. I participate because I want to control the sensationalism."

"But do you ever look at it from Natalie's side?"

"Sure I do. I grew up loving her. My wife is her biggest fan."

"Duane, Natalie's death was completely preventable. Noguchi can call it accidental, but undetermined would have fit better. *How* did she get into the water? That's what needed to be answered."

"Choi did the autopsy with two representatives from the sheriff's department present. He did a good job."

"I don't doubt it, but there was much more to explore—a lot of evidence at the scene that spoke for itself. And there was no answer offered for the bruises or the bottle smashing. You've always claimed rough seas, as Wagner told you, causing the wine bottle to fall and break." I explained how the bottle actually broke and what Wagner had said.

"Is that really the way it broke?"

"Yes, Duane, it is."

"You know, Natalie was combing a little girl's hair in the restaurant that night."

"Natalie was enjoying her night, Duane. And in Finstad's book, it says Wagner sent a waitress to check for Natalie after just ten minutes. So why did he wait *four hours* for an official search when she was in the ocean? I just wish you had probed more with Wagner."

"Twice was enough. I went to his home for the second interview. He wasn't drunk, and I didn't think he was drunk the first time."

"He holds his liquor well. He was drunk or hungover."

"He was grieving."

"And he was lying."

"When I interviewed Davern, he was drunk."

"Both times?"

"No, the second was at the attorney's. Dennis kept looking to his attorney for every question I asked. He admitted staying with Natalie then because of rough seas."

"The seas weren't rough."

"Hmmm."

"Didn't Natalie's bruises concern you?"

"They weren't consistent with a beating."

"They weren't consistent with falling in the water, either, but they were consistent with handling. There was a big argument, Duane. Right before she died. A big fight that went from their stateroom to the open deck. Forget about calling Dennis a liar and thinking he's out for a buck. Think about a big fight on the deck, then Natalie goes missing, and Wagner doesn't look for her."

"Davern lied about being under 'house arrest' at Wagner's."

"It wasn't 'house arrest'—it was strong monitoring. Wagner didn't want Dennis exposed, for all of the reasons I'm telling you right now. Dennis—and believe it or not—Marilyn Wayne too—have received death threats. Okay, I don't want to sound too dramatic here, but please, back to basics."

Duane quietly listened to the rest of my overview. Our conversation ended with Duane telling me that if I can convince him with my manuscript being published in a believable format, he would be the first to help us correct history.

"I loved Natalie Wood. She was a beautiful woman," he said.

I called Lyndon Taylor to tell him about Rasure claiming Noguchi had lied about the scratch marks. We could not understand why this had not been a red flag for Rasure. I asked Lyn if he would perform another test. He spent his next visit to his boat trying—without success—to scratch the rubber sides of his dinghy with his fingernails. Even if Natalie had scratched at the dinghy, it is unlikely marks would have been visible. Yet, Noguchi had used this fabricated information to enhance the theory of Natalie having clung to the dinghy, which offered a plausible explanation for her bruises.

Rasure was telling the truth: there were no dinghy scratches.

Dennis was not as willing to warm up to Duane Rasure as I had been. Dennis found it astonishing that Rasure had been offended by Dennis's drunken demeanor and appearance on the morning of November 29, 1981, but had not recognized that Wagner was drunk too. Rasure had sympathized with Wagner and had no concern for Dennis, primarily because Dennis was an employee, and Wagner was a celebrity. Therefore, Dennis had been drunk, and Wagner had been "grieving."

In fact, not only had Dennis been grieving, he had been thrown into a state of shock upon learning that Natalie had died. If he appeared disheveled and confused after his sleepless night, it is because Robert Wagner had revealed a Mr. Hyde persona that Dennis had never witnessed before; he had instructed Dennis to lie, had poured him booze throughout the night, and had asked him to identify Natalie's bruised-up, drowned body. This was a horrific morning for a happy-go-lucky young man of thirty-three.

Rasure had been mentioned in Suzanne Finstad's *Natasha*, but Wagner had nothing to say about Rasure in Gavin Lambert's *Natalie Wood, A Life* (2004), where Wagner admits to some of his previous lies or omissions, most importantly the fact that he had indeed smashed a wine bottle. For decades, in interviews, Rasure confidently had been citing rough seas in reference to the broken glass he had seen in the main salon aboard *Splendour*.

The Mystery of Natalie Wood based on Finstad's *Natasha* aired. The banging dinghy theory ended the movie, thus no mystery was solved.

Robert Wagner, who had refused to cooperate with Finstad's project, was not only a major source for Lambert but obviously a guiding force as well, although Lambert professed that Wagner had little influence over his content. Some rather telling information is offered in Lambert's book. Editor, director, screenwriter, and author Gavin Lambert provided a perfect platform for Robert Wagner's comfort zone. But Wagner's "demon-filled drunken personality" is exposed too.

It was once the norm for Hollywood to protect its stars from scandal twice as cautiously as it protected the ending of the next major film, whereas modern-day celebrities are on their own when they make mistakes in their personal lives.

Today's celebrities seem more willing to admit to their mistakes or faults. The public appreciates honesty and usually forgives and forgets, unless, of course, there are more sinister details involved, as in the case of O.J. Simpson or Robert Blake.

Actor Robert Blake, who starred with Natalie Wood in *This Property Is Condemned* (1966), had been a source for Finstad's *Natasha* and insinuated, ironically, that Natalie's death was suspicious. Just as *Natasha* was released, Blake was arrested and accused of putting a bullet through his wife's head after having dinner at a restaurant with her. I asked Lana Wood if Blake had been a close friend to Natalie, and Lana emphatically answered, "No. Never!"

Robert Wagner's personal friend Gavin Lambert possessed the ultimate experience to mix old Hollywood with the new. Lambert was educated at Cheltenham and Oxford in the United Kingdom. He was deeply involved in Britain's Free Cinema movement and an advocate for strengthening social realism in contemporary movies. An honest man about his identity, Lambert was far ahead of his time in regard to gay rights.

For the first fifty years of filmmaking, homosexuality was rarely portrayed on the big screen. Lambert succeeded in expressing personal sensibilities discreetly and subliminally in his screenplays before a drastic turn in Hollywood censorship made it easier for other gay writers to be direct. Lambert lived his life the way every person—homosexual, heterosexual, or bisexual—should: unashamedly. Still, to be published in his early career, he conformed and had perfected the art of the subliminal message.

One of the unique and honorable attributes of Natalie and R.J. as a Hollywood couple was their willingness to accept all kinds of people into their lives. They had many gay friends, friends of various vocations, friends of differing cultures, politics, and philosophies. They learned and grew from varying their social crowd. Lambert had socialized with Natalie and R.J. and became a family friend, probably more so on R.J.'s side, according to Lana

Wood. Gavin was invited to the last of the Wagners' black-tie New Year's Eve parties and said there was a special "feel" to that party the couple hosted each year. The Wagners always called it a black-tie event because they felt it was a night that people should dress up, but the atmosphere was always relaxed. "If you were invited, you knew you were a real friend," Lambert said. Dennis had been invited to those black-tie parties as well as to many other parties held at the Wagner home.

In *Natalie Wood, A Life*, Lambert also controversially claimed that Natalie frequently dated gay and bisexual men, including director Nicholas Ray, who was once Lambert's lover, and actors Nick Adams, Raymond Burr, James Dean, Tab Hunter, and Scott Marlowe. Perhaps I was looking for the subliminal in this revelation: Was telling that Natalie dated gay men some sort of hint that if indeed she had once caught Wagner with another man (as Finstad had reported) that Natalie shouldn't have been so shocked? Was a name missing on Lambert's list?

While still living in England, his homeland, Lambert wrote numerous screenplays. He became a United States citizen in 1964 and wrote many acclaimed works, including the novel and screenplay *Inside Daisy Clover* (1965). Two of his screenplays were nominated for Oscars: *Sons and Lovers* (adaptation of D. H. Lawrence's classic novel) in 1960 and *I Never Promised You a Rose Garden* in 1977.

In 1996, Lambert wrote the introduction to *3 Plays*, a collection of works by his longtime friend Mart Crowley. Lambert said that Natalie supported homosexual playwright Crowley—a later lover of Lambert's—in "a manner that made it possible for him to write his play *The Boys in the Band* in 1968." Natalie had offered to pay for six months of therapy for Crowley, who later commented during an interview for *Starring Natalie Wood* (a 1988 documentary written by Lambert and narrated by George Segal) that she had owned up to only five months of those payments. The documentary concluded by saying Natalie's career ended when she accidentally died off Catalina Island.

Gavin Lambert died of pulmonary fibrosis on July 17, 2005. He had spent his final years in Los Angeles. He was survived by a brother, a niece, and a nephew, but named his friend and lover, Mart Crowley, as executor of his estate.

Lambert left behind a much less detailed account of his former friend than Finstad presented in *Natasha*, and he applied his knack for the subliminal throughout his work, but few might recognize it. Some of his blatant remarks border on the ridiculous. He calls Lana Wood a "James Bond bimbo"—it was a *character* part. (Of course, Jill St. John, Wagner's current wife, was also a Bond Girl.) Lambert suggests that Lana's book, *Natalie: A Memoir by Her Sister* (1986), was hastily written for nothing but profit.

Others who have written about Natalie Wood—Warren J. Harris, Suzanne Finstad, Thomas Noguchi, Sam Kashner, and Gavin Lambert himself—have all done so for profit. Warren J. Harris's dual biography on R.J. and Natalie read like one long magazine article. Lambert found it acceptable.

Lambert also had a mission in writing *Natalie Wood, A Life*: Robert Wagner said that he would be "at peace" when Lambert wrote Natalie's story. Agenda accomplished.

In Lambert's book, Wagner's jealousy is shown through the story of how he once went berserk when Natalie was filming *From Here to Eternity* with William Devane. Devane's and Natalie's onscreen chemistry bothered Wagner, and one night, witnessed by Mart Crowley and another friend, R.J. accused Natalie of having something going on with Devane. Natalie, furious, went to their room in their eighth-floor hotel suite, and Wagner, totally drunk, bolted toward the window as if to smash through it and plummet to a certain death. Natalie overheard the commotion and came out of her bedroom to tell Wagner he was crazy and to stop. Crowley and the other friend physically struggled with Wagner to keep him from hurting himself, then locked up the windows and doors and put Wagner to bed.

This incident, Lambert states, is told to prove that no matter how upset Natalie and R.J. might become with each other, they would make up. Lambert's purpose backfires here, confirming that Wagner has a history of reacting abnormally to his jealousies, just as he did the night he punched a man in the Polo Lounge, and as he did aboard *Splendour* the night Natalie died.

Lambert says that Wagner claims to have noticed a change in Natalie in 1977: the "career demon" took over, and her career was her only security other than her daughters—as if finding security in her career and in her daughters were a bad thing.

Dennis told me, "It always seemed that Natalie could live with or without R.J., and that R.J. needed Natalie more than she needed him. Everyone in Natalie's world, including RJ, depended on Natalie, for many reasons."

Lambert suggests that Natalie, in the late 1970s, started drinking too much, sometimes losing her temper and sometimes her ability to recall events that took place while she was drinking. That's pretty much the same complaint about R.J. that Natalie had confided to her hairdresser, Ginger. Lambert does confirm that R.J. had a drinking problem and that R.J.'s personality could turn dark when he was drunk.

Guy McElwaine calls Natalie's alleged behavior changes a "psychic infection" in Lambert's account, as he claims Natalie sometimes left messages on McElwaine's voicemail in which she called herself Natalie, Natalie Wood, or Mrs. Wagner, whichever fit the purpose of the call. By identifying herself in different ways, the book asks, had Natalie "started to fracture in the last year of her life?" Lambert then suggests that she had multiple selves, curable only by discovering underlying causes.

To insinuate that Natalie was conflicted and unstable because she used both her maiden name and married name at different times is absurd. Natalie, like millions of people, saw a therapist regularly to deal with her inner struggles, trying to juggle career, home, friendships, family, and motherhood. According to Dennis, she seemed to be handling it all and enjoying herself in the process.

Lambert interviewed Jeffrey Rochford, a chiropractor and founder of the Rochford Clinic, which offers alternative medicine. Rochford literally calls Natalie a drug addict and says she admitted to increasing alcohol and pill use. Rochford had noticed her eyes and claimed her "liver was challenged."

Autopsy results showed Natalie with a perfectly healthy liver.

Lambert says Dennis Davern remained "star struck," and although totally unprepared for what happened that weekend, he had been around long enough to realize the situation was ripe for exploitation.

Dennis never exploited R.J. He kept silent with information that tore his gut apart for four years. Wagner brought Dennis into the world of acting. Wagner insisted Dennis stay at his home. Wagner enabled Dennis in every way for close to two years after Natalie died, then got tired of carrying him. Dennis never asked for anything from Wagner, and Dennis worked at the docks and at the studios, and paid his own way. His need to tell his complete story is to *prove* he did not exploit a terrible event. What happened to the participants aboard *Splendour* on November 29, 1981, happened to Dennis in a personal way, as well.

Liz Applegate, Natalie's friend, told Lambert she knew of Dennis's financial problems, that he owed money to his ex-wife who was out to sue him, and so had reason to sell out to reporters. Dennis was not married when he lived in California. Dennis did not marry until 1993, in Florida. Liz Applegate obviously knew nothing about Dennis's personal life, past or present. Dennis did not offer any information to any reporter until 1985, four years after Natalie's death. What would Liz have known about Dennis's finances then? He never saw Liz after Natalie's funeral. A simple check of official records by Lambert would have proven Davern's single status before 1993.

Lambert tends to group Lana Wood and Dennis Davern together in his account, as though the negative publicity each has received over the years—and the accusations against both of them of being money-hungry—would feed off each other. Dennis worked hard for his pay as *Splendour's* captain. R.J. freely offered Dennis money after Natalie died, but Dennis quickly went to work as a general actor and made his own money. Lana never received one penny from Wagner after Natalie died, with the exception of some support dollars for Mud's illness and then for Mud's funeral. Support for Mud was in Natalie's will.

Lambert claims Natalie left three messages the morning before leaving the Pavilion hotel with Dennis: two to Josh Donen and one to Mart Crowley. In the first message, to Donen, Natalie said she was confused and lost and was on the island with Davern. The next message, to Crowley, said she had had an argument with R.J., went to the island, where Davern slept on the floor, but she was going back to the boat and may need to call again if the arguing continued. The third message, to Donen again, let him know she was back on the boat and all was fine.

If Mart Crowley knew from Natalie's message that there had been arguing and trouble aboard *Splendour*, serious enough that Natalie spent the night on the island with Dennis, why did he not come forward and alert the authorities to this knowledge? Natalie told Dennis, on the Saturday morning at the Pavilion, that she had only tried to contact Lana and her friend, Peggy.

Then Lambert's writing gets interesting. In both Finstad's and Lambert's books, the account remains the same about how Natalie and Christopher got to Doug's Harbor Reef Restaurant. Both authors write that Natalie and Christopher went ashore in the dinghy to the bar and that Natalie left a note for R.J., who woke up from a nap and got mad about it. Then Wagner and Dennis took a ship-to-shore boat to the restaurant to follow. Here, with an opportunity for Lambert (and Wagner) to show that Natalie operated the dinghy on the very day of her death, the point is ignored. Lambert leaves it alone, as if it is further strengthened by Finstad offering the same information.

That's not the way it happened. Natalie did not operate the dinghy to get to Doug's, and Walken had no clue how to operate it or maneuver his way around. It was Natalie and Christopher who took a shore boat to the island, and although Wagner was upset about it, he was still feeling guilty over creating the argument the night before, so he kept quiet. Dennis and R.J. took the dinghy to join Christopher and Natalie hours later. R.J. knows this but apparently did not correct Lambert.

As Lambert gets deeper into the weekend of Natalie's death, the details he or "someone" doesn't want published are conveniently explained by use of the "Hellman syndrome," a quote by Lillian Hellman offered by Lambert: *Much of what appears perfectly clear when you're drinking never appears clear again, probably because it never was.*

Wagner admits he doesn't recall Walken throwing a glass to the floor at the restaurant and Natalie following suit. Davern does not recall that incident either. Only Walken has previously explained this glass-breaking scene.

In Lambert's assessment of Marilyn Wayne and John Payne, who each heard a woman's cries for help, Lambert cleverly quotes Wagner as claiming to have heard no voices from another boat. Lambert says that Wayne's account in the *L.A. Times* left the sheriff's department unconvinced, and they ignored it.

"She's gone! She's gone!" R.J. apparently cried to others besides Dennis. Lambert writes that this was what R.J. cried to Mart Crowley with his call to inform Crowley of Natalie's death. Lambert does not mention that these were the same words R.J. had cried to Dennis. Nor does he tell of Wagner sending a car when Dennis returned from the island after identifying Natalie's body. He doesn't mention that Dennis was driven immediately to Wagner's home to speak with attorneys. Nor does he tell that Dennis stayed by Wagner's side at the funeral, at the gravesite, and then, at Wagner's request, was a houseguest at Wagner's home for three months after Natalie's death. Lambert doesn't mention that Wagner gave Davern a general-extra acting job on *Hart to Hart* and paid for Dennis's membership in the Screen Actors Guild, nor that Wagner took Dennis to his own psychiatrist with him for joint and single sessions. Dennis maintained *Splendour* for Wagner until 1984—*three years after Natalie's death*. Why doesn't

Lambert explain why Wagner would have done all of these favors
for "delusional Dennis"?

Just as Lambert claims, Natalie's death was ruled
accidental, and the case was closed on December 12, 1981.
Lambert then says the sleaze mongers found it "mysterious" that
R.J. and Walken both fumbled their accounts to police. Lambert
claims it would have been even more "mysterious" if Wagner and
Walken had offered straight-up answers and "precisely" agreed on
the events of that night. Hellman syndrome prevails.

Prevalent, subliminal tactics carry over in Lambert's book
to the use of photographs. A picture of Natalie operating the
dinghy doesn't take away the fact that this was not routine for her.
The photograph is a careful close-up so no one can see that
someone was probably right by her side. Another photograph of
R.J. and Natalie standing on the swim step is included. It appears
that Natalie uses her left arm and hand to cling to the *Splendour*
wall in fear. Another photograph is such an insult to Natalie, it's
hard to believe it could have been included. It was taken during
Brainstorm production and shows her dilated pupils and unfocused
attention; the caption, too, enforces the accusation of heightened pill
and alcohol consumption, virtually suggesting "that crazy Natalie."

Another photograph shows Natalie with William Devane
in what Lambert calls an "ocean scene" with them immersed in
what appears to be deep dark water. Nice try, but it's a studio tank
shot. Suzanne Finstad is conscientious enough to mention that this
particular scene was filmed in a studio tank because of Natalie's
fear of water.

While some messages in Lambert's book are cautiously
hidden and worded, some pure carelessness exists too. Wagner
claims he is certain that after they returned from Doug's restaurant,
the dinghy was tied up to port (the left side of the boat, facing
forward), where it would bang into his stateroom's outside wall.
But Dennis is certain he tied the dinghy to the back of the yacht.
Wagner says in Lambert's book that Natalie had untied the *ropes*.
Wagner consistently says "ropes," not "rope," in reference to
securing the dinghy to the yacht—and he is correct: the dinghy was
secured by two ropes.

Several messages may get past even a discerning reader,
but the contemptuous tone when it comes to Lana Wood is blatant.
Lambert makes an awful lot of noise about the Wood sisters'
paternity, obviously meant for the ears of the only person this
information will hurt.

When Lambert names the two most "complex cases" since Natalie's death, it's no surprise to see the names of Lana Wood and Dennis Davern—ironically, the two people Wagner fears the most in bringing true retribution to his "charmed" life and reputation.

Most of Natalie's other friends—Liz Applegate, Peggy Griffin, Mart Crowley, and many more—have all stayed close to Wagner. The two who chose to question his lies—Lana and Dennis—are chastised and insulted throughout Lambert's work.

Lambert begins his book with an unproven claim that Lana Wood and Natalie Wood were fathered by different men, and the same blather is saved for his climax, where he claims Natalie may have had a hint from her mother. Natalie's life ends in Lambert's book with a probable new father. Not with a tragic death.

Lambert tells that Natalie's daughter Courtney once attempted suicide. Lana Wood explained this sad choice of Courtney's to me. An obvious reason for the attempt was clear from the means of this near-tragedy. Courtney had surrounded herself with photographs of her mother, then slit her wrists. This is a terribly sad sight to visualize.

As for Lambert's consistent attack on Lana Wood in his book, Lana told me, "I was so incredibly upset I had to stop reading [*Natalie Wood, A Life*], and will never finish the crap. He [Gavin Lambert] has lied about every single thing he said about me, and therefore, I would assume everything else is a lie too— orchestrated by R.J. I was recently told that R.J. warned Gavin if he ever spoke to me, R.J. would remove his sanction of the book, and tell everyone else not to speak with Gavin, and therefore Gavin would not have a book at all. Where...does this irrational hatred come from? If I am guilty of anything, it is being too complacent and allowing R.J. to get away with everything he has! Gavin is not a dear friend of Nat's. He was an acquaintance that she worked with, and she loved gays! He is a very old aging gay. He is tied to R.J., and I don't doubt that he was compromised."

Under the guise of a biography, Lambert's book contains numerous slurs against Natalie. In her fourth biographer's book— the only one sanctioned by Robert Wagner—a derogatory image of Natalie is presented throughout: the image is exactly what the writer, under Wagner's scrutiny, intended.

Perhaps the most revealing and insulting tactic of all is that throughout the book, Lambert, king of the subliminal, never once refers to Natalie's coat as a down jacket. This omission makes me wonder if king of subliminal Lambert deliberately avoided "down jacket" because he figured it out or if Wagner persuaded him to use parka, as Wagner usually calls the jacket, because Wagner knows: ducks float.

And so do down jackets.

PART FOUR

A Voice for Natalie

And if I pass this way again, you can rest assured
I'll always do my best for her, on that I give my word.

—Bob Dylan ("Shelter from the Storm")

Chapter 39

After Suzanne Finstad's and Gavin Lambert's Natalie biographies were released, I felt defeated. History had been rewritten. I feared that the two well-established authors had done irreparable damage to Dennis's credibility. Finstad's book had turned Dennis into an accomplice: a spineless drunk who went along with Wagner's foul choice to watch Natalie Wood die a torturous end by the water she deathly feared. Lambert's book presented Dennis as a delusional, money-grubbing, profiteer who ran with an opportunity to exploit an "accidental death." Both portrayals of Dennis were inaccurate.

When Dennis and I discussed Lambert's book, we were distraught over the distorted truth and the lies it contained, and we believed the authorities should have been concerned with its contents. The authorities question why Davern has not "come forward?" They have never asked that same question of Wagner and Walken. No doubt, Wagner has good reason to hide his truth, but Walken is fully aware that Wagner became maniacal after the group returned from Doug's Harbor Reef. For that matter, the people Natalie had left voice messages for from the Pavilion Lodge in Avalon—Mart Crowley and Josh Donen, according to Lambert—knew of trouble brewing on that fatal cruise. No one has "come forward." When Marilyn Wayne "came forward" she was ignored.

During one of our conversations about Lambert's book, I asked Dennis again about those words he had said to me in New York. "Den, please explain what you meant when you once told me, 'He put her coat on her.'"

"Marti, it's what I think. When I review everything that happened so fast that night, I keep coming up with Wagner having something to do with that coat. I didn't put the music on until they took the fight to the deck. They were screaming at each other, and Natalie was not wearing her coat on deck. I believe if she had put her coat on to leave, she would have put on clothes too. And the way the fight had burst onto the deck, and the way they were still going at it, I can't see her stopping to say, 'Oh, hold on R.J., I'm chilly, let me go get my coat.'

"After Natalie was missing, R.J. told the harbormaster she was wearing her nightgown. He purposely didn't mention that she was wearing her jacket. That would have meant he knew more about what happened than he was owning up to. R.J. was with her when she went into the water. He knows I heard the fight on deck. He knew I was suspicious when he told me the dinghy was missing. Wouldn't he have noticed her red jacket missing from the stateroom—the only room he checked? I believe he knew exactly where that coat was: on Natalie's body. But he didn't say one word about the coat that night. That's why I think he had something to do with putting it on her—that he probably is the one who fetched it."

"Den, I still want to clear up all of the published lies, to tell your story."

"Do you know what I want, Marti?" Dennis asked, his voice stern.

I waited.

"I want to make a call to report a *murder*."

Despite all the years I had tried to convince Dennis to place exactly such a call, I convinced him to wait. I asked, "Den, did you actually see how Natalie got into the water?"

"No."

"Did you hear her calling for help?"

"No. I would have saved her."

"Well, Marilyn Wayne *did* hear cries for help at the exact time you were on the bridge. It all fits. You didn't hear Natalie because you played music. Marilyn heard Natalie *and* the music. Let's prove that you didn't know Natalie was in the water and then present what you *did* see and hear. There will always be the mystery of how Natalie actually got into the water, but it doesn't take a rocket scientist to figure that out. Wagner was in a real predicament with what to tell authorities. He couldn't make up a lie about Natalie accidentally falling because then the bruises and his delay in calling for help would've come into play. Celebrity worked in Wagner's favor. There wasn't much he could say without incriminating himself, so he said as little as possible and still does to this day. But he tells about the bottle smashing—I'd be so angry if I were on the police force in L.A. and following this man, but no one seems to care."

Dennis listened to me in utter silence. Then he asked, "How can I die, Marti, without helping Natalie? I didn't help her that night, or the morning after, because I helped R.J. instead. It took a lot of years for me to realize it, but when R.J. didn't want to search for her—and I let him convince me it was because of their star status—that's when Natalie was suffering. I need to help Natalie now."

"Exactly. He didn't pour you drinks and wait hours to call for help for no reason. He panicked. He needed time to think about what to do—to save himself and his image, just like he told you."

"Marti, he was the most suspicious-looking character I've ever seen. He reeked of guilt that night. When the guy from the island showed up, R.J. started screaming at him to 'find her, where is she?' Why didn't he scream that to me?"

"Den, your story is the only thing that makes sense to me."

"I can disprove anything Wagner says," Dennis said.

"You don't have to disprove anything, Den. So, before you make a phone call, let's take a breather."

Dennis had never used the word *murder* before. Lambert's book had reignited his anger and frustration, and I knew he needed a few weeks to deal with his emotions. I also knew that if he made a sudden, sensational accusation now, after twenty-two years and in an emotional reaction to Lambert's book, Dennis's credibility would again be questioned. His truth needed to be told in its entirety with as much objectivity as I could manage, not in an emotional burst that would be either discounted or exploited.

Our breather turned into months, then years. Our busy lives kept getting busier, and although we were disappointed in ourselves for what seemed like our retreat after Lambert's book, we had scarce moments in conversations that always reminded us of our unfinished business. We called each other for occasional family updates, but not until 2008, when the legend of Natalie Wood found *us* again, did we make an important decision.

In February of 2008, I let Dennis know that my twin brother Jimmy passed away of a heart attack. I was upset because Jimmy had called me just days before his death, but I had said I would get back to him. "You just never know what link it is in the chain of events that will lead to regrets," I told Dennis. "It's so sad that Natalie didn't listen to your suggestion to postpone that cruise."

Dennis replied, "Don't beat yourself up over not taking Jimmy's call. I still think about what I could have done differently the night Natalie died. Sometimes it feels like that part of my life happened to someone else. I'm so sorry I didn't tell what I knew immediately. I had nothing to lose, but I sympathized with all that Wagner had to lose. I *still* dream about her sometimes."

Although I cried for the loss of my twin, I smiled for Dennis's life. His family of five was enjoying their new house in a beautiful gated community. His and Ellen's third child, Emily, was almost nine years old. Dennis's marina business was busier than ever, and he had worked on a few boats in Costa Rica, the country he so admired when *Dizzy Izzy* moored there for a few days in 1975.

I had watched Robert Wagner on the television sitcoms *Hope and Faith* and *Two and a Half Men*. Occasionally, I saw him in late-night, reverse-mortgage commercials and in others where he conveniently mentioned Natalie Wood for advertising augmentation. Wagner seemed to have regained his momentum and has become rather good at debunking the occasional hint that he is culpable for his late wife's death, and he seems smug in his belief that nothing can ever topple his little empire of lies. But the name, Davern, must linger in his thoughts.

I blamed a shabby investigation for Wagner's celebrity growth. Celebrities sometimes do bad things, and we cannot continue to feel as though it is our faux pas to call them on it.

Christopher Walken has maintained a positive spin with his impressive range of talent. Walken has carved a prominent niche in show business, and his continued popularity leaves him virtually unscathed by the Natalie Wood tragedy.

I learned that Wagner lost his highly publicized 2000 lawsuit to Aaron Spelling Productions and sold his house soon afterward. He and wife Jill St. John spend their time mostly in Aspen these days. Socialwhirl.com featured a photograph of Wagner and wife smiling and chatting at an Aspen art museum affair with CBS news anchor Katie Couric. I doubt that these A-class journalists who occasionally find themselves in Wagner's company ever get the urge to ask him for an in-depth interview about November 1981.

On *The View*, in 2004, I watched as Barbara Walters warmly introduced Robert Wagner to the show as a guest. Although Walters had wanted an exclusive interview with Wagner after Natalie died, she coddled Wagner's latter day grief by rushing and hushing her voice when she brought up Natalie in his presence.

As R.J. Wagner spoke of having an affair with Barbara Stanwyck on *The View*, hosts Meredith Vieira, Barbara Walters, Star Jones, Joy Behar, and Elisabeth Hasselbeck lapped up the details. Wagner said he was twenty-two and Stanwyck forty-five when this love relationship occurred, and at that detail, the audience applauded vigorously, as if in appreciation for Wagner having bestowed the generous gift of his young self to the older Stanwyck. When asked how the affair was kept hidden, Wagner said they had been careful.

Magazine articles from Wagner's early days in Hollywood tell of his "love for Natalie." A Louella Parson's column from 1957 states that Wagner telephoned her—the queen of Hollywood gossip—to tell her his relationship with Natalie was his first time in love. *Life's* DVD *Great Loves* shows Wagner claiming Natalie was his first love.

But now, Wagner's story changes. Maybe Stanwyck was his first love. Maybe his first love was Natalie. As Wagner himself has lamented, it seems you can say anything you want about someone after she or he is dead. Wagner constantly presents different stories, and no one calls him on it. Just as authorities looked the other way when there was a need to probe further on the morning of November 29, 1981, journalists continue to neglect the essence of their work with their softball Wagner interviews.

It is Dennis, to this day, who bears the brunt of shame for Natalie's death.

Chapter 40

Dennis called me in late February 2008, distraught and insulted, and asked how he might be able to get something erased from the Internet. He explained that the husband of his wife's friend had Googled Dennis's name, and the very first thing that appeared said, "Dennis Davern was a scum bag...."

I explained that it would be virtually impossible to remove the comment but that I might be able to contact the source to see what it was about. I Googled Dennis's name, and the "scumbag" comment came up. A click took me to its origin—a site called the Death of Natalie Wood Discussion Forum at Network54.com.

I contacted Gail, the author of the scumbag post. She had already changed her mind about Dennis after having read Lambert's Natalie biography, and she apologized for her insult to Dennis, claiming that "ignorance was bliss" for her in reference to Natalie's death.

Gail's knowledge of Natalie Wood's life astounded me. She regularly exchanged anecdotes and information about Natalie at several Internet forums and was known by most fans as the "Natalie historian." Gail and I became quick friends. I enjoyed the stories she shared in her e-mails, such as this one: "Did you ever hear the story of when Natalie met San Francisco Mayor George Moscone? She was in a restaurant in 1979. He saw her, walked up to the table, introduced himself, and flirted with her. What did she do? She flirted right back! Men simply adored her. She was a woman who liked being a woman. And then, then there is Isaac Mizrahi, the designer. He said, 'How can I make anything as beautiful as Natalie Wood? That's what keeps me up at night.' This is how she is remembered."

Gail Abbott, a wife, mother, and young grandmother, lives a private family life in the Northeast and wants to keep it that way, but her thirst for justice in the Natalie Wood saga connected her to Natalie's legacy. Gail was making sure Natalie would never be forgotten—introducing Natalie to young fans, giving Natalie a voice, promoting Natalie's films, and remembering the vibrant, happy Natalie. She told me, "When I heard she was gone, my first thoughts were of her children and her mother. I wondered what her last thoughts were. I also hoped that she was happy at the end of her life. When the Internet became popular, it was wonderful to be able to talk to others who felt as I did, but there is a division:

the people who believe that Robert Wagner would never have harmed his wife and those who believe he was at the very least culpable because of bad judgment. At first, I believed in R.J. When the *Vanity Fair* article came out, I ignored it. When Suzanne Finstad's *Natasha* came out, I bought it and loved it, but I would not read the dark water chapter. I wanted to believe with all my heart that Robert Wagner would never have hurt Natalie, but his delay in searching for her haunted me. Then I was aghast at the obvious agenda involved in Lambert's biography. He was trying to dust off the dirt that Finstad threw on Wagner in her book. R.J. allowed Lambert to show Natalie in the worst light. 'Natalie liked to swish her tail'—that made me sick. The way Lambert portrayed her, she looked like nothing more than a burden to Wagner. It breaks my heart that she has not had a voice. She was robbed of that as she was robbed of so much more, robbed of seeing her beautiful daughters grow into women."

Many of the posts at the Death of Natalie Wood Discussion Forum analyzed details of the November 1981 weekend; other posts were lengthy scenarios, including one that absurdly theorized why and how Dennis Davern is the more likely suspect and very well could be Natalie's killer. Dennis was now being accused of murder! I went on a month-long Internet surf and knew for certain that it was time for truth. Wagner was planning to release his autobiography in September 2008. It was time for Natalie's voice. She deserved her turn. And Dennis deserved his.

Since the two Wood biographies have been published, the word murder has popped up often enough in discussions of Natalie Wood's death to warrant taking another legal look at the case, but Lambert's book remained the lingering tone.

Dennis and I were fully aware that many people would resist believing a "nobody" like Davern over a celebrity like Wagner. I trusted in my conviction that telling the truth mattered.

I called Dennis and said: "It's time to finish our something big. It has never been more necessary."

From the time Geraldo Rivera contacted Detective Salerno in 1992 and suggested the Wood case be reopened upon the opinions of three attorneys, I had wanted to follow up with a phone call to Salerno. Now, I felt compelled to talk with the former lead detective of Natalie Wood's case—the man who had officially closed the case.

On April 4, 2008, I gathered the courage. Salerno had retired, but I hoped to obtain contact information from the Los Angeles County Sheriff's Department. I was a bit stunned when a Frank Salerno answered my call. The voice sounded far too young to be the Frank Salerno who had worked the Wood case in 1981. He explained he was the junior Frank Salerno and had followed in his father's work. He seemed to pick up on my sense of urgency, despite my calling about a twenty-seven-year-old case, and I trusted he would urge his father to call me immediately, as he said he would.

Fifteen years earlier, Frank Salerno's words in the letter from Wagner's attorney: "The case speaks for itself" motivated me. My stomach clenched. This was going to be a no-holds-barred conversation.

I did not want to point fingers or put Salerno on the defensive. After all, Salerno had not been hands-on with the case. He had trusted in Rasure and Hamilton's investigation, as sergeants usually do of their trusted detectives. I needed to approach the subject with Salerno as "the case that got away from them" rather than as "the case they had bungled." Rasure had been manipulated.

While waiting for his return phone call, I Googled Salerno. Frank Salerno Sr. had helped to nail the Hillside Strangler and the Night Stalker, two infamous, demented killers. I learned he had once acquired the nickname Honest Frank.

Now retired from the department, Salerno is president of his own private investigation company called Salerno & Scully Investigations, offering detective, guard, and armored car services, in Encino, California. I looked at Salerno's photograph online, and even though Chuck Esser—who had passed away—and Salerno physically look nothing alike, that hardened, familiar penchant for justice is evident. To calm my nerves, I told myself to talk with Salerno the same way I used to talk with Chuck.

My phone was not ringing, so I called the number of Salerno's business location. After two messages to Salerno, my phone finally rang. Salerno said he did not recognize my name, and I was relieved. He playfully asked, "Should I recognize it? Do you have a bad reputation or something?"

I chuckled and answered, "No, but I was definitely misunderstood once in reference to the Natalie Wood case. Before we talk, please trust that my flip remark was nothing more than a retort to a deceitful producer. I would like to talk about Wood's death for a manuscript. I just read some things about you—"

Frank said, "I hope good things."

"Yes, all good, but there's one case that did get away from you. But, please, hear me out, because I don't blame you. Your detectives on the case were deceived."

"How were we lied to, Marti?" Salerno asked, then said, "Call me Frank."

I told Frank about the socks and the floating jacket and mentioned that Wagner deliberately delayed in calling for help "to protect his image." I mentioned how Marilyn Wayne had been ignored. I told about Dr. Lyndon Taylor's drift tests. I explained the stateroom argument that carried out to the deck. I explicitly got the point across that Wagner was with his wife on the deck when she went missing.

Frank asked, "Are we talking homicide?"

I curbed my personal opinion but answered honestly: "Well, I'm talking a lot of circumstantial evidence that could point in that direction to a motivated prosecutor, but, really, I think a defense attorney could prevail, as usual in celebrity cases. But, there's more..."

"Tell me," Frank said, and not in a patronizing way.

I rushed through some details for Frank and became breathless at points, but I don't think I sounded nervous—the conviction in my voice stayed constant. I was still no more than that New Jersey nobody unless Frank would give my words consideration. After telling about the bottle smashing and the fight, I said, "If you took me on as a client and listened to my information from a private investigator angle, you wouldn't doubt a word. So, please listen new."

Salerno chuckled, but it was the kind of chuckle meaning, "You might be right." He said, "Go on. I'll listen."

And he did. He listened first with courtesy, if not believability, and as my information continued—Den going to the stateroom, Den seeing R.J. and Natalie on the deck, the fight that sounded physical—Frank, I think, started to believe.

Then Frank interrupted. "Who saw that bottle smashing?"

I answered, "Natalie, Walken, and Davern." I could sense his anger. I paused, then said, "You're probably stewing most about Walken. Wagner would have had good reason to hide it. Dennis was the common participant, but Walken having covered it—"

"Rasure saw the broken glass," he stated.

"Wagner told him 'rough seas,' yes."

"Well, no one would admit to the bottle at this point," Frank surmised.

"Wagner already admitted it," I told him.

"What?"

"In Lambert's book. Wagner confesses to breaking the wine bottle in anger."

"He actually admits it?"

"Page three-eleven, Frank. Wagner tells about the argument and picking up a wine bottle and smashing it on the table, because Natalie was 'swishing her tail.' That's how he talks about his late wife to this day."

And then it hit me. I was always so upset and frustrated because the former detectives on the Natalie case never seemed to be "sparked" by new information. Of course, Geraldo had informed them of the 1992 *Now It Can Be Told* episode and had presented his information with a plea to reopen the case, and Salerno's comment that the case "speaks for itself" was justified because of the mistakes Dennis and I had made through our nervousness on that hacked tape. But Frank Salerno had not read the *Vanity Fair* article, Suzanne Finstad's book, or Lambert's. It was everyday people, slighted by lack of initial details, who followed the Wood case, not those who had worked it and closed it. If the case had stayed open long enough, the contradicting statements that soon came from the participants—the cruise survivors— perhaps would have driven the detectives in the right direction. Detectives take enough unfinished work home with them, let alone having to drag home *closed* cases.

And Frank must have known exactly what I was thinking, because his next question was, "Why hasn't Davern come forward?"

I explained the myriad reasons. Confusion. Fear. Natalie's girls. The threats. Wagner's control. "Wagner watched over Davern until he thought he reached a safety zone. Dennis was always afraid of being accused, too, especially after the Finstad book that claimed he saw Natalie in the water too."

"Did he?"

"Absolutely not. We're arranging for polygraph tests soon. Dennis only followed his attorney's advice. When Natalie was missing, Wagner kept pouring booze and told Davern he needed to protect his image."

Frank almost moaned.

I next told Frank all the details about the stateroom fight, Natalie's bruises, the banging dinghy theory, Marilyn Wayne's account, Natalie's floating coat, information about the dinghy being tied with two ropes, and the fact that Wagner was with Natalie up to the moment of her disappearance.

Salerno went dead silent.

He finally asked, "Where was Walken?"

"Sleeping. He went to his cabin after the bottle smashing."

Frank backed up as he absorbed my information. "How long did Dennis work for Wagner afterward?"

"Two years, up until the boat was donated. In the meantime, Wagner gave Dennis a recurring acting job on *Hart to Hart*."

I sensed this information bothered Frank, as his breaths went deeper.

I then explained how Dennis's attorney ridiculed Rasure. "Why on earth would an attorney in such a tragic case laugh at Detective Rasure, as if he were the old cowboy detective, easy to deceive?"

I could almost hear Salerno seething.

"This is the case that needed to be kept open longer, Frank," I finished.

I was not trying to impress Salerno—I just wanted him to believe. He was so quiet that I could not tell what he was thinking. That made me nervous, but then he asked, "How did the dinghy get released?"

"Only Wagner knows how Natalie got into the water. And only Wagner knows how the dinghy got released. Dennis didn't see the dinghy being released, but he heard sounds, and he went down to the deck at that time. Only Wagner was on deck then."

This is where I lost Frank.

"How does one *hear* a dinghy being untied?" he asked.

"Dennis knows. You get used to sounds you've been around for years."

Frank didn't respond.

I then told Frank I would like to talk with Rasure again but couldn't locate him. Frank said he would contact Rasure for me and have Rasure call me.

I closed by saying that I doubted anything would officially come of the case over a quarter century later, but I believed an official inquiry should be considered. I assured Frank that Dennis was willing to cooperate. I insisted that Dennis had never lied. I was not seeking absolution for Dennis's mistakes, but wanted to impress upon Frank the bigger mistakes. I think Frank understood.

Before letting me go, Frank asked, "Why didn't Dennis look for her?"

I explained again that Wagner had demanded Dennis to stay put. Wagner was worried about bad publicity, and he probably needed time to figure out an acceptable lie before authorities showed up. Wagner immediately went to work on Dennis and convinced him that Natalie was in the dinghy. Although Dennis suspected worse, he had no choice but to wait it out.

Before ending the conversation, I told Frank about Wagner's autobiography. "It will include more lies," I said.

Frank said he would need to review a lot of things but for me to "keep working." I hoped that meant he would pay close attention.

Many people have difficulty comprehending the official answers to the mystery of Natalie Wood's death. I do not believe that authorities had looked for every possible explanation to support "accident." I believe that everyone accepted Natalie's death as accidental because it was incomprehensible to believe otherwise. Natalie and R.J. were considered the perfect Hollywood couple. They were gentle. They were happy. No inconsistency in that everlasting love of R.J.'s and Natalie's had ever been publicly proclaimed after their second marriage. No one knew of or really suspected trouble in their paradise. Therefore, how could Natalie Wood's untimely death have been anything *but* accidental?

That was the mistake in thinking that everyone made. Natalie's death scene was far more indicative of foul play than of accident, but the mainstream media that had always offered us the wisdom and endurance of R.J.'s and Natalie's love could only remain impartial.

The investigation into Natalie Wood's death was botched because we had all been previously impressed with something far too good to be so suddenly false. There was utter disorder in the attempt to reach a logical explanation in the days following Natalie's death. No one seemed driven to collect details of this incomprehensible death. It was easier to let Natalie "rest in peace."

But somehow, Natalie Wood ended up in the water she feared her entire life. *Common sense*—all I had to go on when I started my quest for truth—added to all I have learned since, screams out for a closer, professional look into Wood's death.

Detectives got lost in the delegation of duty and information. A coroner shuffled his findings, ignoring the public to provide a satisfactory report for the celebrity community, to save his job.

But bodies never lie—the truth was right there in Natalie's bruises and in her attire. Natalie's body spoke volumes. No one listened, but Natalie's lifetime mantra will always remain *her* cry from the grave: "I'm deathly afraid of water that is dark."

Chapter 41

On May 6, 2008, I received a call from Dennis. Ruth Davern, his mother, had passed away at the age of eighty-eight. Ruth's obituary captured the essence of this gracious woman I had known for almost forty years—a very thoughtful and generous person, always taking time to ensure that everyone around her was taken care of. If anyone needed anything, she would do whatever she could to satisfy their needs. Ruth loved to sew, knit, quilt, and crochet. Her many handcrafted baby items were donated to local hospitals and her Raggedy Ann and Andy dolls put smiles on many faces on Christmas mornings. Ruth's generosity was a gesture Natalie Wood once told Ruth was one of the kindest things she could imagine.

I was glad I had a set of Mrs. Davern's dolls at home, just as I was certain that Natalie's daughters appreciated having something their mom had needlepointed, perhaps one of Natalie's pillows.

When the funeral parlor quieted for Ruth's eulogy, granddaughter Amy started to read the verse on Ruth's funeral card, Linda Ellis's world-famous poem "The Dash." I paid special attention this day to the many poignant lines, but it is the end of the verse that delivers the most impact:

So when your eulogy's being read, with your life's actions to rehash,

Would you be proud of the things they say about how you spent your dash?

As I stood at Ruth's gravesite in the pouring rain, I bowed my head and thought about her "dash." She had been my refuge on a long-ago night in Florida, the first night I had met Dennis.

Natalie's gigantic "dash" in a shortened life weighed heavily on me this day. Natalie had loved her husband. You could see it in her eyes when she looked at him, in photographs and in interviews. Dennis maintained that Natalie and R.J. had adored each other.

Part of Natalie's dash included a friendship with the son of the woman being buried this day. Mrs. Davern had always spoken of Natalie's and her son Dennis's friendship with pure pride. And she had every reason for that pride.

I looked over at Dennis, standing in the rain, as he said goodbye to his mother. His dash needed to be understood.

I met up with Dennis at the wake, and we talked about getting together again soon for something long overdue—Dennis's polygraph test.

The American Polygraph Association believes that scientific evidence supports the high validity of polygraph examinations. However, a valid examination requires a combination of a properly trained examiner; a polygraph instrument that records as a minimum cardiovascular, respiratory, and electrodermal activity; and the proper administration of an accepted testing procedure and scoring system.

The American Polygraph Association has a compendium of research studies available on the validity and reliability of polygraph testing. The eighty research projects published since 1980 provide an average accuracy of 98 percent.

For Dennis's test, the polygraphist's solid reputation was our primary concern. I found Howard Temple's listing at Accredited Polygraph Service online. Mr. Temple, a member of the American Polygraph Association, has worked in the private sector of the polygraph industry since 1971. He has also served as a polygraph advisor/vendor for the city of Bloomfield, New Jersey, for over twenty-five years. He received his training at and was subsequently employed by the prominent Backster School of Lie Detection. He has additional training in voice stress evaluation and psychological stress evaluation.

Mr. Temple has conducted examinations for a wide variety of clients, including law enforcement agencies at the local, state, and federal levels; private industry in the manufacturing, retailing, financial, and legal fields; and for private citizens.

Over the course of his career, he has served as an expert on several major television and radio news broadcasts. He has lectured at colleges, law enforcement agencies, and private industry on the use of the polygraph machine.

I called Howard Temple and was glad to learn that he had licenses in states where he adminstered polygraph tests requiring licensing, including Pennsylvania.

Dennis flew in from Florida, and we met with Mr. Temple on June 19, 2008, at a Marriott business meeting room at the Newark Airport.

I had written a synopsis of what Dennis and I hoped to accomplish and had devised a list of questions for Mr. Temple, but as we studied the list at our meeting, Mr. Temple explained that some of the questions could be considered "interpretive." He suggested we change the questions to follow an "issue format" for a more precise reading.

He asked why investigators on the scene at Catalina had not asked some of the questions he now asked. Dennis and I felt that Mr. Temple doubted us as we told him about the weekend Natalie Wood died and the events that had led us to arrange a polygraph.

Dennis became nervous as Mr. Temple's questions became harder. We were his clients, but he treated us as if the cops had just delivered us for an interrogation. His attitude seemed intimidating, but Dennis and I realized that Mr. Temple's doubt was exactly the reason Dennis was taking a polygraph in the first place.

Mr. Temple seemed awed that R.J. and Natalie had fought on the back deck and then she just went "missing." He asked, "Okay, she could have fallen in, but then, why wouldn't Wagner save her or call for help?"

He asked Dennis if he ever saw Natalie in the ocean. (No.) He asked if Dennis ever saw Natalie swimming, wading, or even touching the water. (No.) He asked Dennis if he was scared that night. (Yes.)

Mr. Temple's most accusatory question was, "Why a twenty-seven-year wait?" Dennis explained that he had made a terrible mistake in covering for Robert Wagner, had even lied for him at the scene, but that there had been many reasons for that choice.

I explained that Dennis had not actually waited twenty-seven years and informed Mr. Temple of the various media interviews and the *Vanity Fair* article. I explained that Dennis is a topic of controversy and has been accused not only of trying to profit from Natalie's death but also of being an accomplice or an actual murderer. We explained that the combined *total* of Dennis's "profiteering intake" amounted to Howard Temple's standard fee for three weeks of work. Therefore, only a manuscript could explain "the delay" and rumors reasonably. "Dennis needs to surmount this story, and Natalie deserves her justice," I said.

Then Dennis said something that touched my heart. "It's the kind of story that never goes away. A year or two can pass, then boom, there she is, walking down the dock, smiling at you when you're ready to fall asleep, and you know you just have to do this for her."

After an hour of discussion, Mr. Temple said that Dennis's story was far more complicated than he had realized. He considered certain details bordering on "criminal" and could not comprehend how such a story could end up in a meeting room in Newark, New Jersey, for "testing." He asked to postpone because the nature of Dennis's experience required that Mr. Temple develop a new set of questions, leaving nothing for interpretation, because the test could not consist of what Dennis "believed" or what Dennis "thought," even if Dennis's beliefs stemmed from experience. The test must confirm information only relating to what is *fact*. "If you want the real deal," Mr. Temple said, "we can't do this test today. It's just too complicated."

I was extremely disappointed. We had a window of only four hours, because Dennis had booked a return flight for later that same afternoon. I asked if we could ask just the first three questions on the list: the ones that dealt with noninterpretive fact.

"Leave the room," Mr. Temple told me.

I looked at him, confused.

He smiled. "I'll ask the first three questions, since you both went through a lot to be here today. But there can be no distractions. Take a walk, and we'll call you when we're finished."

Dennis looked nervous but determined. I left the room and went outside the hotel for a breath of air. I sat on a bench and watched the planes taking off just a short distance away. About thirty minutes later, my phone rang. Dennis said, "Come on in, Mart."

I walked into the small meeting room, and there was an ink-filled scroll of paper on the table filled with green and red blotches. I picked it up and looked at it. Mr. Temple smiled. "That's the start-up sheet," he said. "Here's the results sheet. Dennis passed each question."

Howard Temple had asked:

Did you tie the dinghy with two lines at the stern (rear) of Splendour *after you returned from dinner at Doug's Harbor Reef the night of November 28, 1981?*
Davern answered: *Yes.*

Did you hear Robert Wagner and Natalie Wood having a huge argument in their master stateroom that carried outside to the rear deck of Splendour *near 11:00 p.m. on the night of November 28, 1981, and was Robert Wagner with his wife from his smashing of a wine bottle in the main salon until the time he told you she went missing?*
Davern answered: *Yes.*

Did you see or hear Natalie Wood in the ocean the night of November 28, 1981?

Davern answered: *No.*

Dennis had now passed a scientific test that substantiated the fact that Wagner was with Natalie the night she died right up until she disappeared—a noninterpretive fact that Dennis knew to be true. This result enforced that Robert Wagner had to have seen how Natalie got from the boat to the water. Wagner had not "discovered" Natalie missing. Wagner is fully aware of how and why Natalie Wood left *Splendour*.

And, finally, that Dennis passed the question of whether or not he had seen or heard Natalie in the water while her husband still fought with her, as claimed in Finstad's book, was cleared up. Dennis had not been a spineless wimp who obeyed Wagner at the expense of a life, nor was he anything remotely resembling an accomplice.

Many people have a scenario for Natalie's last moments, but Dennis was at the actual scene. All of his senses had absorbed what transpired that night. He witnessed partly with his eyes and partly with his ears everything that had happened up until Natalie was no longer on the boat, and then he was the *only* person with Wagner until a call for help was placed hours later.

Mr. Temple seemed to change his impression of us after Dennis passed the test. Polygraphists are called upon for all sorts of bizarre cases, and Howard Temple had come up against his share of people who think they can "fool the machine." As an experienced professional, however, he knows it is virtually impossible to beat the test. And one thing was obvious to Howard Temple: Dennis was not the kind of person who could fool a machine. Mr. Temple, who picked up on our every inflection while prepping us, impressed me as a conscientious professional who, by this time in his career, could probably detect with accuracy who was lying and who was being truthful even without a polygraph machine. We arranged to rewrite the remaining questions in an "issue format," and we would reschedule.

As I drove Dennis back to the airport, he described the testing. Mr. Temple had asked him to face the wall and to answer with a simple yes or no. Various sensors were attached to Dennis's body, and Dennis was "strapped in." Mr. Temple first asked general questions for a warm-up, and he told Dennis afterwards that it is crucial to get a feel for the person being tested.

Dennis and I met with Howard Temple again on July 3, 2008, at his office in Pennsylvania. We discussed all of the issue-formatted questions for Dennis's test. Mr. Temple eliminated a couple of questions, claiming they were slightly interpretive, but approved the rest. He dissected every single question, every single word, to be certain nothing could be misconstrued. For example, we could not say that Dennis's girlfriend screamed "in fear"—we could only say that she screamed. Fact versus interpretation.

Soon, we were down to the final list of Howard Temple's questions:

Issue 1: *Robert Wagner suddenly decided to move the yacht* Splendour *to the Isthmus on late Friday night, November 27, 1981. Natalie Wood left the yacht with you, and you spent the night with her at the Pavilion Lodge (in Avalon), where you talked, listened to her express anger at her husband, drank wine, and then you slept with Natalie in her bed, with no sexual contact. Is this accurate?*
Davern : *Yes.*

Issue 2: *The cruise resumed on the morning of Saturday, November 28, 1981, and after Natalie made breakfast aboard* Splendour, *later that afternoon, Natalie and Christopher Walken went ashore and you and Wagner followed a few hours later in the dinghy to meet them at Doug's Harbor Reef Restaurant for cocktails and dinner. Is this accurate?*
Davern: *Yes.*

Issue 3: *After the bottle smashing (by Wagner) on November 28, 1981, Christopher Walken retreated to his cabin and stayed there. You did not see Walken leave his cabin until early morning, November 29, 1981. Is this accurate?*
Davern: *Yes.*

Issue 4: *When Wagner followed Natalie to their stateroom after the bottle smashing, you heard loud cursing and yelling, and what sounded like things being thrown or pushed around emitting from their stateroom on November 28, 1981. Is this accurate?*
Davern: *Yes.*

Issue 5: *After Natalie was missing on the night of November 28, 1981, Robert Wagner told you he did not want to search for her because he needed to protect his image and did not want to draw attention to the situation, so he did not agree to your suggestion to turn on the searchlight. Is this correct?*
Davern: *Yes.*

Issue 6: *After Natalie Wood was missing from the yacht* Splendour *on Saturday night, November 28, 1981, Robert Wagner asked you that very night to say nothing to anyone but attorneys about what you had seen and heard. Is this accurate?*
Davern: *Yes.*

Issue 7: *In the months following Natalie Wood's funeral, Robert Wagner paid for your attorney and for your therapy with his therapist. Is this accurate?*
Davern: *Yes.*

Issue 8: *After Natalie Wood's funeral, you stayed at Wagner's home in a monitored atmosphere for months. Wagner's employees would drive you to your fiancée's house. One night, while visiting your fiancée, Wagner's bodyguards physically removed you from your girlfriend's house and dragged you down the sidewalk, while your girlfriend screamed. Is this accurate?*
Davern: *Yes.*

Issue 9: *Reporters sought you for interviews since Wood's death. Not until 1985 with the* Star *magazine did you approve an interview. In all following interviews you granted, you told the truth with details you offered about Natalie's death, and you have been truthful with Marti Rulli through the years she has worked on a manuscript about Wood's death. Is this true?*
Davern: *Yes.*

Issue 10: *In discussing Natalie Wood's death in January 1992 in what you believed was a private setting on the* Now It Can Be Told *magazine show, you and Marti Rulli were discussing facts about the story, and about why you wanted to discontinue the interview. Is this accurate?*
Davern: *Yes.*

Issue 11: *You did not release the dinghy,* Valiant, *from the* Splendour *after Natalie Wood went missing from the yacht on November 28, 1981. Is this true?*
Davern: *Yes.*

Issue 12: *There is an investigator named Peter Rydyn who calls himself "the Retributor." You have no knowledge of this person and have never had any contact or interaction with this person. Is this correct?*
Davern: *Yes.*

Dennis passed every question truthfully on Howard Temple's polygraph machine. Dennis was not lying about any of the issues. Dennis was not lying about what he had experienced, heard, seen, and told about Natalie Wood's suspicious death.

Dennis passed his two polygraph tests.

* * *

Howard sent us his verification:

Re: Capt. Dennis Davern — (Captain: *Splendour*) Former Pleasure boat belonging to Robert Wagner & Natalie Wood

On June 19, 2008, and again on July 3, 2008, a series of polygraph examinations were conducted on the above named subject at his own request and the request of Marti Rulli.

The Intent of these polygraph examinations were to determine whether or not Capt. Davern was being truthful in his statements regarding the mystery in the death of Natalie Wood in November 1981.

Prior to submitting to the polygraph examinations, Capt. Davern explained the circumstances as he recalled surrounding the mysterious death of actress Natalie Wood and his theory as to what actually occurred on that November 1981 weekend.

Prior to submitting to the polygraph examination, the entire process was explained to Capt. Davern to his complete satisfaction. He also agreed to the placing of the necessary objects on his person to enable this examiner to perform several series of polygraph examinations.

Prior to the actual administering of the polygraph examinations, all of the questions were reviewed with Capt. Davern to his complete understanding and satisfaction.

After reviewing this series of polygraph examinations that were given to Capt. Davern, it is this examiner's opinion that Capt. Davern's numerous polygraph exams showed no indications indicative of deception to the list of questions. This is an indication that Capt. Davern was being truthful in his recollection of the facts surrounding the death of Natalie Wood during the weekend of November 27, 28, 1981. It is therefore this examiner's opinion that Capt. Davern was being truthful in his ability to remember the facts as he stated them in the questions.

Chapter 42

I had read Wagner's book, *Pieces of My Heart*, and was intrigued with his admission of obsessive love and jealousy for Natalie. He claims he had once waited with a gun for Warren Beatty outside of Beatty's house over his jealousy of Warren and Natalie.

Wagner's information about Natalie's death—touted as the "final word"—is constructed of lies even with documented records to prove him wrong, yet none of his details were verified or fact-checked.

But the most disturbing thing I took from Wagner's account was his description of the wine bottle smashing. He describes it by saying he smashed the wine bottle after Walken said Wood should devote more time to her film career, but the most startling of claims is that Natalie was *not* in the room when he broke the bottle. He finally admits to having broken the wine bottle and to yelling out in anger, but he changes the dynamics of the entire scene. Not only does he remove Natalie from it altogether, he claims that he yelled at Walken: "Why the fuck don't you stay out of her career?" (Close, but not quite "So, what do you want to do to my wife? Do you want to fuck my wife? Is that what you want?")

Wagner is still manipulating Davern by toning down the rage that accompanied the bottle smashing and by changing the number of witnesses to it. A logical reason for Wagner having confessed to the bottle smashing is that Davern and Walken had *both* witnessed it.

Another stunning and revealing little story in Wagner's autobiography bothered me tremendously. He tells of a nameless photographer who had snuck a photograph of an ailing David Niven and published it worldwide. Wagner says in his book that he and some others made sure it would be the last shot the photographer would take in a long, long time. He offered no elaboration.

How arrogant of Wagner to admit such an episode and to expect readers to cheer his implied violence. Dennis feared exactly such violence for decades, which is why, whenever he came close to revealing the whole truth, he would balk or say he had to leave the country. Dennis still fears for his physical safety. November 28, 1981, left Dennis with no doubt as to what Wagner's anger can lead to.

On October 13, 2008, a Monday, I reached Frank Salerno after a dozen or so attempts since the previous Thursday, anxious to let him know that Dennis had passed all polygraph testing. I explained about Wagner telling a new version of events that contradicted what he had told Rasure at Natalie's death scene, but Salerno said that he didn't want to get involved.

I pressed for an explanation, and Salerno said, "The investigation was based on what the three survivors of the cruise told Rasure, and it's not uncommon for stories to change years later, but that all three stories have changed years later is something of interest." Apparently not of interest enough for him to listen further. When I told him that Dennis had passed polygraph tests to verify his truth, Salerno said he was impressed but, polygraph test aside, he still chose to let the Natalie case stand.

I gave Salerno every opportunity to read what I had discovered throughout my amateur investigation that would put the professional one to shame. Again, Frank just wished me luck. I made one last appeal to his conscience by reminding him of his reputation—his penchant for justice. He paused and said that maybe my work might impress the sheriff's department later, but that he couldn't offer any help. I was terribly disappointed.

It is undeniable, given all of the contradictory statements Robert Wagner has made in published sources since 1981, that the man is a liar. Yet law enforcement officials, writers, interviewers, journalists, and friends continue to overlook his deceptions. Not one interviewer has asked Robert Wagner about Dennis's presence on *Splendour*.

If Wagner has indeed "gone over it and over it" with Walken, as he claims, then Walken could likely have been asked by Wagner to go along with the lies. Dennis and I had not included the bottle smashing in the initial polygraph test because Wagner had owned up to it. But since Wagner has changed his wording of the event from "So, what do you want to do to my wife? Do you want to fuck my wife?" to asking Walken to stay out of Natalie's career, it was imperative that Dennis be asked on a polygraph machine about the bottle smashing.

But first, upon excellent advice, I called Dennis to ask the ultimate of him.

"Den, what do you think about being hypnotized?" I asked, "Just so we leave no stone unturned. If there's anything you've subconsciously blocked, now would be a good time to search for it."

"Make an appointment and let me know," Dennis said, "I'll book a flight."

Dennis was willing to be scrutinized with polygraph tests, hypnotism sessions—whatever it took to prove he is telling the truth. I admired his determination.

I made an appointment with Dr. Jaime Feldman, a forensics hypnotist. Since 1990, Dr. Feldman has been the director/certified instructor of hypnotherapy at the Institute of Hypnotherapy in New Jersey. He is also the certified instructor for basic and advanced hypnotherapy for the American Board of Hypnotherapy, the International Medical and Dental Hypnotherapy Association, and the International Association of Counselors and Therapists. For 18 years, he has also been the director/doctor of clinical hypnotherapy, Dynamic Hypnotherapy Associates, Inc., New Jersey. He is a certified/registered doctor of clinical hypnotherapy with the American Board of Hypnotherapy, National Guild of Hypnotists, International Association of Counselors and Therapists, American Institute of Hypnotherapy, and International Medical and Dental Hypnotherapy Association. Dr. Feldman has been featured on *The Montel Williams Show* on three separate occasions.

In the early afternoon of October 21, 2008, I picked up Dennis at the Philadelphia International Airport. We had a couple of hours before our appointment with Dr. Feldman, so Dennis's sister, Rita Knapp, and her daughter, Amy Knapp, met us for lunch. Of course, conversation centered around Dennis's hypnosis session. Both Rita and Amy approved the choice, and Amy, who is a senior attorney at a Moorestown, New Jersey, firm, told us, "Remember one important thing, both of you: truth is its own defense."

Dr. Feldman began the session by explaining the basics of hypnosis. Then we explained to Dr. Feldman the essentials of Dennis's story and our reason for being there: to see if Dennis could recall anything more through hypnosis. Dennis told Dr. Feldman all that he recalled about Natalie's final weekend.

Dr. Feldman performed a few tests with Dennis to see if Dennis was a "willing participant." He explained that the presession tests prove whether or not a patient is unknowingly adverse to suggestion. Dennis was not. Dr. Feldman was satisfied with the results of the pretesting.

We went into a dim room with two comfortable recliner chairs. I sat in one and Dennis in the other. Dr. Feldman reclined our chairs (he said I should be comfortable too). Dr. Feldman sat near Dennis, and I sat to the side to watch and listen (with a notebook in my lap). Dennis stared at a moving spiral until his eyes became heavy and he was asked to close them. The doctor spoke his techniques into a microphone as Dennis closed his eyes and listened. About 15 minutes into the session, Dr. Feldman asked Dennis to open his eyes after suggesting that he wouldn't be able to do so. I saw Dennis struggling to open his eyes, but he couldn't. Dr. Feldman took Dennis "deeper" into the hypnosis, then began asking questions.

Dr. Feldman in no way suggested anything to Dennis but instead guided him to what he referred to as "significant events." The first event began with the Wagner party of four leaving Doug's restaurant on the night of November 28, 1981. Dennis talked about how drunk everyone was, including himself, as they boarded the dinghy to travel back to *Splendour.*

The next significant event took Dennis to the main salon. Dennis said there was laughter—Natalie was laughing at something Chris said. "Then there was anger." He recalled words but didn't want to talk about them because of what happened next.

The bottle smashing. Dennis said Wagner yelled out, "Do you want to fuck my wife, is that what you want?" He described the wine bottle shattering into pieces after Wagner slammed it on the coffee table. Dennis recalled the rage on Wagner's face. Natalie said, "This is absurd!" She wouldn't tolerate Wagner's outburst and went to her room—alone.

The next significant event went to the argument in the Wagner stateroom. Dennis heard the bumps and the yelling and the curse words. He appeared to be disturbed at this point, and said, "There's fighting, physically and yelling, and things being knocked over." Dennis hesitated, then added, "I knocked on the door to ask, 'Is all okay?'"

"And what happened?" Dr. Feldman asked.

Dennis's face took on a miserable expression, and he said, loudly, "I don't want you here."

"Who said that?" the doctor asked.

"R.J. He asked me to leave."

Dr. Feldman repeatedly asked Dennis to forward to the next significant event, but Dennis stayed quiet. "What's the next event, Dennis?" the doctor asked again and again.

Dennis finally said, "I looked out the window and saw Natalie on the deck in her nightgown."

"What happened next, Dennis?" the doctor asked.

Dennis's hands shot up and his face twisted. This was intense to watch, but he said nothing. I wondered if all of his years of suppressing that horrible night, not being able to talk about it without being condemned, worked on his mind at this point. Something was working his mind, and he wouldn't utter another word. I thought about what Paul Davern had said to me in the hotel room, two decades ago, "Den will take a lot to his grave with him."

Suddenly, Dennis blurted, "There was fighting and arguing and loud voices."

"What then, Dennis?" Dr. Feldman repeated.

"Natalie was gone," Dennis answered.

"And the next event?"

Dennis was getting disturbed, and I began to worry, but I trusted Dr. Feldman. "I checked the boat like R.J. asked. There was something bad but I wasn't thinking. I did as told. I wanted to call for help, but R.J. said, 'No!' It was bad, but he waited a long time to call for help. I knew something was wrong, but he was stalling. He wanted to keep the help away."

Dr. Feldman turned at this point to look at me. He shook his head. Then he asked Dennis to forward to the next significant event and asked him, "Did you ask R.J. about Natalie."

"Yes, she was missing. Like R.J. said."

"Did you feel that R.J. was being truthful?"

"No. He was hiding something. Not truthful. I wanted to call for help. I can see them, see the picture. Natalie was yelling. It was physical."

"Where do you see Natalie?"

"On the deck, in her nightgown. Don't see her jacket. I see the front part of her nightgown. I went away for a minute. All gone. She's gone. I went down. I looked on the boat for her. No dinghy. I just sat there."

"And next?"

"It was daylight and other people around. A lot of people started coming onboard. They got together with R.J. Natalie was dead."

Dr. Feldman looked at me and whispered, "I think this is enough." It was clear that Dennis should be "awakened." He did not appear relaxed. His demeanor was troubled, and when Dr. Feldman asked me if he should go on, I shook my head.

Dennis awakened and said he felt okay. We thanked Dr. Feldman and assured him we were thoroughly pleased with his efforts during the session. But our day was not done. We left the doctor's satellite office in Moorestown, New Jersey, and drove straight to Richboro, Pennsylvania, where Howard Temple was waiting to hook Dennis up to his polygraph machine again. We had a couple of things to confirm in light of Wagner's new version of what was said when he broke the wine bottle.

On the drive to the polygraphist's, I asked Dennis about seeing Natalie on the deck during the fight.

"Marti, when I saw Natalie on the deck during the session, which I always knew I had, I saw her in her nightgown, standing starboard. She was scared. She must have known it wasn't a good place to be because of how crazy R.J. was."

"Meaning she was as far away from the swim step as possible, right?"

"Yes. I think he went for her coat right after that last glance of mine. That's what came into my head when the doctor just had me under."

"Why didn't you say it?"

"Because I didn't see it, but I believe he got her coat and then helped her or saw her go overboard at that very minute, just after eleven. He knew she was in the water. I have no doubt about that now."

Mr. Temple seemed pleased to see us again but got down to serious business immediately. We explained about the hypnosis session and about how Wagner's account of breaking the wine bottle differed from Dennis's. I asked Mr. Temple if he could also ask Dennis about seeing Natalie on the deck in her nightgown. He attached the machine apparatus to Dennis, and I left the room.

Question 1: On the night of November 28, 1981, in the main salon where Wagner, Walken, Wood, and you gathered, did Robert Wagner scream, "Do you want to fuck my wife, is that what you want?" when he smashed the wine bottle?

Dennis answered yes. And passed.

Question 2: On the night of November 28, 1981, after the argument between Natalie Wood and Robert Wagner carried out to the deck, did you see Natalie on deck wearing her nightgown?

Dennis answered yes. And passed.

When I returned to the room, Mr. Temple told me that he had asked the two questions in three different formats, and Dennis had passed all three versions.

I thought about Private Investigator Milo Speriglio telling me the key was with Dennis, and the *Now It Can Be Told* legal panel suggested the same: Lyndon Taylor's "evidence tests" and Marilyn Wayne's exact timing with Dennis's "truth"—Natalie's cry from the grave. This 27-year journey had brought us into an era of scrutiny. Some Internet visitors resent exposed truth and call it conspiracy, while others plead for answers. It's an era when accused killers write books purporting, "If I did it, here's how" or their defenders sell us "Hellman Syndrome." It was imperative that Dennis be scrutinized, too, and that's why we were first to volunteer for a polygraph test and even go one step further with a professional hypnotist as witness to validate Dennis's truth.

If Detective Rasure had asked only one vital, immediate question, "Where was the dinghy tied and with how many lines?" it may have eliminated the fabricated "banging dinghy" theory from ever coming into play, leaving one last illuminating question: "Then why did Wood leave the yacht in a nightgown?" That question may have led to exposing the true words behind the broken wine bottle and to a bit more scrutiny of the lost half hour that became the mystery of Natalie Wood's death. The medical examiner's office should have actually pursued a psychological report. Those official departments may then have closed in on the case up until Natalie's final minute aboard *Splendour*. But, that was 1981 when the weapon of an ocean seemed to negate a forensics pursuit. Rasure and Salerno both told me they might reconsider Natalie's case. I don't know what that may take, but after this full day with Dennis, I thought back to his 1983 middle-of-the-night phone call.

Not once since then had I doubted my friend's honesty, but only now did all of his truths converge with the conviction that I had done my utmost to tell this story. I had patiently learned details from a man whose emotions choked him every time he spoke of the tragedy. I had scrutinized every bit of information Dennis revealed, looking objectively to corroborate or disprove it. I had read hundreds of reports and articles, listened to interviews, considered rumors and opinions, identified discrepancies and contradictions in the accounts of Wagner and others, and carried out my own investigative experiments. The polygraph felt like the final step. I was done.

I carry a terrible image in my mind of Natalie, struggling in the unforgiving sea. Her eyes are wide and pleading: *Don't let me die like this!* And the only thing I can offer her, through Dennis Davern, is this book: her voice, her truth.

Chapter 43

Robert John Wagner lied from the moment Natalie Wood went missing to the moment he approved the final draft of his 2008 autobiography.

Robert Wagner's manipulations started from the moment he told Dennis Davern that Natalie was missing and have lasted through his *Pieces of My Heart*. From refusing to allow the concerned Davern to go into search-and-rescue mode when Natalie was no longer on the boat to reducing Dennis to a boat caretaker in his autobiography—and all of Wagner's lies and subliminal tactics in between—Wagner has provided a far greater answer to the mystery of Natalie Wood's death than anything Davern has ever offered.

Wagner had manipulated Don Whiting, Paul Wintler, Doug Oudin, Doug Bombard, Duane Rasure, and everyone else involved directly or indirectly with the events surrounding Natalie's death.

Wagner had ignored Marilyn Wayne, who came forth with startling information, but Wagner was not interested in hearing from the woman who had heard what were most likely Natalie Wood's last words: "Please help me, I'm drowning."

Wagner, who knew—and told Doug Oudin—that Natalie was in her nightgown claimed he hadn't considered the possibility of the "banging dinghy" theory until after learning that Natalie was found in her nightgown.

Wagner has never talked in depth—even in his autobiography—about the night Wood died. To talk about her death in detail would conjure far too many questions for Wagner's comfort zone.

The only person alive—Robert John Wagner—who undoubtedly knows how Natalie Wood got into the water, will obviously never talk about it, so exactly how Natalie got into the water may never be known, but what is known is that Wagner was with her when the "mystery" was born. What is known is that Wagner argued terribly with his wife. He was raging mad and acted upon the rage by taking a marital fight out to an open deck on his yacht. His wife was in her nightgown, arguing with him. Minutes later, she was in the water—wearing her coat—and crying to be saved.

The "mystery" of Natalie's death would not have been too difficult to solve, certainly not for a police department and a medical examiner's staff, had they *pursued* every angle of the case *together*. Many novices have no trouble solving it through the use of common sense. It seems the public is all that Natalie has left.

Wagner has never addressed his drastic delay in searching for Natalie. No one asks him for details. His fans defend that waiting for hours is logical, even though the number one rule in boating is to call for immediate help when someone is missing. Dennis Davern knows the proper procedures to follow when someone is missing from a boat. Wagner's refusal to allow Davern to search for Natalie indicates that he did not want his wife to be helped: perhaps not ever to be found. Natalie's jacket kept her afloat, helping her to be found shortly after a proper search.

Wagner then still balked on calling for professional help when harbormaster Doug Oudin pleaded with Wagner after three o'clock in the morning to allow him to call the Coast Guard. The harbormaster waited for Wagner's approval.

Avalon Sheriff Kroll saw the inside of *Splendour*—the broken glass, the master stateroom in disarray—and ignored it.

While Baywatch divers hunted for Natalie beneath *Splendour*, diver Roger Smith said he was angry that professional help had not been called for sooner. Smith had asked Bombard not to touch Natalie's body. "Homicide might be involved," Smith had said. Smith obviously suspected something sinister.

Everyone's peculiar deference to Wagner carried on throughout the morning, as each and every official in contact with Wagner after Natalie's bruised dead body was found felt the loss of this remarkable woman and thus related to the pain they believed Wagner endured. Everyone allowed the man with the "most pain" to direct the aftermath of his wife's death. Wagner's grief was apparent to Duane Rasure, and although Wagner had primed Davern on what to tell authorities and on what not to offer, Rasure had been so overwhelmed with Wagner's suffering that he let it slide when Davern reacted to Rasure with nervousness, offense, and outright lies. Rasure got mad at the "lanky, drunk guy from New Jersey" instead—and has stayed mad at him.

Wagner wanted off the island. A private helicopter was summoned. Wagner did not want to be interviewed by Rasure. Rasure let him go home. Legal assistance was ready and waiting for Wagner and Davern at Wagner's front door. It's what money can buy. All of the right people made the wrong decision to allow Robert Wagner to direct a crime scene.

Celebrity privilege was indeed alive and thriving on the morning of November 29, 1981, at the Isthmus of Catalina Island aboard the moored boat, *Splendour*. Celebrity "get out of jail free cards" may as well have been issued. Years later, when Davern told the truth, he was threatened with criminal charges and jail time if he changed the story that the attorney provided by Wagner had prepared for Dennis in 1981. Years later, that same attorney cooperated with Davern's choice to speak with a writer from *Vanity Fair*.

Wagner's grief, which so swayed Rasure, was probably real. The magnitude of what had actually happened to Natalie— and that two young daughters were left behind to deal with a lifetime of pain—must have hit him hard. Natalie was gone forever. As he claims in his book, "his knees went out." It was Davern who had held him up.

After years passed, it became easier to convince himself that his anger and actions were justified. And to write the autobiography he presents in 2008 shows that he thinks he is utterly immune to doubt and suspicion. He had wanted to stop books and movies and other people from telling about their lives. He had asked people in show business to stay away from people he disliked. He wants the laws changed so that no one can reveal his true colors after his demise. He thinks he has gotten away with his part in Natalie's death. And he indeed had a big part in it. He smashed a wine bottle, screamed profanities, and fought a deadly argument with Natalie after she had gone to their stateroom to go to bed. She would have awakened the next morning if only her husband had left her alone. He took the fight to the back deck, and minutes later, Natalie was no longer on board. In 2008, Wagner presents his autobiography because he is still trying to direct a horrible story and still trying to create an image he has successfully pulled off with many, despite that many of his lies have been exposed.

Not one part of Davern's story has ever been exposed as a lie. In fact, over time, Wagner has only corroborated Davern's truth. Wagner evades Natalie's death by saying he has nothing to prove. Wagner has worked hard to protect his own image and while doing so has affected the image of an innocent "caretaker"— his boat captain—the person who wanted to immediately try to save Natalie.

Since Natalie's death, Wagner has been sheltered by his insider network of secrecy and privilege for so long he appears to believe in the image he has created for himself. He has never had to bear the brunt of a direct, in-your-face accusation or questioning. His media buddies and selected interviewers tiptoe around him as if a twenty-seven-year-old death can still shatter him. Interviewers start their questions with their sympathetic eyes and condolences even decades later, as if Wagner is still the victim of love lost and innuendo. Wagner interviewers rarely express sympathy for Natalie's experience. It is Wagner they have coddled, while Natalie is the truest victim.

Dennis knows the truth. Dennis says, "My first reaction was that Wagner had everything to do with Natalie's death, and it is my belief to this day that Natalie is a victim of her husband. I saw too much that night to ever believe it was an accident. I witnessed R.J.'s drunkenness, I witnessed R.J.'s anger and outburst. I heard the stateroom fight and saw that it carried over to the back deck. I know that Wagner was with Natalie when she left the boat. Wagner *knows* how and exactly *why* she left the boat."

Medically, Natalie drowned.

Dr. Choi performed the actual autopsy. Drowning by undetermined cause would have been a more accurate description of Wood's death. No one knew how or why she had left that yacht, and the banging dinghy story—what has become the standard answer—was concocted. Noguchi has the world believing that a wet down jacket weighs 40 to 50 pounds and will drag a person down in water. This misinformation is even posted on a nurse's training Web site.

Almost three decades have passed, and the mystery of Natalie Wood's death is as prominent as ever. Two of the 1981 cruise survivors continue to lie. Natalie's family still suffers. Fans talk about her every single day on the Internet.

Incomprehensible. The entire Natalie Wood case has been a perpetual train wreck.

Natalie Wood experienced one of the most traumatizing deaths imaginable. After Robert Wagner smashed the wine bottle, Natalie Wood's next half hour included a convoluted, horrendous succession of events that she would not survive.

* * *

Floating. Floating. Floating. In her buoyant red jacket, alive. Floating. In the dark water she feared her entire life. She calls out for help. She has hope.

She cries, "Help me, someone help me, I'm drowning...."

"Hold on, we'll get you," she hears a debased voice say.

She continues to plead for help.

She hears the loud music coming from *Splendour*.

She wants to be back in her stateroom. Safe in bed. This cannot be happening.

She recognizes the help of her buoyant red jacket. It offers her a shred of hope. But she is drifting away from the swim step. The coat keeps her from going under, but it is also keeps her from where she wants to go. Back to her *Splendour*.

How can this be happening?

She is shocked. She is in the water.

She tries to keep her nose and mouth above the cold water's surface. The jacket helps her effort. She is amazed at how the jacket makes it easy to hold her head high. But she is filled with panic as the nearby boats fade in the darkness.

She desperately wants to be saved, but she has been pleading over and over, and she is still in the water, drifting away from safety.

It gets colder. She feels pins and needles, then can barely feel her hands. The numbness is terrifying.

She drifts farther away from *Splendour*, floating, beyond help and hope.

She will never see her daughters again.

Acknowledgments

Over several decades, a lot of names have accumulated to thank for support, assistance, and the production of GNGS.

Thank you to the entire Rulli, Carter, and Davern families. Thank you especially to George Rulli, for taking so many of Dennis's late night calls, and for believing. A special thanks to the late Paul Davern and to the late Matthew Davern Sr. and Ruth Davern.

Thank you to the late James Walker Dill, the late Jenny Carter, and the late James Walker Carter. Thanks Dave and Shirley Carter, and all family members: the Haines family and the Bice family.

Thank you to friends Arnold and Carol Felderman, Tim and Grace St. Clair, Laura DePew, James and Cheryl Cronce. Thank you to my kids (Billy, Matt, and Jeannine, and all of their partners and offspring since watching me start this project on a typewriter in 1983 at our dining room table). Jessica West, just by being born, created a turning point for this work.

Thank you to Author George Carpozi, who wrote the bestseller *Poison Pen*, for helping me to humanize the glorified Hollywood couple, Natalie Wood and Robert Wagner. Brian Haugh (*Star* reporter) and George Carpozi (*Star* senior editor), thanks for asking the questions needed. Thank you to writer, producer Steve Dunleavy for all of his valid questions.

For my growing support in the 1990s, heartfelt thanks to dear friends, Frank "Buddy" Greco and wife Mary Sumption-Greco, and John Levandowski for endless nights of debate and discussion over GNGS. Thank you to the late Billy Sumption, a truly perceptive individual who eased my worries over a media blunder. And, thanks to Geraldo Rivera for trying to get the authorities to listen to the three respected attorneys who pleaded for another professional look into Natalie Wood's death.

Thank you to Paul Rovner and Glenn Cochran, two really decent attorneys.

I am grateful for the support of the Mooney/Costigan family and their extended families. And, a forever deep gratitude to Bob Mooney, who to this day has never once said, "Please stop talking about this."

Thanks to all my work friends and colleagues throughout the years.

Undying appreciation is offered for my preview readers throughout the decades who all helped by asking the right questions and by offering honest evaluations. Each helped to grow this project: Carol Felderman, Mary Greco, Josephine Mooney, Ellen Davern, Carrie Rivera, Alicia Ellis, Chip Reid, Renaldo Manuel Ricketts, Mimi Mukherjee, Sue Yared, Debbie Huddleston, Attorney Amy Knapp-Georgiades, Kristy Rulli, Matt Rulli, Joseph Cantito, Gail Abbott, and author Stephanie Shanks-Meile.

Thank you to the late Rita Vermeer, to John Tonnessen, and Erik Holtz for the "test."

Thanks to Ryan Lesinski who in an off-matter way helped to figure it all out, "on paper."

Thank you to the late Chuck Esser, a dedicated, professional detective and friend who saw through the professional mistakes made on November 29, 1981.

For support in the 2000s, I thank author Suzanne Finstad for her amazing work in *Natasha* (2001) and Sam Kashner, author of March 2000 *Vanity Fair* article "Natalie Wood's Final, Fatal Hours." I thank Lana Wood, a true help in understanding her sister, Natalie. Thank you to Marilyn Wayne.

I thank my professional help in the literary world: David Stanford, the late Private Investigator Milo Speriglio, Mark Ebert, Jay Acton, Stuart Miller, Richard Curtis, and the professional, helpful staff at Phoenix Books and Audio, especially Darby Connor and Dan Smetanka. Thank you to Michael Viner for his vision.

Thank you to Ann Rule and Dominick Dunne, just for writing the kind of books they write. Thank you to detectives Duane Rasure and Frank Salerno, and to Coroner Noguchi. Their careers are respectable, and I hope they respect my efforts.

The professional help of Howard Temple and Dr. Jamie Feldman is greatly appreciated.

Finally, to all authors who get the job done alone: I admire you, but GNGS was not written "alone." My undying gratitude is offered to:

Carol Lallier: the true turning point for this project that had become a part of me, as well as me a part of it. Carol's expert editorial work and sharp writing skills helped to transform a manuscript filled with holes to a compelling revelation. She always knew exactly what I needed to say. I thank her for her integrity and talent, and for helping this project to evolve with substance.

Mary Sumption-Greco: the person always right-on with her appraisals after reading many, many presentations. Mary led me to my confidence, to what GNGS needed.

Mark Weston: the most impressive teacher, playwright, and author. Mark's assistance awakened the emotions needed to humanize the people presented in GNGS. Mark's simple advice and editorial assistance was pinnacle. ("Ya gotta believe!" Tugger had a great friend in Mark!)

Dr. Lyndon Taylor: When all seemed lost, I met the most important part of this story: the man who worked for it as if all justice in the world would be gone by tomorrow. Lyn brought justice to this story with over five years of hands-on effort, by testing, by calculating, and by summarizing. Our world is a better place because of people with Lyn's intelligence and integrity. Because of Lyn, I have no doubt of our ultimate goal.

Gail Abbott: The "finishing touch"—my backbone in the homestretch. No one knows more about Natalie than Gail, a true "Wood Historian" who keeps the memory of Natalie alive. She is a natural part of this legendary subject. Odd how we met, but I will always value our friendship.

Dennis Davern: Dennis may not have keyboarded the GNGS chapters, but he is the truest author of this story. Dennis, I thank you for your courage, your willingness to be scrutinized, your ability to overcome all obstacles, and for your truth. I am sorry for all you had to endure since November 1981. You deserved so much better.

Thank you to all who believed, and to those of you willing to try.

Marti Rulli